Robert Hillenbrand
was educated at the universities
of Cambridge and Oxford. Since 1971 he has taught at the
University of Edinburgh, and in 1989 was made Professor of
Islamic Art there. He has travelled extensively throughout the
Islamic world from Morocco to Southeast Asia, and has held
visiting professorships at Princeton, Los Angeles, Dartmouth
and Bamberg. He is the author of over a hundred publications,
including books on Persian painting
and Islamic architecture.

WORLD OF ART

This famous series
provides the widest available
range of illustrated books on art in all its aspects.
If you would like to receive a complete list
of titles in print please write to:
THAMES AND HUDSON
30 Bloomsbury Street, London WC1B 3QP
In the United States please write to:
THAMES AND HUDSON INC.
500 Fifth Avenue, New York, New York 10110

Printed in Slovenia

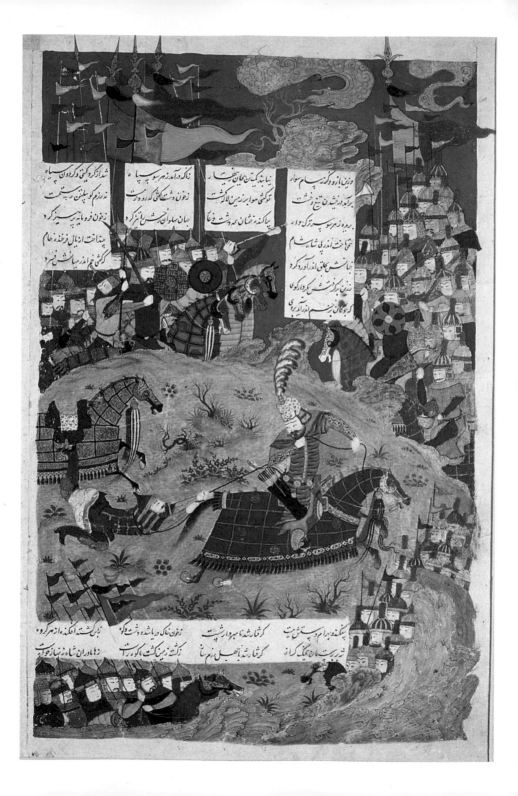

Robert Hillenbrand

Islamic Art
and Architecture

270 illustrations, 80 in color

THAMES AND HUDSON

For Margaret and Ruthie,
with love and thanks for years of encouragement

FRONTISPIECE Rustam lassoing Kamus. Firdausi, *Shahnama*, probably Tabriz, *c.* 1505; attributable to Sultan Muhammad. Rustam, the hero of the *Shahnama*, the Persian national epic, is distinguished by the tiger skin that he wears over his body armour and his leopard's-head casque crowned by a mighty seven-fold plume. Note the floating text panels and concealed grotesques in the landscape.

ACKNOWLEDGMENT I owe a great deal to Dr Barbara Brend, who read the text with painstaking care and unstintingly provided many pages of suggestions for its improvement. The book is much the richer for her efforts.

First published in paperback in the United States of America in 1999 by Thames and Hudson Inc., 500 Fifth Avenue, New York, New York 10110

Library of Congress Catalog Card Number 97-60274
ISBN 0-500-20305-9

Printed and bound in Slovenia

Contents

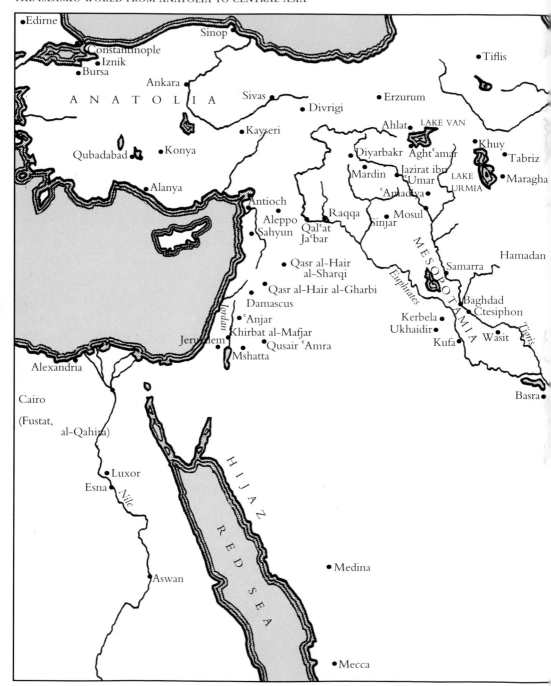

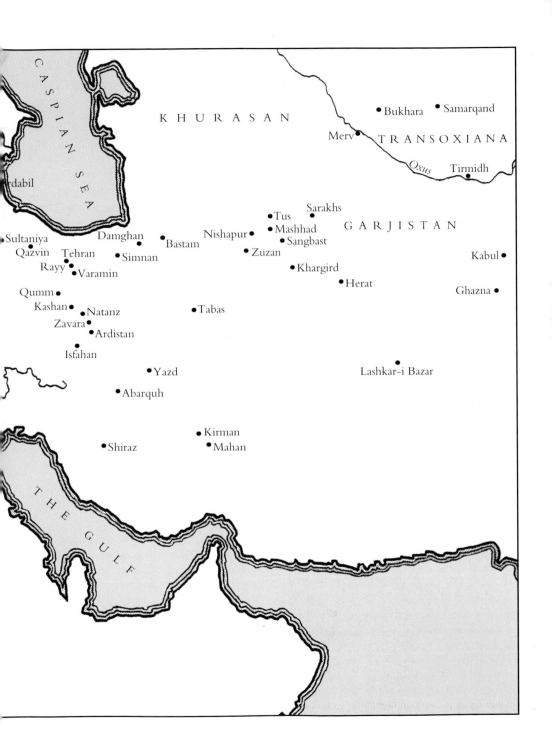

Introduction

Any attempt to make sense of Islamic art and architecture as a whole while retaining a chronological framework runs the risk of distortion. Bias of several different kinds is hard to avoid. It is simply not possible to be equally well informed and equally interested in all aspects of the subject. The need to consider in some detail the early centuries of Islamic art is made imperative by the major impact which work of this period had on later art. But a great deal of this early art has perished, and to do justice to what survives in the context of its own time and of subsequent periods demands a closer and more detailed focus than is appropriate for the more numerous examples of later art. Some degree of over-balance is therefore inevitable.

Certain art forms such as calligraphy or textiles continued to be produced in most parts of the Islamic world from early times, but they are not of equal significance in each area or period. Thus the absence of a discussion of, say, Tulunid woodwork, Maghribi pottery, Timurid textiles, Spanish metalwork or Ottoman Qur'ans should not be interpreted as a signal that they did not exist, have not survived or are of peripheral interest. It is simply that it seemed best to reserve a discussion of certain media for those periods in which production was of the most significant scale and quality. Similarly, the art of entire dynasties – Ghaznavid, Turcoman, the *beyliks* of Anatolia, the *muluk al-tawa'if* of medieval Spain – is virtually ignored. Such omissions are dictated by the rigorous word limit and the need to see the wood rather than the trees. In other words, the option of trying to say something, however little, about almost everything, and thus writing a rather bland and trivial text, was rejected. It seemed preferable to single out key objects and monuments for relatively detailed scrutiny, in the hope that they would provide a means of entry into the school or style that produced them. This book, then, is more a study of the peaks than of the valleys; its colours are intended to be bold and primary.

A secondary aim has been to set the various schools and types of Islamic art in a reasonably full historical context so that the images are not, so to speak, trapped in limbo. Specialists will have to console themselves with the thought that this book was not written with them in mind. It is truly no more than an introduction to a vast field.

Moreover, the very fact that a book with the all-inclusive title of *Islamic Art and Architecture* can be written – whereas the books on western European art in the World of Art series are of a very much more specialized kind, and are often devoted to a single school, or even artist – is a reminder that the volume of scholarship consecrated to this field is tiny in comparison with that available for European art. Basic guides to the territory therefore still have their function. But it would be a serious mistake to assume from that disparity that there is any less 'going on' in Islamic than in European art. You just have to dig rather deeper for it.

NOTE CONCERNING DATES

For the sake of simplicity and consistency, year dates are shown in accordance with the Gregorian calendar, but with occasional mentions of their equivalents in the Muslim calendar (based on the lunar cycle) in connection with specifically dated buildings or works of art. Muslim years are calculated from the date of the *hijra* – the Prophet's journey from Mecca to Medina – in July 622.

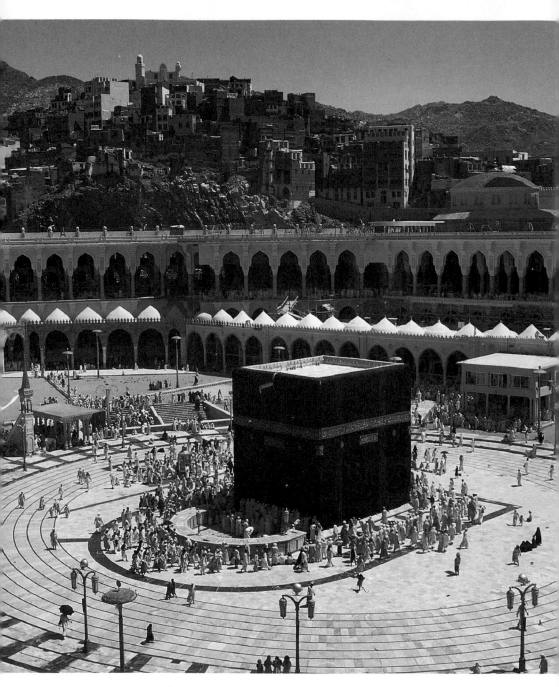

1 The pivot of Islam. The Ka'ba in the Masjid al-Haram, Mecca: principal Islamic shrine and the goal of Muslim pilgrimage. Frequently restored, it contains the Black Stone, the directional focus for Muslim prayer, and is covered – 'like a bride' according to medieval poets – with the *kiswa*, a silken veil, now black but formerly in many colours.

CHAPTER ONE

The Birth of Islamic Art: the Umayyads

The genesis of Islamic art is customarily linked with, indeed often attributed to, the whirlwind military conquests of the Arabs following the death of the Prophet Muhammad in AD 632. Such an idea is plausible enough. The creation of a world empire, the proclamation of a new faith, the formation of an art that bears its name – all seem to belong together. But do they? Is there a causal connection, and – if so – what is the exact chronological sequence? Dazzling and exciting as the spectacle of the Arab conquests is, it in fact has relatively little to do with the early years of Islamic art. Yet the formative nature of those early years is plain. What, then, is the precise connection between the seismic political events of the seventh century and the earliest Islamic art?

The answer to such questions demands a refinement of the chronological and geographical focus. To view early Islamic art as even approximately representative of an empire that stretched from the Atlantic to India and the borders of China is grossly to misunderstand its context. In the two generations which saw the Arabs flood out of their desert homeland and overrun all of western Asia and North Africa there was, it seems, neither the desire nor the time to foster artistic expression. That was to be the achievement not of the first conquerors themselves but of their grandchildren. At all events, no major building or artefact survives from these early years. This sluggish start may owe something to the fact that in this period the nascent Muslim state was being ruled from Arabia, an environment in which the visual arts, though by no means absent – as recent excavations at Qaryat al-Faw (frescoes of royal scenes) and elsewhere (figural sculpture) have shown – nevertheless had no very significant role, though architecture flourished. Arabia certainly lagged far behind the Levant. Similarly, there can be no question of a 'universal' Islamic art at this early stage. The horizons of that art were effectively limited to Syria. The rest of the Islamic empire might as well scarcely have existed at all, except insofar as works of art or craftsmen from outside Syria were active within that province and thus exerted external influence on the art produced there.

These remarks might lead one to expect a somewhat parochial quality in the earliest Islamic art, and also a certain timidity or lack of purpose. Yet this is not so. Such characteristics might well have marked the very first monuments which the Muslims erected, for example in Fustat, Basra and Kufa – although there is no way of clinching this, for they have not survived. But if Islamic art was slow to start, it was quick to gather speed. Certainly the first major monument to survive, the Dome of the Rock in Jerusalem, radiates assurance. A new art has arrived. It established itself quickly and, for all that numerous experiments and changes of mind can be detected during the rule of the Umayyad dynasty (661–750), the pervasive confidence of the age remained undimmed.

This confidence, one of the most striking features of Umayyad art, was founded on several interrelated factors. Chief among them, perhaps, was the astonishing military success of the Arabs in their foreign campaigns. To their enemies they must have appeared to bear charmed lives, their winning streak seeming unassailable for much of the Umayyad period. Decade after decade the borders of the *dar al-islam* steadily expanded, until in 732 – exactly a century after the Prophet's death – the Arab defeat at Poitiers in central France signalled (though only with the hindsight of history) the end of substantial territorial gains for some centuries. But the splendid confidence of the Umayyads was not based entirely on military success abroad; it was founded also on the ability of the new dynasty to survive numerous challenges from within. Such challenges were at their most dangerous in the first thirty years of Umayyad rule. It may be no more than a coincidence that this same period was singularly barren so far as the production of works of art was concerned. Yet it is probable that the outburst of building activity which followed the consolidation of Umayyad power and the dynasty's triumph over its internal enemies should be seen at least partly in a political light – in this particular case, as a celebration of Umayyad dominance. This propaganda dimension was frequently to reappear in Islamic art, especially in architecture, although it tended to be of secondary rather than primary significance.

Allied to the understandable confidence generated by spectacular military successes at home and abroad was a confidence based on a sense of secure dynastic power. The Umayyads had abrogated the primordial Islamic notion of an elective succession to the caliphate and replaced it by the dynastic principle. The internal political turmoil of the later seventh century was in large measure caused – and maintained – by that action. Once victorious over their enemies, however, the Umayyads were able to indulge a heady consciousness of family power for which history can offer few parallels. For several caliphs – notably ʿAbd al-Malik, al-Walid I and al-Walid II – this sense of dynastic pride found its most public expression in ambitious building campaigns. The caliphs Sulaiman and Hisham were not far behind, and other princes of the royal family, such as al-ʿAbbas b. al-Walid and Ghamr b. Yazid, followed suit. Indeed, to judge by the quantities of religious and secular buildings erected in Syria between 690 and 750 under the direct patronage of the Umayyad royal house, architecture speedily became a family business. The immense financial resources of the Islamic state, whose exchequer was swollen by the accumulated booty of the Arab conquests and by the taxation revenue which came pouring in thereafter, were at the disposal of the Umayyad builders. Thus ʿAbd al-Malik was able to set aside the tax revenues of Egypt for seven years to pay for the Dome of the Rock, while his son al-Walid I devoted the entire tax revenue of Syria for seven years to the building and embellishment of the Great Mosque of Damascus. There was thus both the will and the means to embark on grandiose building projects.

Enough has been said to account for the superb self-confidence which triggered and then fuelled the massive building programme of the Umayyads. Yet the geographical location of these buildings also requires explanation. Given that they are to be found, with very few exceptions, exclusively in Syria, how was an undue parochialism, peculiarly inappropriate to a world empire, avoided? The answer is three-fold. First, Syria under the Umayyads was beyond compare the most favoured land in the Islamic empire. Its inhabitants enjoyed privileges and concessions denied to those from other provinces. Its principal city, Damascus, was from 661 the capital of the empire. Here was established the Umayyad court and administration, when these were not to be found toiling in the wake of semi-nomadic caliphs. The massive caliphal investment in agricultural installations – canals, dams, wells, gardens and so on, culminating in the planned but abortive diversion of the River Jordan itself – made Syria perhaps even exceed Iraq as the richest province in the empire. Thus abundant wealth complemented its political prestige.

Parochialism in Umayyad art was further discouraged by the practice of conscripting labour and materials from other provinces. This custom ensured that Syrian material culture would be metropolitan. The caliphs could dip at will into an extensive labour pool within their own domains, and could supplement this by importing still more craftsmen and materials from outside the Islamic world, notably from Byzantium. The chance survival of a cache of papyri from Aphrodito in Upper Egypt documents the workings of an Islamic corvée system − essentially the *leiturgia* practised by Rome and Byzantium − in the early eighth century. The local governor, one Qurra b. Sharik, was responsible for sending a specified number of men to work on the Damascus mosque, and he had to provide money to cover their living expenses too. Such documentary proof of the corvée system can be supplemented by literary references − for example, al-Tabari mentions the activity of Syrian and Coptic workmen in the building of the mosque at Medina − and, above all, by the evidence of the buildings themselves. Stucco sculpture of Persian type, Iraqi techniques of vault construction, mouldings from south-eastern Anatolia, a figural style closely paralleled in Coptic sculpture − all furnish unmistakable evidence that the style and building practice of Syria was enriched by ideas and traditions from much further afield. There was no danger that the local Syrian craftsmen would cling to their own traditions and thus risk stagnation.

Finally, the position of Syria, both geographically and politically, militated against parochialism. The province was uniquely placed to draw inspiration from the major cultures newly yoked together to form the Islamic empire. To the north, west and south-west lay lands in which Graeco-Roman culture was dominant and which were either Byzantine or, like Egypt and North Africa, had recently been wrested from Byzantine rule. To the south was Arabia, which at this early stage in Islamic history was still by no means a spent force in religious, cultural or political terms. To the east lay Mesopotamia and Persia, comprising the accumulated heritage of Assyria and Babylon, and of the Achaemenids, Parthians and Sasanians. Here the tradition of world empires died hard, though the horizons of these Middle Eastern states were appreciably narrower than those of the Umayyads.

Within the Umayyad empire, then, which stretched from France to the Indus, Syria was ideally placed to act as a central point from which metropolitan influences radiated to the outlying provinces. No other region of the Islamic world combined such a deeply rooted Hellenism with an openness to the ancient cultures of the Near East. By virtue of its geographical position and its political pre-eminence,

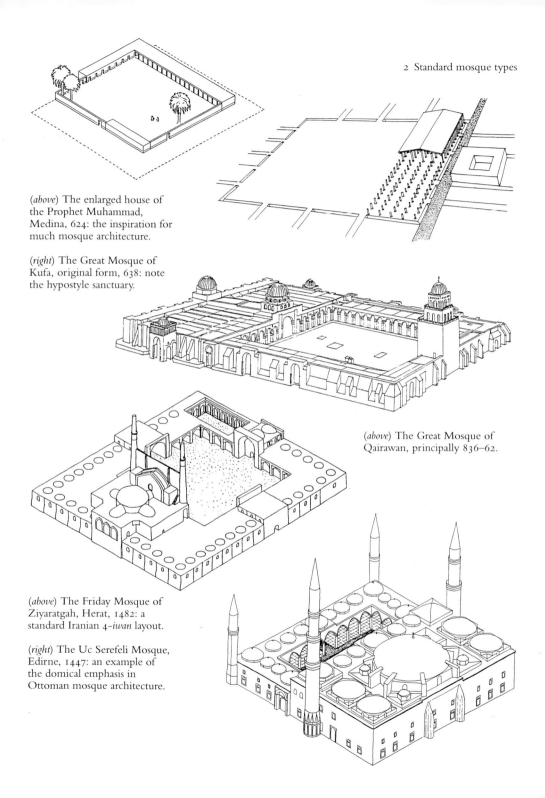

2 Standard mosque types

(*above*) The enlarged house of the Prophet Muhammad, Medina, 624: the inspiration for much mosque architecture.

(*right*) The Great Mosque of Kufa, original form, 638: note the hypostyle sanctuary.

(*above*) The Great Mosque of Qairawan, principally 836–62.

(*above*) The Friday Mosque of Ziyaratgah, Herat, 1482: a standard Iranian 4-*iwan* layout.

(*right*) The Uc Serefeli Mosque, Edirne, 1447: an example of the domical emphasis in Ottoman mosque architecture.

Syria was a natural bridge between east and west, north and south. It was only to be expected that under the Umayyads its art should reflect this unique situation. The fact that those same Umayyads were not a family of local Syrian notables but the representatives of the greatest empire in the contemporary world gave their art a mission of the utmost seriousness. It had a public, an imperial, role. In the immediately pre-Islamic period Syria had perforce been constrained to yield centre stage to Constantinople and even Alexandria, and was thus to a certain extent an eastern appendage of a Mediterranean-centred empire. The emergence of Islam as a world power decisively changed all this and brought Syria its scant century of glory. Umayyad art was the public expression of that glory.

So far as the future of Islamic art was concerned, this was a crucial century, in which the face of the Mediterranean world and the Near East was permanently redrawn. This century established the principle that Islamic art, far from being intrinsically universal, could have (as it certainly began by having) a well-defined regional and dynastic character, a feature which it consistently retained in later centuries. The Umayyad period also ensured that the forms and ideas of classical art, which were much better understood in Syria than in the lands further to the east, would enter the bloodstream of Islamic art. As a result, Islamic architecture tends to feel familiar to a Western observer; it employs, after all, the familiar vocabulary of column and capital, pointed arch and dome, rib and vault. It was under the Umayyads, too, that a distinct iconography of princely life, centring around the formal, ceremonial activities of the monarch and his leisure pursuits, was developed and refined. This set of images was to become a leitmotif of secular art throughout the Islamic world. Similarly, the success of Umayyad solutions to many problems of religious and secular architecture ensured that the building types evolved during this period repeatedly recurred in one guise or another in subsequent centuries. This readiness of later generations to copy Umayyad prototypes was at least partly due to the unique glamour which invested this, the first and most powerful of Islamic dynasties. As already noted, too, the Umayyads recognized the propaganda dimension inherent in splendid buildings and symbolic images; this also was to remain a constant of later Islamic art. Yet this same development was viewed with some mistrust at first, and Muʿawiya, the first Umayyad caliph, when challenged about his taste for ostentation on the Byzantine model, defended himself by asserting that 'we are at the frontier and I desire to rival the enemy in martial pomp, so that he may be witness to the prestige of Islam'.

Finally, the Umayyads' choice of Syria as their power base had tremendous consequences for later Islamic art, since the generative impact of Syria was greater than that of any potential rival among the other provinces in the Islamic empire. Islamic art would have developed in a very different fashion if the Umayyads had settled, for example, in Arabia, in Spain or in India. At the same time, lest too much be claimed for the art of this period, it is worth remembering that some of the media which were later to become most typically Islamic, such as glazed pottery, metalwork, carpets, book painting and textiles, are either totally or virtually absent from art of this period.

What, then, are the principal expressions of Islamic art under Umayyad dominion? The so-called 'minor arts' are quickly disposed of: the textile fragment which, if its attribution to Marwan II is correct, would be datable to c. 750, and whose arabesques and figural style would readily suggest Coptic work but for the Arabic inscription; some ivories for which Coptic and Byzantine as well as Umayyad provenances have been suggested, a controversy which itself sheds much light on the intrinsic nature of Umayyad art; and a little metalwork, much of it also of disputed date and provenance. The so-called 'Marwan ewer' in Cairo may be late Umayyad or early 'Abbasid; but its date, and indeed its provenance, is less important than its form, which is prophetic of much of later Islamic metalwork in that it typifies the preferred Islamic response to the sculpture of living creatures. The body of the ewer is occupied principally by a continuous arcade enclosing rosettes and animals, all lightly incised. A pair of dolphins in high relief support the handle; but the *pièce de résistance* is the fully three-dimensional crowing cockerel, craning forward eagerly with his beak open in full cry, who perches on (and then himself forms) the spout of the ewer. The utilitarian function of such sculpture may well have sufficed, from the standpoint of strict orthodoxy, to justify its otherwise impiously mimetic quality. Several similar but less ornate pieces testify to the popularity of this model. A new chapter in Umayyad metalwork was opened with the discovery in 1985, at the ancient site of al-Fudain, of a square bronze brazier on wheels. At each corner stands a naked girl, sculpted in the round and holding a bird; along the only complete side is a set of panels with erotic images and scenes of revelling. The piece bears close affinities to the sculptures of Khirbat al-Mafjar (see p. 32).

3

4

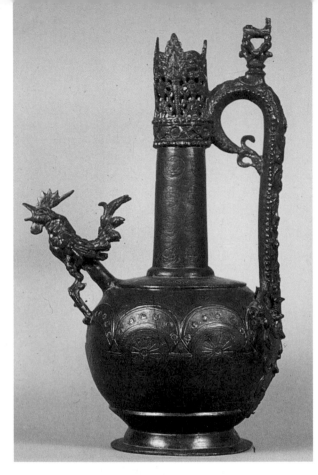

3 (*left*) Engraved base metal ewer
ascribed to the caliph Marwan II,
c. 750, found in Egypt. Its blind
arcades (here with solar rosettes)
recur in *sura* dividers in early
Qur'ans, unglazed clay lamps and
jars, and Umayyad architecture; they
may, like the cockerel, symbolize
light – and even boundaries or
protection. Sasanian and Hellenistic
elements combine with a
distinctively Islamic aesthetic of
all-over decoration.

4 (*below*) Private taste. Bronze and
iron brazier from al-Fudain, Jordan,
before 750. Probably cast by the lost-
wax method. Ceremonial braziers
occur on Assyrian reliefs, but the
griffins with outstretched wings
which form the feet recall Sasanian
metalwork, while the frank sensuality
of these pneumatic figures owes
much to Coptic art and the corner
figures recall the Syrian goddess
Atargatis.

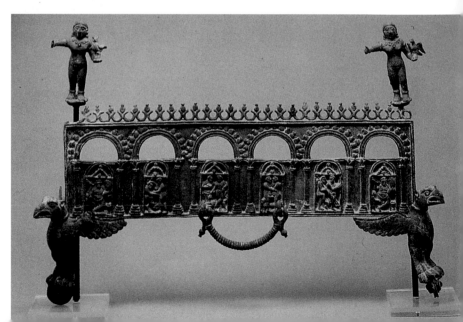

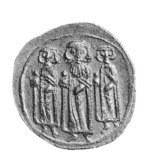
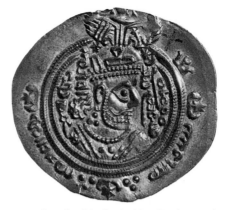

5 Economic interdependence. Money scarcely existed in the Arabia of Muhammad. For this reason, and to maintain economic stability, the Muslims long forbore to replace the existing coinage. They contented themselves with unobtrusive fine tuning, adding Arabic inscriptions and removing religious symbols.

Another significant expression of Umayyad art deserves brief mention here: the coinage of the period. To a quite remarkable degree this coinage mirrors and encapsulates the artistic tendencies traceable in the much more complex field of architecture. Umayyad coins faithfully reflect the long fallow period which preceded the serious involvement of Umayyad patrons with ambitious works of art. The significant innovations in coinage are almost exactly contemporary with the Dome of the Rock (completed in 691). As in architecture, so in coins the evolutionary trend is clear: an initially slavish dependence on classical models gives way to an increasing preference for themes and techniques inherited from the ancient Near East, and the resultant period of experiment produces some unexpected reworkings of old ideas in new contexts. Finally an originally and distinctively Islamic solution is fashioned from these heterogeneous elements. This entire process of acculturation and innovation was, it seems, telescoped into little more than a decade; perhaps the limited physical scope offered by coinage resulted in Islamic forms being introduced at an accelerated pace. The evolution of coins therefore epitomizes a process which in other media, notably architecture, occurred much more slowly and tentatively.

In Iraq, Persia and areas even further east, Sasanian silver coins were copied with virtually no alteration. The favourite design featured on the obverse a portrait head of Khusrau II, one of the last Sasanian rulers before the Islamic conquest of Persia, and on the reverse a fire altar with attendants. Even the name of the Sasanian ruler in the Persian Pahlavi characters was retained, as were the

Pahlavi mint marks, while the date was given successively in the two Sasanian calendars and then in the Islamic or Hijra reckoning. When the Muslim governor's name was given, it was also written in Pahlavi characters. The only distinctively Islamic feature was the addition of pious expressions in Kufic script, such as 'in the name of God' or 'praise be to God'. Thus presumably Persian die makers continued to work under the Muslims. These Arab-Sasanian coins, then, show the willingness of the Muslims to maintain the status quo.

In Syria, with the spectre of a weakened but unconquered Byzantine state just north of the border, the situation was different. Here the Arabs naturally encountered not Sasanian but Byzantine coinage. They were already familiar with this, since the words *dinar* and *dirham* (from *denarius* and *drachma* respectively) occur in the Qur'an. Despite the Greek derivation of its name, the *dirham* mentioned in the Qur'an, in the chapter of Joseph, is probably a Sasanian coin since this was by far the most widespread silver coin in the Near East – the dollar of late antiquity. The Sasanian economy was based on silver just as that of Byzantium was based on gold. Under the

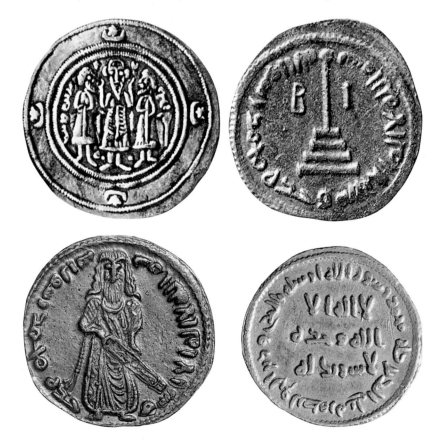

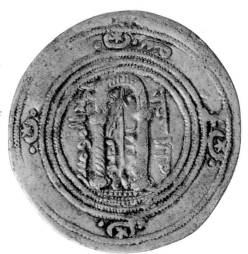

6 A language of symbols. Late 7th-century coins.
(a) Caliph (?) at prayer with attendants. Muslim adaptation of a standard Sasanian type. Silver *dirham* minted by Bishr b. Marwan, 692–3.
(b) Bar-less cross on altar steps. Syrian gold *dinar*, c. 692. The cross was modified, by letters, as here (RI: Rex Ishmaelorum, 'King of the Ismaelites'?), or by a circle, thus creating a Greek *phi*.
(c) Standing caliph with the Muslim creed around the rim. Syrian gold *dinar* minted by ʿAbd al-Malik, 696–7. A response to Byzantine gold issues.
(d) Aniconic epigraphic gold *dinar*, Syrian, 696–7. The forerunner of almost all later Muslim coinage.

7 God's caliph. Silver *dirham*, probably Damascus c. 692. The niche, common in classical and Christian art, here prefigures the *mihrab* and contains the Prophet's lance. The caliph is also metaphorically present through his title.

caliph ʿUmar I, for example, the Syrians paid their taxes in gold while the Iraqis paid theirs in silver. The Arabic copper coin, the *fals*, is the Greek *follis* in disguise; here, too, the Byzantine designs were copied. At first Byzantine types were used without any alteration; this was sound economic sense, for the Arabs had long been familiar with these coins in commerce. Indeed, a Syriac chronicle records that when in 661 the caliph Muʿawiya minted gold and silver 'the populace did not accept it as there was no cross on it'. Several well-known Byzantine types were copied, some of single standing imperial figures, others showing the emperor Heraclius and his two sons. Soon, however, tiny but momentous changes were introduced; on the reverse, the cross on a stepped podium lost its horizontal bar, the monogram denoting Christ was deprived of its initial letter and hence its meaning, and the crosses surmounting the imperial crowns were removed. The intention behind these changes was clearly to de-Christianize the coins, but to do so as unobtrusively as possible, retaining their Byzantine look.

By degrees the Muslims embarked on bolder innovations, replacing for example the Byzantine ruler with orb and sceptre by a recognizably Arab figure, bearded, wearing the traditional Bedouin headdress, and clasping a sword – a pose evocative of the caliph delivering, as his office demanded, the *khutba* or bidding prayer at the congregational mosque on Fridays. In other experimental issues this 'standing caliph' was replaced by other images with an even more unmistakably Islamic religious significance, such as the caliph

21

8 (*below*) Imagery of the afterlife. Dome of the Rock: polychrome and mother-of-pearl mosaic. Motifs of secondary importance in Byzantine tradition are now greatly enlarged and promoted to centre stage. Jewelled vases and celestial plants glorify the Rock and create an other-worldly ambience, employing new symbols of power and Paradise.

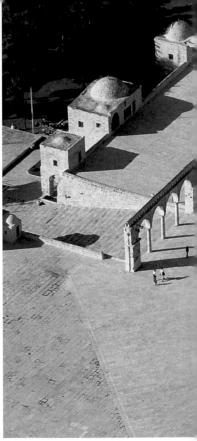

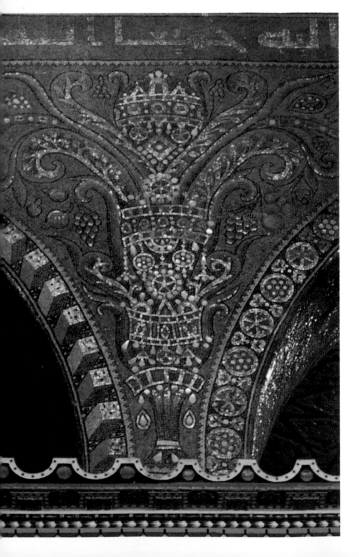

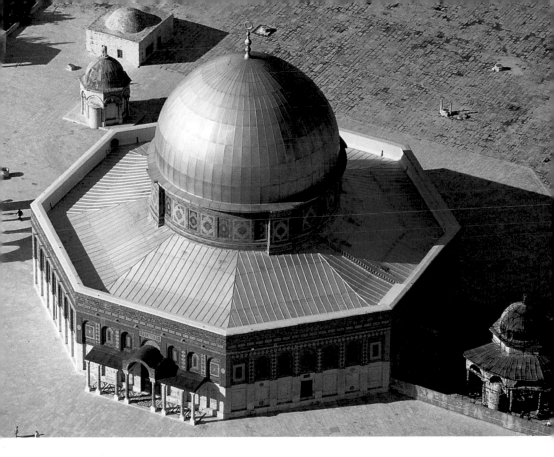

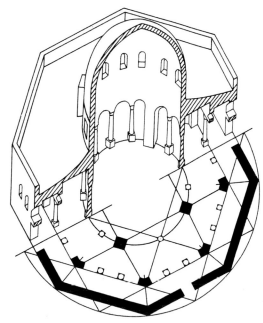

9 (*above*) Islam triumphant. Dome of
the Rock, Jerusalem, completed in 691.
Built on the platform formerly occupied
by Solomon's Temple, it reinterprets a
standard type of Byzantine centralized
commemorative building intended for
pilgrimage. Its central rock evokes
Arabian litholatry, associations of the
Creation and the Last Judgment, and
Muhammad's Night Journey to Heaven.
Tilework replaced the external mosaics
between 1545 and 1552.

10 (*right*) Dome of the Rock: three-
dimensional cutaway view revealing the
underlying geometry of the plan.

flanked by attendants and with his hands raised in prayer, or a *mihrab* enclosing the Prophet's lance. Finally, in a far-reaching currency reform which extended to most of the Islamic world and was carried out between 695 and 697, all figural images were expunged, to be replaced by the quintessential Islamic icon: Qur'anic epigraphy. In these coins, which were minted in their millions, inter-confessional rivalries took on a new and explicit edge. A direct attack on the Christian doctrines of the Incarnation and the Trinity can be seen in the words emblazoned on the field of these coins: 'There is no god but God; Muhammad is the Messenger of God. He has no associate; He does not beget, nor was He begotten.' Seldom in world history has the propaganda potential of coinage been so fully exploited.

Despite the unquestioned significance of Umayyad coins as historical documents, and the curiosity value of the minor arts datable to this period, there can be no doubt that the intrinsic nature of Umayyad art can be gauged only by means of the architecture of the time. Sadly, some of the finest Umayyad mosques have vanished, like the Mosque of the Prophet at Medina, constructed in 707 on the site of his house (see p. 15) as part of a far-sighted programme of major mosques at sites of key importance; in its time this must have rivalled the very finest of Umayyad religious monuments. Others have been totally rebuilt, like the Great Mosque of Aleppo, built by the caliph Sulaiman, or the Aqsa mosque in Jerusalem, possibly founded by al-Walid I. Nevertheless, two supreme masterpieces of religious architecture do survive. They show that, while early Islamic art was still in the thrall of the Byzantine and classical heritage, the Muslims were already developing their own visual language and were well able to use inherited forms for their own ends. These buildings confidently proclaimed that the new faith had come to stay in the formerly Christian strongholds of the Near East.

8–10 The Dome of the Rock in Jerusalem was completed after a turbulent decade in which the Umayyads briefly lost control of the Hijaz, and with it the holy cities of Mecca and Medina, and survived further serious challenges from religious opposition groups. This particular historical background has prompted some scholars to explain it as a victory monument and even as a place of worldwide Muslim pilgrimage to supplement, if not to supplant, Mecca itself. Yet its site and its form also suggest other interpretations. It stood on what was incontestably the prime plot of real estate in all Jerusalem – the vast high platform on which Solomon's Temple had rested, shunned by Jew and Christian alike since the destruction of that

Temple by Titus in AD 70. It marked an enigmatic outcrop of rock traditionally associated with the Creation itself and with the near-sacrifice of Isaac by Abraham, the prelude to God's covenant with man. Later Muslim belief identified this as the place of the Prophet's Ascent to Seven Heavens (his *mi'raj*) in the course of his miraculous Night Journey. In form the building is a domed octagon with a double ambulatory encircling the rock; in essence, then, a centralized structure of a type long familiar in Roman mausolea and Christian martyria. The choice of form probably stems from a desire to upstage the nearby domed church of the Holy Sepulchre, perhaps the most sacred shrine of Christianity, also built over a rock; the diameters of the two domes differ by only a centimetre. Nevertheless, the earlier building was confined within the urban fabric of Jerusalem, while the Dome of the Rock enjoyed, as it still does, a matchlessly uncluttered and highly visible site. In much the same way, the quintessentially Byzantine medium of wall mosaic was used to decorate the interior and exterior of the Dome of the Rock on a scale unparalleled in any surviving earlier Byzantine church. The pervasive motifs of jewelled plants, trees and chalices have been interpreted as references to Muslim victory, Solomon's Temple and Paradise itself, while the earliest epigraphic programme in Islamic architecture comprises lengthy Qur'anic quotations exhorting believers and attacking – as did contemporary coins – such Christian doctrines as the Trinity and the Incarnation.

The Great Mosque of Damascus (705–15) offers the natural 11–14 pendant to this great building – again, a royal foundation occupying the most public and hallowed site in its city. Here too its topographical dominance has clear political overtones. It too is of impressive size and splendour, and uses Qur'anic inscriptions (now unfortunately lost) for proselytizing purposes. The caliph al-Walid I purchased the entire site, comprising the walled enclosure of the temple of Jupiter Damascenus and the Christian church of St. John the Baptist within it, and forthwith demolished that church and every other structure within the walls. The revered model of the Prophet's house in Medina – the primordial mosque of Islam – as refined by slightly later mosques built in the garrison cities of Iraq and elsewhere, seems to have inspired much of what now followed. An open courtyard filled most of the rectangle created by this wholesale demolition, with the covered sanctuary of the mosque on its long south side. Yet this arrangement is not entirely Muslim. It boldly recast the standard components of a typical Christian basilica to

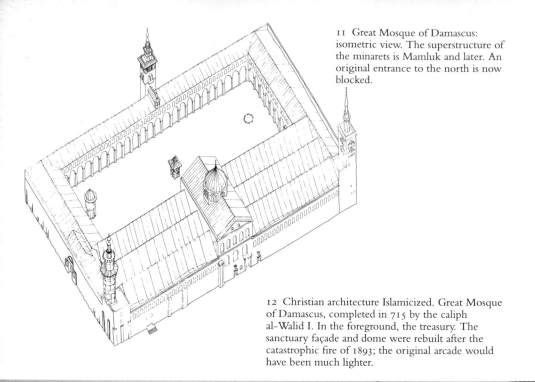

11 Great Mosque of Damascus: isometric view. The superstructure of the minarets is Mamluk and later. An original entrance to the north is now blocked.

12 Christian architecture Islamicized. Great Mosque of Damascus, completed in 715 by the caliph al-Walid I. In the foreground, the treasury. The sanctuary façade and dome were rebuilt after the catastrophic fire of 1893; the original arcade would have been much lighter.

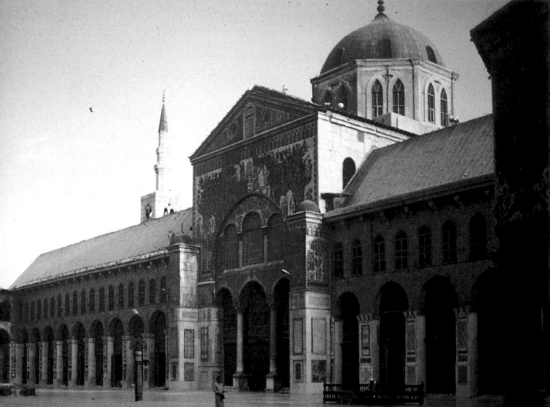

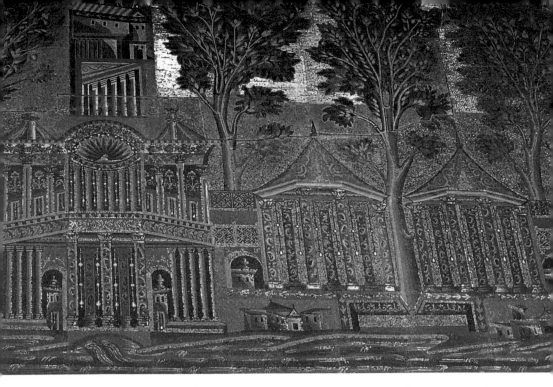

13, 14 (*above*) The new Rome? Great Mosque of Damascus, mosaic on west wall. This fantasy architecture uses – no doubt for political purposes – a Roman, not a Byzantine, vocabulary. (*below*) A world transfigured. Drawing of the landscape panorama in the Great Mosque, showing its full context.

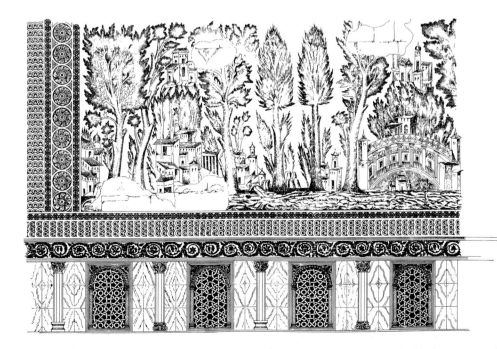

secure a new lateral emphasis in keeping with the needs of Islamic worship. The three aisles remained, but the direction of prayer ran at right angles across them and was marked in elevation by a towering domed gable which clove through the pitched roof to form a central transept. Its façade was a free variation on the standard west front of Syrian churches. This T-shaped partition of the sanctuary was destined to have a long posterity in the mosques of the western Islamic world (see p. 186).

Carved marble window grilles with elaborate geometrical patterns loosely inspired by late antique wall mosaics presage the enduring geometric bias of much Islamic ornament. Quartered marble, so cut that the veining of the stone continues from one slab to the next, formed dados in typical Byzantine fashion. Above them unfolded the glory of the mosque: hundreds of square metres of wall mosaic in the predominantly green and gold tonality already encountered in the Dome of the Rock mosaics. The caliph seems to have obtained artists and materials from Byzantium itself for this great work; certainly the technical standard of the mosaics is beyond reproach. Along the inner wall of the ancient enclosure, above a continuous golden vine-scroll (now lost) which functioned like a religious *cordon sanitaire* for the entire mosque, is unveiled a vast panoramic landscape. Along the banks of a river regularly punctuated by gigantic trees rises a fantasy architecture of villages and palaces in endless profusion. The link with Roman wall-paintings of the type found at Pompeii is unmistakable; but here the idea is put to new and unexpected use, for it strikes the dominant note in a huge monument of religious architecture. Some of these multi-storey structures also evoke South Arabian vernacular architecture. Human and animal figures are conspicuously absent, indicating – as at the Dome of the Rock – that a distaste for figural ornament in a religious context had already taken root. Despite the obvious success of these mosaics as pure decoration, many meanings have been proposed for them: topographical references to Damascus or to Syria in general, wish-fulfilling depictions of a world at peace under Islamic sway, or evocations of Paradise itself. Perhaps such ambiguity is intentional.

Clearly, these two buildings belong together as a considered Muslim response to the splendours of classical and Christian architecture around them, and an assertion of the power and presence of the new faith. The same message issues from the much more numerous desert establishments founded under royal patronage. The Umayyad princes – chafing under the moral and physical restraints of city life, apprehensive of the plague which recurrently menaced those cities, and perhaps atavistically drawn to desert life – moved restlessly from one of these desert residences to another. With a few exceptions – among them a *khan* or travellers' lodging place at Qasr al-Hair al-Gharbi and perhaps one at Qasr al-Hair al-Sharqi too, and a miniature city at ʿAnjar laid out on a Roman grid plan – these foundations fall into a well-defined category. Here, too, pre-Islamic forms are pressed into service.

Yet much more than mere imitation is involved. Where the Dome of the Rock sedulously copied Christian martyria and the Damascus mosque reworked the Christian basilica, the desert residences radically refashioned inherited forms. They combined two familiar building types whose origins are Roman, not Byzantine – and this association with the remoter but more prestigious *imperium* (rather than its still unconquered successor) is surely significant. The two building types in question – the *villa rustica* and the frontier fort – are intrinsically unrelated and are thus quite naturally segregated in their parent culture. This unawaited combination springs from the need, peculiar to this group of patrons, to integrate two essentially dissimilar functions. These residences served at once as the nerve centre of a working agricultural estate, in which the caliph was – so to speak – lord of the manor, and as outward symbols of conspicuous consumption and political power. The shell of the Roman frontier

15

15 Roman authority. Qasr al-Hair al-Sharqi, main gate of caravansarai or palace(?), *c.* 728. The projecting towers, arcuated lintel and alternation of stone and brick are all Roman; the central machicolation copies local models.

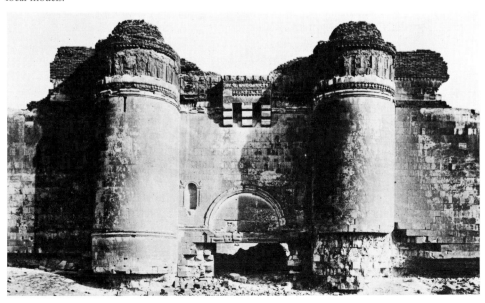

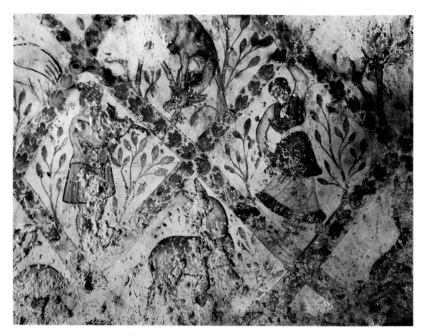

16 Rustic idyll. Qusair ʿAmra, hunting lodge and bathing establishment, early 8th century. Vault fresco with human and animal figures in a lozenge pattern adapted from classical floor mosaics.

fort, complete with salient gateway, corner towers, battlements, and even its favoured Roman dimensions, was retained. But now it was shorn of virtually all its functioning defensive devices, and contained both luxury royal apartments and service quarters grouped in two stories around a central courtyard. Qasr al-Hair al-Gharbi, Usais and Khirbat al-Minya all attest this type.

A rather different kind of establishment is represented by a pair of
16 sites north-east of ʿAmman in the Jordanian desert – Qusair ʿAmra and Hammam al-Sarakh. These also make free with a classical building type – in this case, the bath. In approved Roman fashion, cold, warm and hot rooms, all variously vaulted, succeed each other. The novelty lies in adding a ceremonial vaulted hall, complete with royal niche, to this humble ensemble and thereby exalting it to a new dignity. Qusair ʿAmra is especially notable for its matchless series of wall-paintings, the most extensive sequence of true frescoes to have survived from the late antique and early medieval world. Shot through with techniques and iconographical allusions of classical origin, they celebrate the pleasures of wine, women and song – to

30

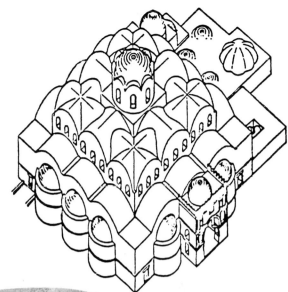

17 Concert hall? Khirbat al-Mafjar, bath hall, c. 740. The 21 vaulted spaces gave this chamber a magnificent acoustic; its patron, al-Walid II, loved to hear performances of poetry and music. The cross-in-square format and the vaulting system are taken directly from Byzantine church architecture; some parody may be intended.

18 The Umayyad world view. Khirbat al-Mafjar, mosaic in *diwan* (retiring room) of palace, c. 740. A hunting scene linked to late antique floor mosaics by theme and technique alike is transformed into a powerful allegory of a world divided between Muslim and infidel. Here presumably sat the caliph, dispensing justice: reward on his right, punishment on his left.

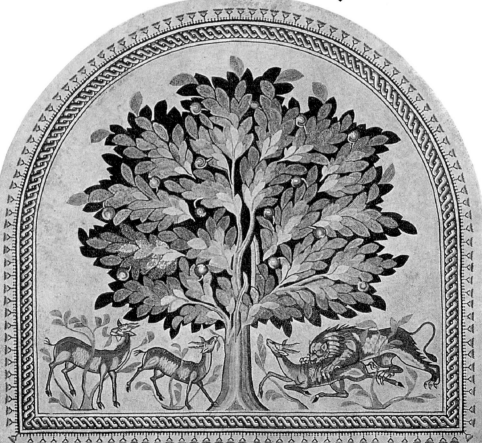

say nothing of the dance, the bath and the hunt – in a remarkably uninhibited idiom. Among several images in a more serious vein, some of them with Solomonic echoes as at Khirbat al-Mafjar (see below), a scene of six kings in submissive pose, identified by inscriptions as the monarchs of the earth, is especially notable. It symbolizes the entry of the Umayyads into the exclusive club of world leaders, and implies the dominant role of their dynasty in that club. The epicurean lifestyle conjured up by the main body of frescoes has to be seen within the context of this overt bid for imperial status. Thus political concerns infiltrate even the carefree atmosphere of this remote hunting lodge, to which the anonymous prince occasionally repaired for a few days of recreation – there was no provision for him to live at this site permanently.

17, 18   At the very end of the Umayyad period, in response to the increasingly extravagant ambitions of the playboy caliph al-Walid II, greatly enlarged multi-functional palaces were built. Khirbat al-Mafjar (unfinished; before 743) is a free variation on the loosely planned agglomeration of discrete units found in the Roman and Byzantine palaces of Tivoli, Piazza Armerina and Constantinople. Here, in the fertile valley of Jericho, and linked by little more than their proximity within an enclosing wall, are disposed a palace, a mosque, an underground bath with shower, a courtyard with an imposing central *tholos* (a circular colonnaded structure) over a fountain, and finally the jewel of the site – a huge domed and vaulted bath hall, a precocious forerunner of the Byzantine cross-in-square church. A peerless array of thirty-nine adjoining panels together create the largest single floor mosaic to survive from the medieval or indeed the ancient world, and provide a fitting match for the spatial subtleties of the elevation. Other amenities include a bathing pool, a plunge bath which held wine, a luxurious royal retiring-room perhaps used for private audiences, for banqueting or as a tribunal, and finally a splendidly appointed latrine designed to accommodate some thirty-three visitors at a time. Fresco and tempera paintings and, above all, stucco carving of unexampled vigour and resource complemented the splendours of the architecture and floor mosaic. The sculptures of athletes and serving girls in particular seem to epitomize the *joie de vivre* which the entire establishment exudes.

19, 20   Mshatta is altogether more sober, not to say gloomy. Its size – 144 m (472 ft) per side – is unprecedented among Umayyad palaces and greatly accentuates its sombre, dominating impact. Though it was never finished, enough survives to reveal the basic principle of its

19 Totalitarian architecture.
Ground plan of the palace of
Mshatta, Jordan, c. 744. The side
tracts are a speculative
reconstruction.

20 A petrified textile. Filigree
ornament is at odds with the
fortified air of the Mshatta palace
façade. Solar rosettes – a Sasanian
theme – stand proud of a thicket
of classical vine-scroll ornament
compartmentalized by a zigzag
moulding adapted from Christian
Syrian architecture.

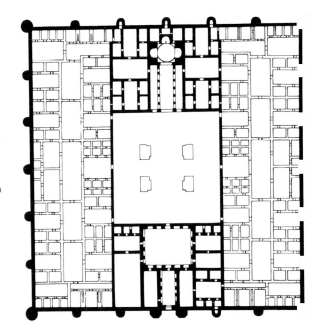

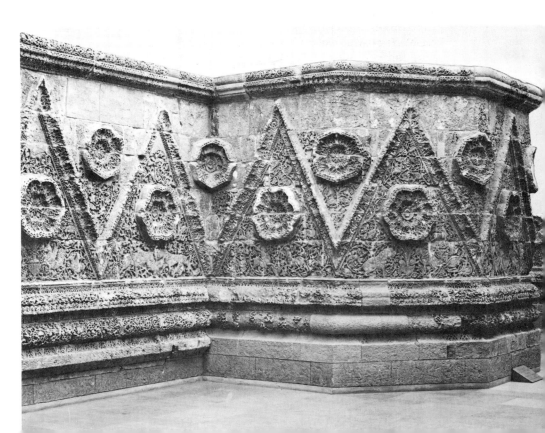

layout – a sequential subdivision into three parts on an ever-diminishing scale. An iron logic governs the working out of this scheme. While the caliph's own quarters, at the far end of the central tract, were no doubt as lavishly appointed as their counterparts in other Umayyad palaces, they are not enough to explain the overwhelming scale of the ensemble; indeed, they are sufficiently small to underline the fact that this was no mere pleasure palace. The key to the building, therefore, must lie in the side tracts, which were scarcely begun when work on the whole complex was abruptly stopped. Their huge size suggests that Mshatta, unlike the other Umayyad residences, was intended to accommodate large numbers of people – perhaps the entire Umayyad court complete with administration and bodyguard, or even pilgrims returning from the *hajj*, the pilgrimage to Mecca, though this is less likely since it would happen only once a year. If Mshatta really was a palace city it would be the natural precursor to the Round City of Baghdad, built barely a generation later (see pp. 40–1). Whatever its function, there can be no doubt that Mshatta draws inspiration from the tradition which produced Diocletian's palace at Split, itself no villa but the apotheosis of the *castrum* or Roman military camp. Once again, then, the source is Roman rather than Byzantine. Yet Mshatta is no mere copy. Its tightly regimented square design is subtly orchestrated to assert the absolute power of the monarch; the language of military architecture is made to serve the ends of political propaganda. Not even the celebrated carved façade which extends along the outer face of the central or royal tract, and that tract only, can mask this grim political message.

What conclusions as to the nature of Umayyad art can be drawn from the material surveyed in this chapter? Three consistent characteristics can be isolated: it is eclectic, experimental and propagandist. The eclecticism is easily explained. The fact that Umayyad art developed in Syria meant that it was open to the influence not only of the local school of late antique art but also to the art of contemporary metropolitan Byzantium, Coptic Egypt and Armenia, and of course imperial Rome, whose monuments were ubiquitous. Borrowings from the East – Mesopotamia, Sasanian Iran, Central Asia, even India – waxed as classical influences waned in response to the increasingly definitive alignment of the Umayyad state towards its eastern territories. Given the relatively primitive stage of artistic expression which characterized much of the Arabian peninsula in pre-Islamic times, there was no question of the Umayyads importing their own ready-made indigenous Arabian art into Syria. Thus they

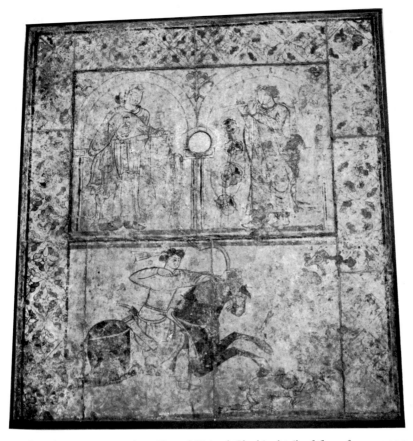

21 Conspicuous consumption. Qasr al-Hair al-Gharbi, detail of floor fresco, *c.* 725. Regimented and abstracted floral rosettes frame three scenes: a beribboned prince hunting gazelles, using stirrups and a compound bow; a flautist and lutanist; and a groom in a game park (not shown). All this reflects Sasanian rock reliefs and silverware, with their iconography of pleasure, and the increasingly Eastern orientation of Umayyad art.

had perforce to adopt the initially alien styles of the people they had conquered. Their practice of conscripting labour from provinces outside Syria ensured the meeting of widely divergent styles.

This helps to account for the second hallmark of Umayyad art – its experimental nature. Virtually limitless funds were set aside for architectural projects; and the speed with which they were completed shows that large teams of workmen laboured side by side. Naturally they learned from, and competed with, each other. It is thus scarcely surprising that, in the heady atmosphere created by a continuous building spree, and in response to the urgings of patrons who delighted in all-over decoration, the sense of restraint integral to classical art and its descendants was soon thrown off. Experiment became the watchword. It has its serious side, as shown in the austere geometric wall-paintings of Hisn Maslama, an Umayyad residence and settlement on the Euphrates in Syria. But in general one is struck by the infectious gusto of Umayyad decorative art, especially its figural stucco and painting, where the effect is heightened by bold, even garish, colours. Unshackled by convention, open-minded, endlessly inventive, artists delighted to turn old ideas to new account, equally ready to trivialize important motifs by dwarfing them and to inflate essentially minor themes so as to lend them an unexpected significance. Umayyad artists were far less inhibited than their contemporary counterparts elsewhere in the Mediterranean world. Hence they freely combined themes and media which tradition had hitherto kept apart; at Mshatta, for example, brick vaults of Sasanian type are found a few feet away from a classically-inspired triple-arched entrance in cut stone. Transpositions are equally common: cornice designs are used for plinths, epigraphy overruns both capital and shaft of a column and patterns normally created by quartered marble are imitated in plaster. In this high-spirited and often vulgar art, parody is never far away.

Yet alongside this robustness, this often wayward originality, Umayyad art consistently strikes a more serious note. Virtually all the significant buildings to survive were the result of royal patronage, and their political and proclamatory dimension cannot be ignored. Sometimes, as in the references to Paradise in the lost inscriptions of the Damascus mosaics, or in the frontal attacks on Christianity in the inscriptions of the Dome of the Rock and later Umayyad coinage, the message is religious. More often it is political, asserting – as in the ground plan of Mshatta – the lonely pre-eminence of the caliph, or – as in the floor frescoes of Qasr al-Hair al-Gharbi – Umayyad dominance over east and west alike. The apse mosaic in the *diwan* at Khirbat al-Mafjar goes further still in its unmistakable warning of the sudden death which awaits the enemies of Islam. It is peculiarly fitting in this context that it should be Umayyad Syria, not Rome or Byzantium, that can claim the most extensive programme of wall mosaics and the largest single floor mosaic to survive from ancient or medieval times. From ʿAbd al-Malik onwards, the masters of the new Arab *imperium* needed no instruction in the prestige value of such glamorous decoration.

21

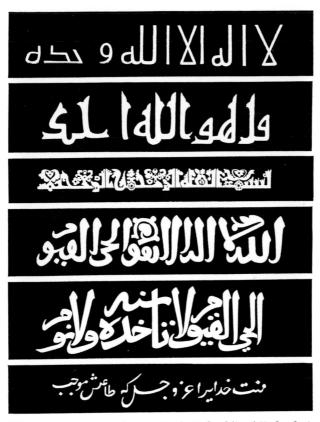

22 Types of Islamic writing (*top to bottom*): simple Kufic; foliated Kufic; floriated Kufic; *naskhi*; *thulth*; and *nasta'liq*.

The historical and geographical setting of Umayyad art made it inevitable that some of the directions it took turned out to be dead ends. Such classical or Byzantine borrowings as figural sculpture and wall mosaic, for example, struck few chords in later Islamic craftsmen. Yet it was the Umayyad period which integrated the classical tradition into Islamic art, which devised some of the basic types of mosque and palace destined to recur repeatedly in later generations, which established the sovereign importance of applied ornament – geometric, floral and epigraphic – in Islamic art, and finally which showed that a distinctive new style could be welded together from the most disparate elements. In so doing it moulded the future development of Islamic art.

37

CHAPTER TWO

The ʿAbbasids

The Umayyad ruling class had been a tiny Arab minority, maintained in power only by its military strength and riven internally by religious and tribal disputes which hastened its downfall. Tolerance of other religions and dependence on *mawali,* non-Arabs who had turned Muslim, were therefore political necessities. Victimized by illegal taxation, reduced status in the army and the racialist scorn of the Arabs, the *mawali* manifested their social and economic grievances by participating in a series of uprisings that in 749 culminated in a brilliantly orchestrated revolution that toppled Umayyad power and championed the cause of those descended from the Prophet's uncle, al-ʿAbbas. The new ʿAbbasid dynasty vaunted these blood links with Muhammad and claimed to usher in the true Islam based on universal brotherhood irrespective of race.

Politically, the change of dynasty marked the eclipse of Syria and a consequent weakening of Greek influence in the burgeoning Islamic culture. It also signalled the end of purely Arab dominion. The foundation of a new capital, Baghdad, at the eastern extremity of the Arab-speaking world, epitomized this process. Its site near two major rivers suitable for sea-going traffic – the Tigris and Euphrates – made Baghdad a much greater mart than Damascus had ever been, and its huge volume of trade opened it to very diverse influences, from China to black Africa. Such trade benefited from the adoption of Arabic as a lingua franca throughout the empire. Nearby, there still stood the palace of Ctesiphon, the Sasanian (ancient Persian) capital whose legendary splendours were now arrogated to Baghdad. Persian costume became fashionable at the ʿAbbasid court, the Persian New Year was celebrated and Baghdad became an intellectual centre where the philosophical and scientific heritage of the ancient world was to be translated into Arabic, the prime language of culture as of religion, and thence transmitted via Muslim Spain throughout Europe. Such features of Sasanian government as the court executioner, the intelligence service and the formal periodic review of the army were now introduced. The new Persianized administrative system hinged on the vizier, a post which was often hereditary and gradually came to erode the caliph's power. But in the first century of 'Abbasid rule that power was absolute, as the chilling anecdotes of contemporary chronicles testify. To the Western world, the figure of Harun al-Rashid – who sent his contemporary Charlemagne an elephant – has always symbolized the oriental potentate, and it is the golden prime of eighth-century Baghdad that is celebrated in the *Arabian Nights*. There can be no doubt of the immense cultural superiority of the Muslim East over western Europe at this time. Court life attained an unequalled peak of sophistication and luxury in manners, costume, food and entertainment.

This gilded world was underpinned by a complex financial machine to which capital investment, liquidity and long-term credits were familiar concepts. As late as the eleventh century a Saljuq vizier could pay a boatman on the Oxus with a draft cashable in Damascus. Wars of conquest had now ceased, along with their attendant booty, but the resultant Pax Islamica allowed the collection of revenue and the expansion of trade to proceed smoothly. Perhaps the major distinguishing feature of the early 'Abbasid empire was thus the immense wealth that it commanded. But this idyll was short-lived. Squabbles over the succession pinpointed much deeper rifts, for example between Arab and Persian, and between the various religious groupings. Gradually the extremities of the empire – in Spain, North Africa, Central Asia and Afghanistan – gained autonomy. Iran in particular saw a blossoming of national sentiment which found expression in literary controversies with the Arabs, in heterodox religious movements and – under the Samanid dynasty in particular (819–1005) – in a revival of pre-Islamic Persian culture. Meanwhile, in Baghdad the caliphs' increasing reliance on slave troops of Turkish stock caused so much local unrest that in 836 they moved their capital northwards to Samarra, a move which led to their eventual domination by these Praetorian guards. This situation was formalized in 945 when the Persian Buyid dynasty, whose Shi'ite rulers functioned as mayors of the palace, dealt caliphal prestige a catastrophic blow by assuming direct control of the state. Nevertheless, a cosmopolitan Islamic civilization had been made possible by a basic unity of language, faith and religious institutions which exists in large measure to this day, transcending ethnicity and diverse political systems. It was only after 945 that the political divisions of the Islamic world between east and west began to take final shape.

The shift in the centre of gravity from Damascus to Baghdad involved not merely a geographical adjustment of five hundred miles. It had potent repercussions in politics, culture and art. Baghdad became, in a way that Damascus had not, an Islamic Rome. It absorbed ideas, artefacts, and influences from the East – from the Iranian world, India, China and the Eurasian steppe, and then exported them, transformed, throughout the Islamic world, stamped with its own unique cachet and glamour. Nine-bay mosques in Afghanistan and Spain, Baghdadi textiles laboriously copied in Andalusia, even down to the inscription identifying the piece as 'made in Baghdad', Iraqi stucco forms in Egypt and Central Asia – all attest the unchallenged cultural dominance of Baghdad. The cumulative gravitational pull exerted by the eastern territories broke the grip of Mediterranean culture, and specifically of Graeco-Roman classicism and its Byzantine Christian descendant, on Islamic art. Classical forms can still be dimly discerned on occasion – the triumphal arch underlies the portals of 'Abbasid palaces, and all three styles of Samarran stucco are foreshadowed in early Byzantine art – but they have undergone a sea-change. New contexts and new functions transform them.

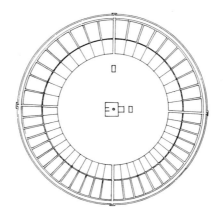

23 The caliph as cosmocrator. Round City of Baghdad, 762: reconstruction drawing. The 9th-century historian al-Ya'qubi calls Iraq 'the navel of the earth' and Baghdad 'the centre of Iraq'; at its heart was the caliph's palace.

In architecture, the process of change is exemplified in the Round City of Baghdad, founded in 762. This concentric circular design was probably derived from such Sasanian models as Firuzabad, Darabjird and Merv. Housing for the citizens occupied the outer perimeter while the caliph's palace, oriented to the four points of the

40

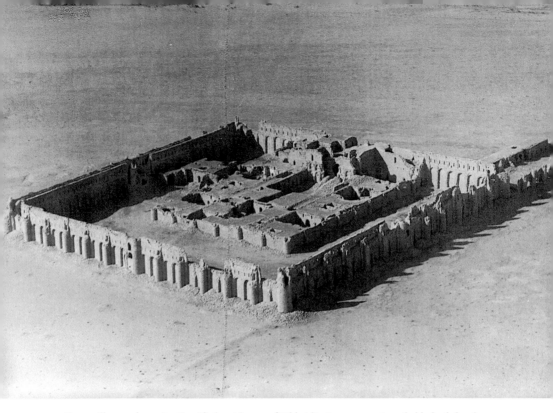

24 From villa to palace-city. Fortified residence of Ukhaidir, Iraq, *c.* 775–6, probably built by the governor of Kufa, ʿIsa b. Musa. Desert now surrounds it, but extensive traces of cultivation explain its name of 'the little green one'. It betrays a typically ʿAbbasid obsession with security and ceremonial; its design looks both to Syrian and Iranian traditions for inspiration.

compass and dwarfing the Friday mosque beside it – Caesar took precedence to God here – was located at the dead centre of the city and girdled by a largely empty precinct. This powerful symbol of cosmic dominion and royal absolutism owed little to the Graeco-Roman world but had a long pedigree in the ancient Near East. All this splendour has left not a wrack behind.

For surviving ʿAbbasid architecture in Iraq one must turn to the palace of Ukhaidir, generally dated *c.* 775–6. Flamboyantly isolated, it evokes in equal measure the despotic and the pleasure-loving charac-ter of the dynasty. Despite the palace's gigantic size (175 × 169 m, 574 × 554 ft), its living quarters are cramped, thereby perpetuating Arab tradition; but its luxurious amenities and ceremonial aspect are strongly Persian in flavour, notably in the interplay of *iwan*s and

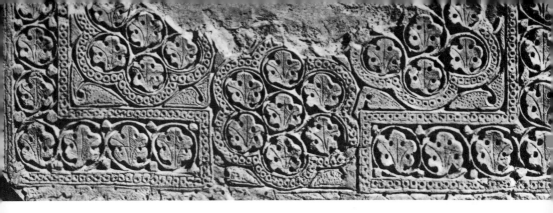

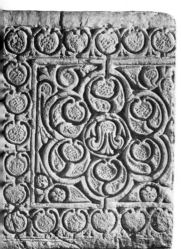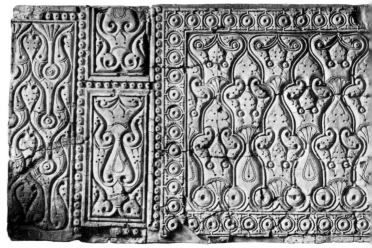

25, 26, 27 An Islamic aesthetic: all-over decoration. Samarra, stucco wall panels, 9th century. Three styles occur contemporaneously, despite differences of conception and technique. The first (*top*) uses a broadly naturalistic classical vocabulary of five-lobed vine leaves and tendrils arranged in rows or circles. The second (*above left*) flattens, abstracts and geometricizes this idiom. The third (*above right*), now moulded, not hand-carved, has a quilted and sculptural quality; its abstract, tactile forms are at once suggestive and ambivalent. In all three, equal attention is given to precise rendering of detail and to the overall design.

large courtyards, and in the use of ornamental brickwork, numerous small domes and ingenious vaults. Although this palace embodied such advanced military features as continuous machicolation and a portcullis, the difficulties of supply and an inherent inefficiency of design make it hard to imagine how it actually functioned. This concept of the palace-city was perpetuated in the following century at Samarra, with its numerous sprawling official residences laid out in

42

ribbon development and galvanized by remorselessly axial planning, for example by the use of the familiar three-tract design borrowed from Umayyad palaces (see p. 34). Proportional ratios (often 3:2) and strict axiality hold these structures together. Inferior building materials − principally mud-brick − are disguised by lavish revetments, and less important wall surface were covered at top speed with stucco. These palaces were rendered independent of the outside world by integrating gardens, domestic housing, military and administrative quarters and royal compound within a single but vast walled enclosure.

It was at Samarra that Islamic art came of age, and from that centre it spread virtually throughout the entire Muslim world, also influencing local Jewish and Christian art. The new aesthetic is perhaps best expressed by the wall decoration most fashionable in Samarra in 25−27 palaces and houses alike: polychrome painted stucco, both carved and moulded. Three major styles have been isolated: their chronological order is disputed, but their roots in the transformation of classical naturalism and in the two-dimensionality of early Byzantine art is plain. In the first, the surface is divided into polygonal compartments, with borders of pearl roundels. Each compartment is filled with vine stems bearing lobed leaves or with fancifully curved vegetal elements too stylized to equate with any actual plant. In the second style, this tendency is accentuated to the point where recognizably natural forms disappear. The borders become plain and the compartments themselves more varied. The Chinese motif of *yin* and *yang* appears frequently. Finally, in the third style, the decoration is not painstakingly carved by hand but is rapidly applied by moulds in a rigorously abstract bevelled style capable (like wallpaper) of indefinite extension. The motifs themselves are more loosely and flowingly arranged, and are more varied − spirals, lobed designs, bottle-shaped forms and other motifs no longer dependent on vegetal life. This style established itself rapidly and was still full of life five centuries later. The labour-saving properties of the moulded bevelled style were ideally suited to the mushroom growth of Samarra, and the humble mud-brick of which even the palaces were mostly built was cheaply and effectively disguised by this mass-produced decoration. Its abstraction and its even patterning fitted it for any number of architectural contexts − walls, columns, arches, window grilles − and the 'Samarran style', especially in the bevelled technique, soon penetrated the so-called 'minor arts' too.

The Samarran palaces show how the secluded, relatively small-scale splendours of the classically-inspired Umayyad desert residences

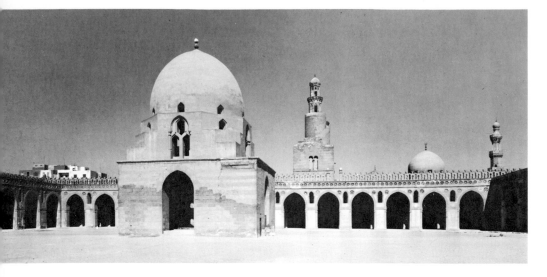

28 Courtyard of mosque of Ibn Tulun, Cairo, 876–9 (the foreground dome dates from 1296). Its essence is Iraqi: outer enclosure, brick construction, piers with engaged columns, crenellations, stucco ornament and minaret. The pointed arch serves as a leitmotif. The mosque was connected by a broad road to its patron's palace.

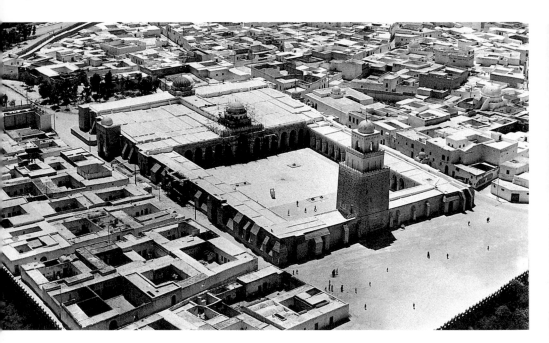

29 The mosque in its urban setting. Great Mosque of Qairawan, Tunisia, mostly after 862, aerial view. The raised and domed central aisle owes something to the Damascus mosque, but the T-shaped plan of the sanctuary is already distinctively Maghribi, while the 2:3 proportional ratio and the huge axial minaret derive from 'Abbasid Iraq.

gave way to vast urban palaces, or rather palace-cities, conceived on the Perso-Sasanian model, where massive scale is the dominant factor. Gigantic scale also characterizes many of the major mosques (Samarra – the largest mosque in the world – and Abu Dulaf in Iraq; Ibn Tulun in Egypt; Tunis and Qairawan in western North Africa). Powerful bastions militarize the mosque, which can even be interpreted (as in the case of Qairawan) as an emblem of *jihad*. Nor is this the only symbolism at work. Recent research has revealed that certain columns looted from predominantly Christian buildings and reused in the Qairawan mosque were colour-coded and so placed that the red and blue columns respectively outlined in simplified form the ground plans of the Dome of the Rock and the Aqsa mosque, the major religious sanctuaries of Umayyad Greater Syria. Thus in the Tunisian capital worshippers could make a regular symbolic pilgrimage to some of the holiest spots in the Islamic world.

28

29

30 The interplay between metropolis and province. Hajji Piyada Mosque, Balkh, Afghanistan, probably 9th century. This diminutive nine-bayed multi-domed mosque without a courtyard may reflect a lost Iraqi prototype; certainly its abundant stucco decoration faithfully mirrors the idiom of Samarra. The stumpy piers have Sasanian antecedents.

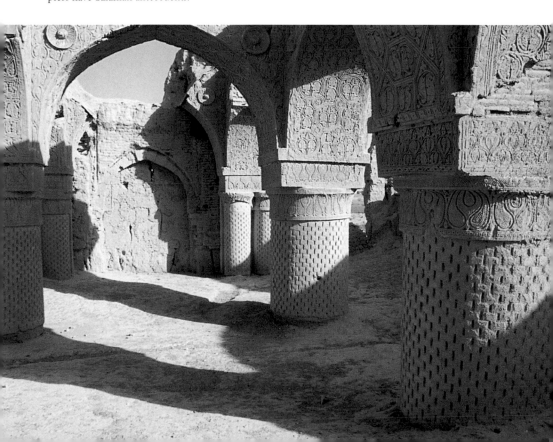

In some instances, these 'Abbasid mosques are surrounded by further enclosures which serve to mediate between sacred and profane space. Typically, they were built on the sites of new Islamic towns and thus catered for the whole population – hence their great size, which often brings monotony and repetition in its train. Monumental minarets proclaim the Islamic presence but they often assert an axial and *qibla* emphasis and serve as reminders of royal power. The forms of these minarets have a complex heritage; some derive from Graeco-Roman lighthouses, others (e.g. Harran) from Christian campaniles, and yet others from ancient Mesopotamian ziggurats or temple-towers. They demonstrate both the absorptive and the creative transforming power of 'Abbasid art. These building projects were huge; the historian al-Ya'qubi notes that over 100,000 men were recruited for the construction of Baghdad, and the city of Ja'fariya near Samarra, whose ruins cover 17 square kilometres (6.5 square miles), was completed in a single year (AD 859). Schemes of this magnitude could only have been organized by a corvée system (see p. 14). This system had a significant by-product: native craftsmen learnt the traditions of their imported fellow-workmen. Forms of varied foreign origin were at first juxtaposed and then, within the course of one or two generations, blended. This blend was in turn exported by the new generation throughout the Islamic world.

30 Hence the basic similarity of style which underlies provincial variations in early Islamic art.

31 The figural iconography of Samarran palaces such as Jausaq al-Khaqani attests the gradual consolidation and refinement of a cycle of princely pleasures – music, banqueting, hunting, wrestling, dancing and the like. These are to be interpreted not literally but as a sequence of coded references to a luxurious royal lifestyle that was summarized by the eleventh-century Persian poet Manuchihri in the rhyming jingle *sharab u rabab u kabab* – 'wine and music and meat'. This cycle was assiduously copied by 'Abbasid successor states or rival polities from Spain (Cordoba and Játiva) and Sicily (Cappella Palatina, Palermo, see pp. 68–72) to Armenia (the palace chapel at Aght'amar) and Afghanistan (the palaces of Lashkar-i Bazar). It occurs on marble troughs and ivory boxes, on brass or bronze buckets and ceremonial silks, on the exteriors and interiors of Christian churches, and of course in numerous palaces. The figural type popular in these paintings – characterized by pop-eyes, over-large heads, curling love locks, scalloped fringes and minuscule feet – had an equally wide dissemination.

46

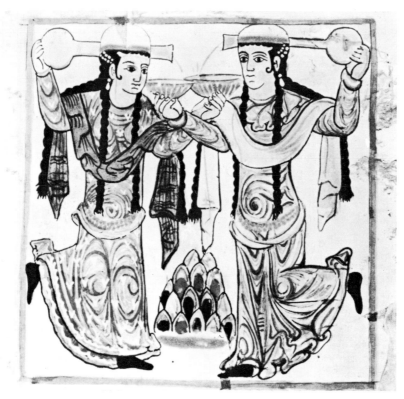

31 The courtly ethos. Restored wall painting from the Jausaq al-Khaqani palace, Samarra, 836–9. The early ʿAbbasid period saw the apogee of wine poetry (*khamriyya*); many such poems praise the cup-bearer. The kiss-curl, the scalloped fringe and the agitated hem find parallels in Central Asian art possibly brought to Iraq by Turkish slave troops.

The immense financial resources of the early ʿAbbasid empire generated luxury arts galore. Rock crystal workshops flourished in Basra. Gold and silver vessels with figural decoration including hunting scenes and dancing girls are described in the Bacchic poetry of the court laureate Abu Nuwas. Surviving wares, mostly in the form of plates, dishes, jugs and ewers – mainly of base metal alloy such as brass or bronze but sometimes silver, and occasionally even gold – display a somewhat degenerate Sasanian iconography of fabulous beasts, royal *diwan* scenes and princely hunters. Some important bronze sculptures (serving for example as aquamaniles or incense burners) depict birds and beasts of prey. Medieval texts mention

32

47

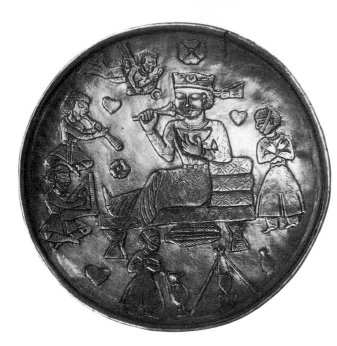

32 (*left*) The princely cycle. Silver-gilt dish, Iran, perhaps 9th century. Details such as the piled-up cushions, bench throne, musicians, putto, ribbons, and the courtier with hands crossed on his chest, his face masked so that his breath does not pollute the royal presence, derive from Sasanian art but are already coarsened.

33 (*below*) The word as benediction. *Ikat* cotton cloth with applied gilt decoration, Yemen, 10th century. The text reads 'Glory is from God. (?) In the name of God. And the blessing of God be upon Muhammad'. Such striped cottons (*burud*) were a Yemeni speciality; the Persian 11th-century traveller Nasir-i Khusrau wrote of San'a' that 'her striped coats, stuffs of silk and embroideries have the greatest reputation'.

presentation gold medals of prodigious size minted by the Buyids, but the surviving pieces are much smaller. Their iconography, however, is significant; it includes images of princes seated cross-legged and entertained by musicians, portrait busts of rulers wearing crowns of pseudo-Sasanian type, mounted horsemen and the ancient royal motif of the lion bringing down a bull. Some bear Pahlavi

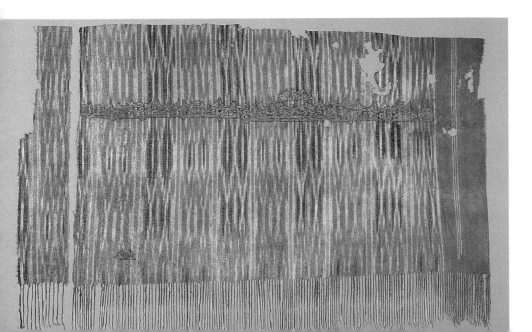

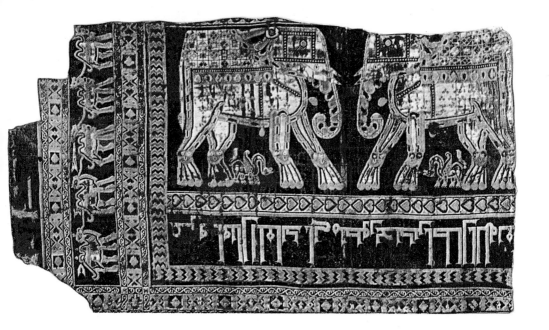

inscriptions and use the ancient Persian title *Shahanshah*, 'King of Kings'. All this indicates a radical departure from the aniconic norms of Muslim numismatics.

But the art form *par excellence* was textiles. Byzantine ambassadors marvelled at the 38,000 precious hangings displayed to them in a caliphal palace. Such textiles played a key role in architecture, for

33

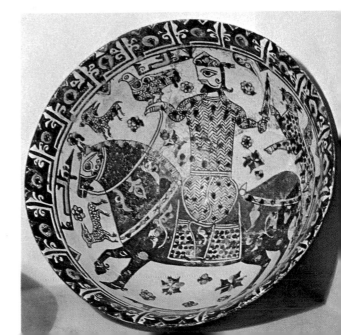

34 (*above*) The word as official livery. Part of the St Josse silk, Khurasan, before 961. The inscription wishes 'glory and prosperity to the *qa'id* Abu Mansur Bukhtegin, may God prolong (His favours to him?)'. The two small dragons crouching at the feet of the elephants evoke China, the camels wear Sasanian ribbons, and the patron is a Turk: a remarkable mixture of sources.

35 (*right*) *Haute vulgarisation.* Slip-painted bowl from Nishapur, Iran, 10th century. Sasanian silverware favoured hunting scenes; that theme is much reduced here, and barely makes sense, thanks to the rearing leopard, the falcon and the farrago of inscriptions, leaves, rosettes and animals that fill the field. But a distant echo of Sasanian majesty is discernible.

they were used not only as wall decoration which could be regularly changed and so transform the spaces thus hung, but also to partition rooms, to curtain off private spaces, and to bedeck key areas like entrances. They formed a crucial element in public ceremonies and parades. Above all, they were a form of liquidity thanks to their portability and their sometimes prodigious cash value. Copious literary references testify to the hundreds of different centres throughout the length and breadth of the Islamic world which specialized in given types of textiles and indicate that this was the most prestigious art form of the time.

Palace and other government-run workshops known as *tiraz* produced textiles (also called *tiraz*) bearing laudatory or benedictory inscriptions with the name of the ruling caliph, making the courtiers who wore them walking advertisements for their monarch – an Islamic form of livery. Other silks were pictorial, like the so-called St Josse silk woven in Khurasan before 960 for the Samanid *amir* Abu Mansur Bukhtegin. Affronted elephants whose aberrant form betrays Chinese rather than Indian influence take up the field, while Bactrian camels and cockerels pace the borders, supplemented by a benedictory Kufic inscription in lapidary style. This silk is typical of many formal pictorial silks from Sasanian and Islamic Iran, Iraq, Syria and Byzantium which found their way westward and were preserved in church treasuries because they were used to wrap relics. Foremost among the themes of such Islamic pieces were heraldic images in roundels, among which lions and eagles took pride of place. Moulded cameo glass with relief inscriptions and lustre painting typified the technical advances achieved by Islamic craftsmen. Nearly all the objects in precious materials such as ebony, ivory and alabaster described in medieval texts have vanished, but they must be borne in mind in reconstructing the ambience of ʿAbbasid art. Thus it is all the more regrettable that the fullest sequence of any imperial ʿAbbasid art form should survive in the humblest material of all – pottery – which thereby, *faute de mieux*, takes on a defining role in modern perceptions of ʿAbbasid art. This assuredly leads to a grossly distorted view of what courtly ʿAbbasid art was really like, yet this material does provide a paradigm of the radical innovation which characterized this period.

Indeed, the ninth century sees the beginning of the long and distinguished tradition of Muslim ceramics. Strangely enough, there is no feeling of hesitation in these early styles; the technique and decoration are equally assured, and several major varieties of ceramics are encountered in this first century. This immediate maturity is puzzling. It is true that the rather earlier Nabatean painted pottery of the Levant does have some striking connections with 'Abbasid wares (as in the use of the 'peacock's eye' motif), and that lead-glazed wares had already been made in Egypt for a millennium. But the virtual absence of fine Umayyad pottery, together with the fact that glazed pottery – which accounts for most quality medieval ware – though known in ancient Egypt and Parthia, did not achieve the status of a fine art in the ancient world, underlines the lack of immediate precedents for these wares. The earliest Arab pottery, being simply for domestic use, continued this utilitarian bias and was sparsely decorated with simple incised or relief designs.

Under the 'Abbasids, pottery was suddenly promoted to an art form. Why? The impact of Chinese ceramics seems to have been the galvanizing factor. Ample literary references testify that pottery was imported in quantity from China, both overland through Persia – by the celebrated Silk Road – and by the sea route via India; and imported Chinese wares have been found in nearly all excavations on Islamic sites. In the early centuries of Islam, Chinese art had a peculiar cachet: Severus ibn al-Muqaffaʿ wrote 'The Chinese are a nation of artists but they have no other merits', while al-Baihaqi reports that the governor of Khurasan in eastern Iran sent the caliph Harun al-Rashid 'twenty pieces of Chinese imperial porcelain, the like of which had never been seen in a caliph's court before', together with two thousand other pieces of porcelain. The latter were no doubt the product of the Chinese export industry; as is usual in China, the finest pieces are the ones made for home consumption. In the field of ceramics, then, China was held to be supreme. There alone pottery had been cultivated for many centuries as a fine art. Given the prestige attached to Chinese wares, it would be natural for the 'Abbasids to supplement the always insufficient imports of choice pottery by establishing a local industry. Hence, perhaps, the sudden explosion of the ceramics industry in the ninth century. Theological prohibitions might also have contributed in slight measure, for various *hadith*s (sayings of the Prophet) condemn the use of gold and silver vessels. The development of pottery with a sheen imitating precious metals lends some credence to this view. Finally, the advent of Islam led to a much-reduced output in certain well-established media – notably sculpture – which depended on figural motifs. Perhaps the burgeoning quality-ceramic tradition was an attempt, conscious or not, to develop an alternative means of expression for

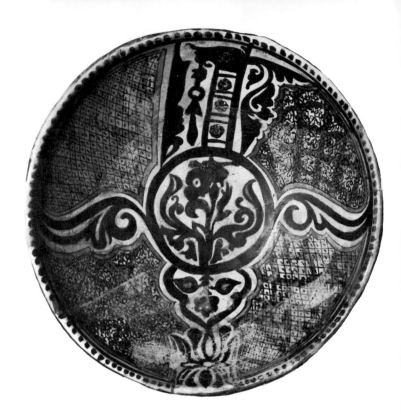

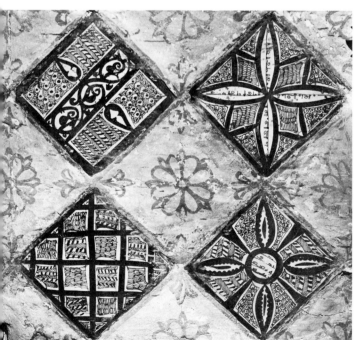

36 (*above*) The lore of the stars. Lustre bowl found in Samarra, 9th century. It depicts Cygnus (the swan), a fixed star from the constellations of the northern hemisphere. The subject–matter implies a cultivated patron. The bird has been transformed into a vegetal design; the busy hatched and squiggly background is typical of lustreware.

37 (*left*) Images of light. Great Mosque of Qairawan, *c.* 836: four of the 139 surviving monochrome and polychrome lustre tiles decorating the *mihrab*. Literary evidence indicates that a craftsman from Baghdad was partially responsible for them; perhaps the remainder were made locally. The *mihrab* itself and the *minbar* were also Baghdadi imports.

this type of subject matter. In all 'Abbasid pottery – whose secular bias requires emphasis – the intention of the potter is clearly to devise colourful and stimulating surface decoration. He was able to use figural motifs, often with a pronounced courtly flavour, as well as geometric designs, epigraphy and a whole range of vegetal orna-   36, 38 ment. With this *embarras de choix* in the field of decoration, it is not surprising that his interest is not focused on technical refinements of body or glaze or on the shape of the pottery itself.

Among apparent imitations of Chinese ware, the most common – perhaps because it was also the cheapest – is the so-called splashed ware that recalls the mottled decoration of certain Chinese ceramics of the contemporary T'ang period and also Liao wares (907–1125). The connection is, however, uncertain because T'ang mottled wares seem to have been reserved for funerary use. One must therefore reckon with the possibility of an independent invention on the part of Muslim potters, even though the parallels with Chinese pieces seem to be too close for coincidence. This lead-glazed ware is also known as 'egg and spinach' after its predominant colours; sometimes it was lightly incised. Chinese celadon, much prized because it was thought to shatter when poisoned food was placed in it, was also widely imitated. But Islamic potters were spurred above all to emulate white Chinese porcelain. Lack of suitable raw material

38 Poetry on pottery. Glazed lustre relief dish from Hira, Iraq, mid-9th century. The Kufic inscription is a couplet by Muhammad b. Bashir al-Khariji (d. 846): 'Do not abandon the hope, long though the quest may endure, That you will find ease of heart, if but to patience you cling.'

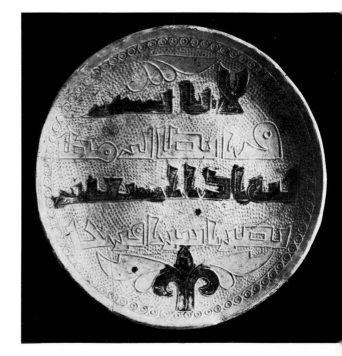

locally meant that the 'Abbasid potters could not reproduce its stone-hard body, but they copied this much-admired and coveted monochrome ware by applying an opaque white glaze to ordinary earthenware. Typically, they did not rest content with this, but began to decorate such tin-glazed ware, which was painted and glazed in one firing. In this technique, the colour is absorbed into the glaze and spreads like ink in blotting paper. This running of the glaze betrays a lack of technical expertise, a deficiency here turned to good account. But the potters were soon able to devise glazes that would not run and so allowed a controlled precision in the application of paint. Much more complex designs were therefore made possible. The Chinese emphasis on form, body, touch – even the sound a piece made when struck – was replaced, at least in part, by applied decoration not encountered in the prototype. This change of emphasis lays bare the profoundly different priorities of Muslim taste.

The major technical breakthrough in this period is the development of a difficult technique entirely new to ceramics (and to glass) – that of lustre. A fragment of Egyptian lustred glass datable as early as 772 suggests that the technique may even have been known in Umayyad times. In such pottery, sulphur and metallic oxides are combined with ochre and vinegar and the mixture is painted on to an already glazed vessel. It is then lightly fired in a reducing kiln in which the metal oxides diminish to an iridescent metallic sheen on the surface, reminiscent of the splendour of precious metals. Such democratization or vulgarization of more expensive art forms and materials became characteristic of Islamic art. The lustre process was difficult: the vessels were liable to overfire, underfire, or crack during the second firing. 'Abbasid lustre has been found as far afield as Samarqand, Sind, Egypt, Tunisia (where over one hundred lustre tiles decorate the *mihrab* of the Great Mosque of Qairawan) and Spain; presumably it was usually the pottery that was exported rather than the craftsmen. The commonest colours are brown and yellow, and at first decoration is extremely simple, consisting mainly of spots, squares and dashes. But after about 900, animal and human figures with a dotted background enclosing the central design become popular. These figures are often grotesquely, almost frighteningly, distorted; often they employ royal or magical themes.

Probably the outstanding achievement of Iranian potters at this time is the Samanid ware associated with Samarqand and Nishapur, though similar wares have been found at numerous other sites in Central Asia, Iran and Afghanistan. The hallmark of this slip-painted

37

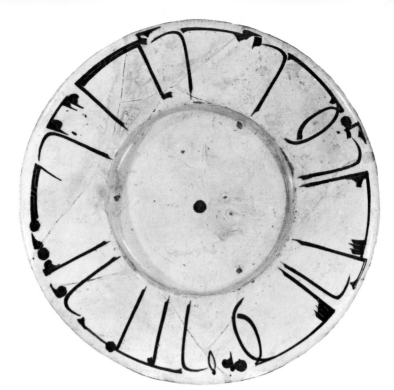

39 Restraint. Dish covered with white slip and painted with brown Kufic inscription; Samarqand, 9th–10th century. In the centre, the Chinese *tai-ki* motif. The text is in Arabic, not Persian (the language of daily life) and reads: 'Knowledge: its taste is bitter at first, but in the end sweeter than honey. Good health [to the owner].'

ware is its stylish, often virtuoso epigraphy, which unfolds in majestic 39 rhythm around the surface of the dishes. The inscriptions are all in Kufic, and this choice of hand itself imparts a certain formality to these pieces, implying that they were intended to be displayed as serious works of art. The numerous varieties of script encountered often point unambiguously to professional calligraphers. But the urge to decorate is at war with the desire to inform. These inscriptions share an almost wilful complexity, as if they were meant to elude ready decipherment. The oracular, gnomic quality of the aphorisms that they express is thus entirely appropriate, though many are of a Shi'ite tenor. As decorative ensembles, these wares are remarkable in their appreciation of void space as a positive factor of the design. Human figures are never found, and birds and animals occur only in severely stylized form. A comparable austerity usually restricts the colour range to cream and dark brown, purple or red, thereby heightening the starkness of the inscriptions. A clue to the origin of this decoration may be sought in Chinese Song ceramics and in contemporary Qur'ans. These dishes apparently offer the first examples in Islamic art of Arabic script being used as the major element in surface decoration, if one excepts coins, where the epigraphy has a mainly utilitarian function. In the stark simplicity of these inscriptions one may recognize at once a minimalist aesthetic and beauty of a highly intellectual order.

Other contemporary work at Nishapur did not share this cerebral quality. Of outstanding interest is a group of wares distinguished by sprawling, cluttered compositions and violent colour contrasts, which usually glory in a bright mustard-yellow. Here the designs are simplified almost to the limit of recognition, but they maintain the directness and vitality of an unsophisticated folk art. Birds, rosettes and scattered Arabic inscriptions that seem to call down a hail of blessings on the owner are all used as space-fillers. Sometimes the design is a bastard survival of the Sasanian royal iconography of the banqueting scene or the hunt, and astrological themes are also found. Such pottery belongs to the so-called 'ceramic underworld of Islam', a category represented by wares from numerous provincial centres. Thus, Sari may have been the centre of production for a type of ware closely akin to folk art in the primitive vigour and garish colouring of its stylized animal drawing. But the commonest category of provincial wares is the sgraffito type, so called after the technique of incising the design into the body before or after glazing. It is found

40 The word as icon. Qur'an leaf with *sura* heading in gold; parchment, perhaps 9th-century Iraq. Red dots indicate vowelling, thin black strokes (made with another pen?) diacritical marks. Spacing between individual letters, sequences and whole words can be very wide and thereby privilege certain syllables.

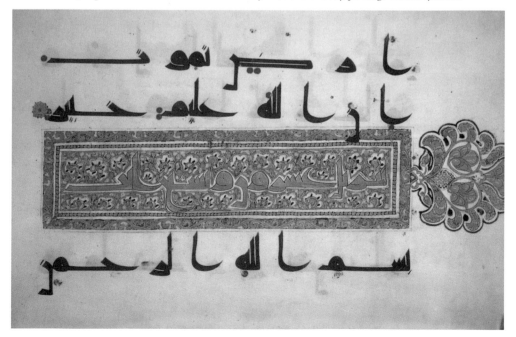

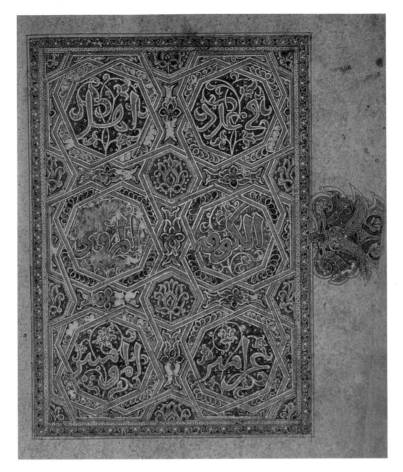

41 The power of the word. Carpet page from Qur'an of Ibn al-Bawwab, Baghdad, 1000–1. The *naskhi* text in interlaced polygons continues on the frontispiece and refers to the Qur'anic word count on the authority of the caliph ('Ali). 42 The book as a holy thing. Wooden cover inlaid in ivory for oblong Qur'an, Egypt, 10th century. In early Islamic art, arcades often denote a boundary or separation, even serving as an augury of Paradise. The solar disc acts as a metaphor of spiritual illumination.

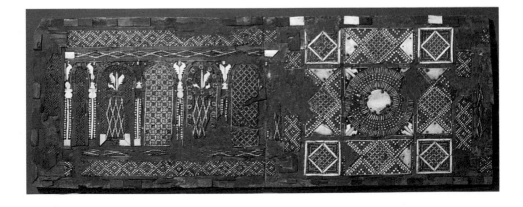

widely distributed throughout north-west Iran. Its decoration frequently apes metalwork, even to the use of the incised lines to prevent colours from running. A particular class of *champlevé* ware, in which the white slip is gouged away to form the design, is associated with the Garrus area in Kurdistan. These varied provincial schools were independent of influences from the court and from abroad, though reminiscences of Sasanian iconography were common. Their subject matter favours single figures of animals and monsters or bold abstract designs.

The other art form which has survived in substantial quantity is calligraphy. It is exercised above all in Qur'ans – the major illustrated secular manuscript of the period is a copy of al-Sufi's astronomical treatise (Bodleian Library, Oxford), dated 1009 and probably produced in Baghdad, with drawings of constellation images in mixed Central Asian and Samarran style. Under 'Abbasid patronage the somewhat haphazard penmanship of the early Hijazi Qur'ans, expressed in irregular letter forms, skewed lines of text, spasmodic illumination and a general indifference to visual effect, was replaced by a solemn discipline appropriate to holy writ and redolent of epigraphy on paper. Horizontal parchment sheets often accommodated no more than four lines of text, thus leading to prodigally expensive Qur'ans of thirty or even sixty volumes. The script would be so spaced, and with letter forms subject to such extremes of stylization, as to slow down recognition of the words themselves: an objective correlative to the awesome enigmas found in the text itself. A supple, flexible system of extension and contraction allowed calligraphers to balance words on a page with the utmost finesse and thus to create striking visual harmonies. Symmetries and asymmetries, echoes, repetitions, and a seemingly endless variety of patterns and rhythms abound. Clearly, therefore, the scribes had ample licence to experiment and were not constrained to limit themselves to a text block characterized by regular, even spacing.

A major benchmark of new developments is the Qur'an on paper which, according to its probably reliable colophon, was copied by Ibn al-Bawwab, the most renowned contemporary master, and written in the *naskhi* (cursive) script which he allegedly invented, in Baghdad in 1000–1 (Chester Beatty Library, Dublin). Its diminutive size cannot mar the well-nigh endlessly varied splendour of its ornamental palmettes, its frontispieces and finispieces conceived like the leaves of doors and structured with a ponderous, recondite rhythm around a theme of interlaced semicircles, perhaps intended to have

40

41, 42

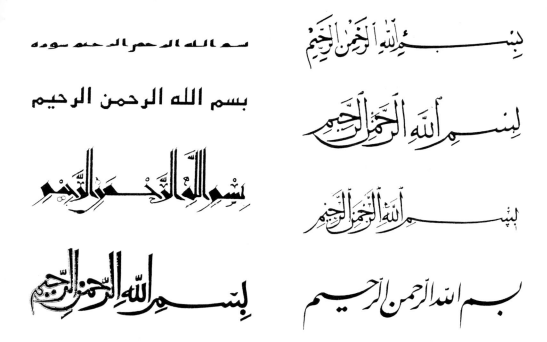

43 'In the name of God, the Merciful, the Compassionate'. Almost every *sura* in the Qur'an begins with this phrase, known as the *bismillah* from its opening three words. Often displayed by calligraphers, in popular belief it has special power as an amulet. Here it is executed in some major Qur'anic hands: (*left, from top*) early Kufic, square Kufic, eastern Kufic, *thulth*; (*right, from top*) *naskhi, muhaqqaq, rihani, ta'liq.*

an apotropaic effect. It should be noted that in manuscripts the so-called 'Kufic' types of script (named after the town of Kufa in Iraq) were restricted to Qur'ans, although they could be used for headings, captions and the like in other manuscripts. This style spread, it seems, throughout the 'Abbasid dominions with only minor local variations. It thus typifies the prestige and paramount authority enjoyed by the art of Baghdad: a fact of life epitomized by the courtier Ziryab, who imported the lifestyle of the Iraqi capital in food, language, clothing and art to far-off Cordoba, the capital of Umayyad Spain, in the tenth century (see p. 175).

In the 'Abbasid period Eastern – including Central Asian, Turkish and Chinese – motifs, techniques and themes begin to infiltrate Islamic art. The political and economic background for this is the shifting of the capital from Damascus to Baghdad, which brought with it a rush of Iranian ideas; the importation of Turkish soldiers who gradually usurped supreme power; and the rapid growth of

59

long-distance trade with lands to the east, both overland and by sea. Islamic art now largely severed its connections with the classical world, and turned its back on the Mediterranean. In architecture, Sasanian forms were dominant for city plans, palaces and mausolea. Baked brick, mud-brick and even stamped earth often replaced stone. Classical ornament of foliate inspiration became ever more abstract and this abstraction – which led, among other motifs, to the arabesque in its final form – became the basis of much later Islamic art. Such classical materials as carved stone and mosaic were largely rejected in favour of stucco, which was to become the decoration *par excellence* of eastern Islam. The unusually yielding quality of stucco made it an excellent testing ground for new techniques and designs. In certain fields such as Kufic Qurʾans and epigraphic pottery – and perhaps also lustreware – the achievements of the ʿAbbasid period were to remain unrivalled; but still more important was the full elaboration of the thematic cycle of court life begun under the Umayyads and destined to be eagerly taken up by later Islamic dynasties. Thus from the point of view of materials, techniques and subject matter, ʿAbbasid art was to offer a much richer quarry for later generations than Umayyad art. It is also to be found over an incomparably wider geographical area. Moreover, it still enjoyed the same advantage of a corvée system which, by making craftsmen mobile, disseminated the latest developments over a wide area. Within the empire, there were no frontiers, a fact which can be explained by a basic unity of faith and political institutions. The division of the Islamic world between East and West was not to become definitive until the Saljuq period.

CHAPTER THREE

The Fatimids

From the death of the Prophet onwards, a body of Muslim opinion held unswervingly – though with many internal divergences of opinion – that supreme power in the Islamic state could be vested solely in a member of the Prophet's own family. The first and obvious such candidate was Muhammad's cousin 'Ali, who by marrying the Prophet's daughter Fatima also became his son-in-law. 'Ali's claims to the caliphate were pressed by the so-called 'party of 'Ali' (*shi'at 'Ali* – whence the term Shi'ite), but after his assassination in 661 the caliphate passed to the Umayyad family. Thereafter, despite frequent and bloody Shi'ite insurrections (of which the most significant, historically speaking, was that of the Prophet's grandson al-Husain, who was killed at Karbala in 680), a pattern that lasted for centuries was established: no Shi'ite ruler wielded enough power to disturb the political status quo. Shi'ite principalities in the Yemen, the Caspian region and elsewhere were protected but also imprisoned by their remoteness.

All this changed with the advent of the Fatimids, who took their name (and claimed descent) from the Prophet's daughter, and who held the belief that the authentic line of *imam*s or rightful rulers had ceased with the death of Isma'il, the seventh Imam. This belief caused them to be dubbed Isma'ilis. The dynasty was founded by a certain 'Ubaidallah who proclaimed himself the Chosen One (*al-mahdi*) and from obscure beginnings in eastern Algeria took over the central Maghrib within a few years. In 921 he set the seal on his conquests by founding a city on the Tunisian coast which he named al-Mahdiya after himself. His successors consolidated their hold on the eastern Maghrib before turning their eyes further afield to Egypt. Eventually they conquered its capital, Fustat, and founded their own capital – al-Qahira, 'the victorious' – nearby, in 969. In so doing they hastened the dismemberment of the 'Abbasid state which had begun with the loss of Spain to the Umayyads of Cordoba in 756.

But the Fatimids were interested in more than merely winning their independence from Baghdad; they sought to supplant the 'Abbasids altogether and to establish a Shi'ite hegemony in the Islamic world. It was this grandiose aim which differentiated them so markedly from the numerous other (and minor) successor states which broke off allegiance to the caliphate of Baghdad in the course of the ninth and tenth centuries. The Fatimids sought to achieve their goal of pan-Islamic domination under the banner of Isma'ili Shi'ism not only by military expansion, especially into Syria and Arabia, but also on the ideological plane. Hence their creation of a corps of missionaries (*da'is*) who were sent throughout the orthodox Islamic world to preach their doctrines in secret. These Isma'ili doctrines offered hope to the disenfranchised and to political dissidents, while their mystical and esoteric flavour exerted a widespread appeal. Not surprisingly, some of the religious zeal of the Fatimids can be detected in their art, especially their architecture, and it has left its unmistakable imprint in over four thousand tombstones of the ninth and tenth centuries whose cumulative evidence suggests that Fatimid missionaries were active in the cemetery area of Fustat and that many of their sympathizers and converts were women (see p. 77). The same zeal found expression, but unfortunately only in an impermanent form, in the royal ceremonies and processions so characteristic of Fatimid court life. These celebrated, for example, the four Fridays of Ramadan, numerous Shi'ite holidays (especially the birthdays of the Prophet's family), the New Year, which coincided with the high-water mark of the Nile, the circumcisions of the royal children, and the Breaking of the Dike, which symbolized the beginning of the agricultural year.

From the art-historical point of view the importance of the Fatimids is due both to geography and chronology – for the art of this dynasty forms a bridge in time and space between east and west in the Muslim world, between the pervasive influence of first Umayyad and then 'Abbasid art and the rather different art of the eastern Islamic world which developed in the wake of the Saljuq invasions of the eleventh century. It was the Fatimids who dominated the southern Mediterranean world, with its millennial heritage of Hellenism, and whose contact with the Christian powers to the north brought fresh ideas into Islamic art. The metropolitan status of Cairo, probably the major Muslim city of the eleventh century, can only have accentuated this internationalism.

Discussion of the evolution and even to some extent the nature of Fatimid art – though not the architecture of the period – has been bedevilled by the extreme scarcity of datable (not to mention actually dated) objects. Only two ceramics, three rock crystals and two woodcarvings are securely datable. The great exception is the *tiraz* textile production of the period, but these pieces are principally of interest for the history of epigraphy. Happily the ceiling of the Cappella Palatina in Palermo, Sicily, which is of immense value as a guide to Fatimid art, can be dated securely between 1140 and 1150; nevertheless, its paintings contain significant European elements which have yet to be sufficiently disengaged from their otherwise Islamic context. The essential danger in dealing with Fatimid art, therefore, is the absence of dated objects to act as landmarks.

In 1068 the Fatimid palace treasury was pillaged by troops whose arrears of pay had driven them to mutiny, an event which brought the contents into the public eye and – even more to the point – the open market. While recent research has raised some doubts about earlier theories which proposed that the dispersal of the *objets d'art* in the Fatimid treasury triggered a democratization of the minor arts, so that an affluent bourgeoisie began to adopt (and, by degrees, to debase) courtly themes, it cannot be denied that the events of 1068 brought into the public domain thousands of objects which had hitherto been kept secluded in the royal collections. Medieval accounts of the fabled contents of this treasury prove beyond doubt that the surviving legacy of Fatimid art is a very pale shadow of its original splendour and multiplicity. But this information has to be used with care. It so happens that the description by al-Maqrizi is more detailed and circumstantial than any other medieval Islamic account of objects of virtu in royal collections. That is why it is so frequently quoted. But it should not be interpreted to mean that such collections were confined to the Fatimids. On the contrary, disjointed snippets of information indicate that the ʿAbbasids of Baghdad and the Umayyads of Spain – to name only two dynasties – also amassed staggeringly rich collections of precious works of art. Similarly, the preference for courtly themes among patrons apparently unconnected with the court is by no means confined to Fatimid art; this tendency is, for example, equally characteristic of the Saljuq period.

Other aspects of Fatimid art, too, require re-evaluation. The much-vaunted realism of Fatimid lustreware, far from being an innovation of this period, has been shown to have much deeper roots in the arts of the Copts and even in the Hellenized late antique world of the eastern Mediterranean than previous scholarship had recognized. Finally (thanks to some crucial re-attributions), a much larger body of Fatimid metalwork is now available for study than was previously the case. Pride of place must go to the numerous small-scale animal sculptures. They include camels, lions, cats, gazelles, rabbits, ibexes, goats and even parrots – the latter functioning as ornaments for hanging lamps. Many such pieces were cast and were therefore presumably made for a mass market.

From the time of the Muslim conquest onwards, a series of independent settlements had been built at intervals of about a century around the site of modern Cairo – Babylon, al-ʿAskar, Fustat and al-Qitaʿi. Al-Qahira supplanted all of these and became the nucleus first of medieval and then eventually of modern Cairo. Its foundation should be seen, like that of Baghdad, al-Mutawakkiliya, al-Mahdiya or Madinat al-Zahra, as an expression of royal aspiration and pomp; an action to be expected of a powerful ruler. That same political dominance was reflected in the location of the court within a ten-

44 The Gate of Victories in the City of Victory. Bab al-Futuh, Cairo, 1087. One of three Fatimid gates built by three Armenian brothers from Edessa, and incorporating the very latest defensive devices, this fortification belongs to a Jaziran tradition best illustrated by the walls of Diyarbakr. It was one of many gates in the palace-city wall.

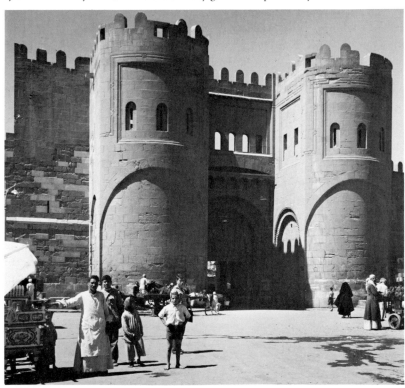

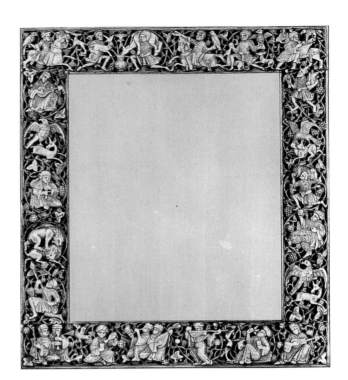

45 Recreation as ceremony. Carved ivory, Egypt, 11th–12th century. Perhaps a Fatimid book cover, ultimately derived from a Byzantine five-part ivory cover. The unbroken continuity of these images aptly suggests the formalized ritual of court life, encompassing both business and pleasure. This is a visual equivalent of the 'delight of days and nights, without surcease or change' mentioned in contemporary textile epigraphy.

gated enclosure walled off from the rest of the city; the palace area inside was cordonned off by chains and still further distanced by a huge cleared space constantly patrolled by guards. The two palaces themselves were a byword for ostentatious splendour, with their gilded marble cloisters, their gardens prinked out with artificial trees of precious metal on which perched clockwork singing birds, their chambers crammed with luxury textiles and above all the great golden filigree screen behind which the caliph sat to enjoy court festivals. Of all these splendours only some fragments of woodcarving remain. They depict scenes of revelry and are in the standard Islamic idiom favoured for such subject-matter (see p. 68). 44 45

Textual sources alone preserve the memory of some of the most spectacular Fatimid treasures, such as a world map woven of blue silk with every feature identified in gold, silver and silk writing. Mecca and Medina, the ultimate goals of Fatimid ambition, were given special prominence. Made in 964, it allegedly cost 22,000 *dinars*. The surviving and similarly coloured Star Mantle of the Ottonian emperor Henry II, made in the early eleventh century in a south

Italian milieu saturated with Islamic influence, perhaps gives some idea of this *tour de force*. Another vanished masterpiece is the *shamsa* (solar rosette) made for the Ka'ba at the order of the caliph al-Mu'izz in 973. It was a sun-shaped object stuffed with powdered musk, containing openwork golden balls which themselves each held fifty pearls the size of doves' eggs – and the whole object was appropriately surrounded by verses from the Surat al-Hajj executed in emeralds with the interstitial spaces in the writing 'filled with pearls as big as could be'. These treasures, which often had a curiosity as well as a purely monetary value, could serve a political role as diplomatic gifts and as instruments for the display of royal power. In Byzantium, too, precious objects were sometimes put to the same uses – for example, the marriage contract of the princess Theophanou, who was despatched from Constantinople in 970 to marry the German emperor, was drawn up in gold lettering on purple-tinted vellum. From much the same time dates the celebrated though now dismembered 'Blue Qur'an', probably made *c.* 1020 in Qairawan –

66

46, 47 A religion of the book. Leaves from the 'Blue Qur'an'; parchment dyed indigo; perhaps Qairawan, *c.* 1020. Qur'an folios dyed saffron, salmon–pink and pale yellow are also known, and presumably derive ultimately from Byzantine 6th-century purple codices. The absolute control of the text block, and the overall symmetry to which individual variations of script are subordinated, bespeak the professional scribe.

though Cordoba has also been suggested – whose gold Kufic script unfolds against a background of indigo-dyed vellum. It is the only such Qur'an known. An almost musical sensibility controls the expansions and contractions of the letters, an aesthetic device here carried to its highest point. Whether these visual rhythms were intended to correspond to the way the text was recited or chanted is a matter for future research. Unfortunately, as yet there is no way of placing the Blue Qur'an securely in its contemporary and probably Fatimid context, given the near-total absence of Qur'ans dated or datable to the Fatimid period.

46, 47

In painting, as with so much else in Fatimid art, the rich literary sources underline how incompletely the few survivals reflect either the splendour or the variety of contemporary production. The caliph al-ʿAmir, for instance, had a belvedere bedecked with paintings of notable poets, each portrait accompanied by quotations from that poet's works. And a competition organized by the vizier of the caliph al-Mustansir in the 1050s between a local artist and an Iraqi rival hinged on their mastery of illusionistic techniques dependent on strong colour rather than three-dimensional space. Both had to depict a dancing girl, but the local man (who won) was to show her entering a niche while the Iraqi tried to show her coming out of it. Al-Maqrizi's account of this incident suggests that one master relied on line while the other preferred to exploit blocks of colour – evidence, perhaps, that at least two quite distinctive styles of painting flourished in Fatimid Egypt. Painted lustre pottery tells the same story. A similar mastery of illusionism is implied by al-Maqrizi's description of a fountain which decorated a mosque.

None of the paintings which graced the Fatimid palaces has survived, but by a curious freak of chance a wonderfully complete cycle – almost a thousand pictures – of royal images, in all probability basically of Fatimid origin, though overlaid at times by influences from southern and western Europe, is preserved on the ceiling of the Cappella Palatina in Palermo. The subject matter ranges widely, and is somewhat unfocused. It gives the impression of an originally coherent cycle of images rendered incoherent by repetition, and diluted by the introduction of non-courtly and even non-Islamic subjects. Nevertheless, the core of the iconographic programme is clear enough: it is the fullest rendition extant of the cycle of courtly pursuits that is known in the medieval Islamic world – though the intention may have been to enrich that general theme by others with paradisal and astrological overtones. Wrestlers, dancers, seated rulers with and without attendants, grooms carrying game or birds, nobles playing chess or backgammon, exotic animals or birds, hunting and jousting scenes, processions, animal combats, men wrestling with animals, races, drinking, music-making – all are promiscuously intermingled. Other scenes plainly do not fit into this courtly category but have apparently zodiacal significance (such as the scene of Aquarius at the well) or are clearly mythological in content, such as the image of the eagle with outspread wings bearing a human figure aloft, or the numerous fantastic beasts: sphinxes, griffins, harpies and animals with two bodies but only one face. Such images draw on a millennial Middle Eastern heritage. Scenes which seem to derive from western sources include one of a man grappling with a lion (Samson), an old man holding a bird (Noah?) and a Norman knight engaged in close combat with a Muslim cavalier. Apparently, then, the artists ransacked the entire repertoire of images available to them, relevant and not so relevant, and used it to cobble together a programme of sorts. The inconsistencies already noted thus fall into place as a necessary consequence of a visual cycle forced to expand far beyond its normal confines.

The honeycomb vaulting of the ceiling's *muqarnas* form ensures a constant variation in the size, shape and angle of the painted surface. But what renders the entire scheme so distinctively Islamic is the way that every inch of the ceiling is painted, to the extent that there is no foil of plain framing bands or of empty flanking niches or spandrels for the larger designs. Instead, the images are crammed into the available surfaces irrespective of whether they fit naturally into them or not. In this respect, the images on the Cappella Palatina roof are treated in a dramatically different way from those of the normal princely cycle, in which each image is given the same emphasis as the next. The form of the ceiling decisively forbids this and imposes on the painters an iconographically uneven handling of their material. Thus on occasion minor elements may be accorded more space than major ones. Even the narrow bands which separate the stars at the apex of the ceiling are made part of the decorative scheme: they bear elaborate Kufic inscriptions invoking benedictions – presumably on the Norman king, Roger II, for whom the chapel was built between 1132 and 1140. Just as at the Armenian church of Aght'amar two centuries earlier, and in a comparable context of a Christian monarchy trying to come to terms with a much more powerful Muslim neighbour, a palace chapel is the setting for a diplomatic visual acknowledgment of the Muslim presence. In both cases the Muslim cycle is set well above the Christian images at the outer limit of visibility, and in both cases it is emphatically secular in tone. This suggests, perhaps, that the prestige of Muslim court life was such that it became the natural target for emulation even by non-Muslim princes who were geographically within the orbit of Muslim power. Much the same process can be traced continuously for centuries in Spain.

What of the style of the paintings in Palermo? Its hallmark is its unbroken fluency. The smooth line is complemented by a capacity to reduce form into rounded masses which flow easily into each other. Simplification is the key to this way of seeing. Often it results in mirror symmetry, but zigzag or diagonally emphasized compositions are also common. Features such as scalloped fringes, large eyes, kiss-curls by the ear all point to the influence of imperial 'Abbasid

50

69

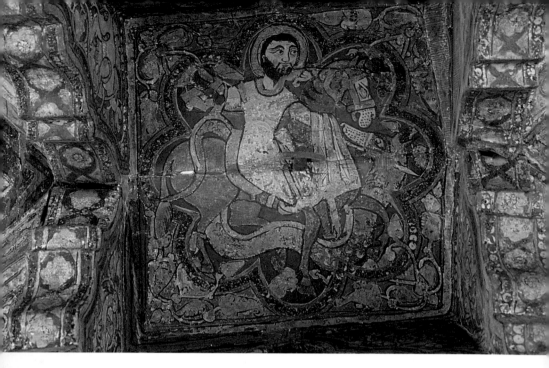

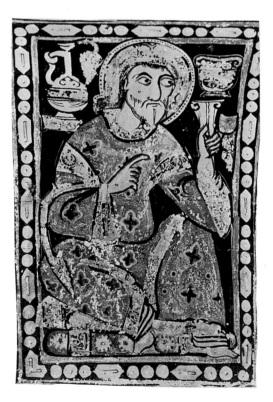

48 (*above*) A Christian story retold. Wall painting from nave roof, Cappella Palatina, Palermo, Sicily, mid-12th century. The equestrian dragon-slayer probably derives from Byzantine or Coptic images of Saints George or Theodore, though Saljuq Turkish sculpture and even the *Shahnama* offer further parallels, sometimes with cosmic or astrological implications, as the dragon's coiled tail suggests.

49 (*left*) The Byzantine saint secularized. Man with beaker, Cappella Palatina. The haggard, cadaverous figure framed by his halo clearly derives from a Byzantine source, and the seated posture is Western. Despite religious prohibitions, ritual drinking on the Sasanian Persian model often marked medieval Islamic court life. The space-filling jug and pot accord with the subject-matter.

50 (*right*) A pluralistic society. Section of nave roof, Cappella Palatina. This, the most highly evolved surviving Islamic wooden roof of its time, is unmistakably Muslim despite its ecclesiastical setting – perhaps, together with the Byzantine mosaics below, a metaphor for religious tolerance. Its trilobed, keel-shaped and segmental arches echo Fatimid and Saljuq architecture.

51 (*below left*) Courtliness commercialized. Wall painting from a bath outside Cairo, pre-1168, depicting a youth seated in Islamic pose (unlike 49) with a beaker. Nearby are depicted affronted birds and a scarf dancer, whose damaged state may reflect the edict of al-Hakim in 1013–14 to scratch out depictions of women in public baths.

52 (*below right*) Soldiers of the Prophet. Outline of a Fatimid design (woodblock print?), 11th century. The tree with birds derives from textile design. An inscription (half-complete?) wishes 'glory and good fortune to the leader Abu Man[sur]' – blessings partially repeated on the sword. Note the chain mail, two-horned helmet and accoutrements of rank hanging from the belt. 14 × 14 cm (5.5 × 5.5 in).

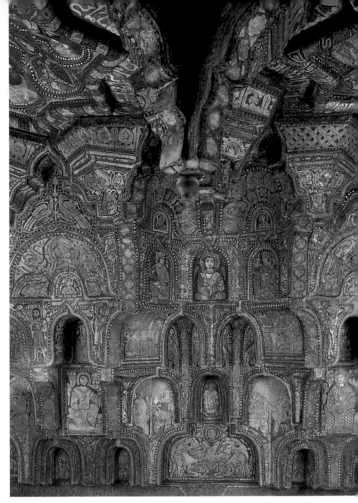

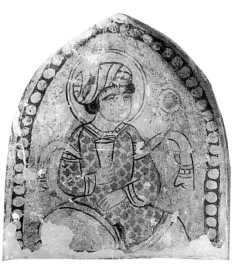

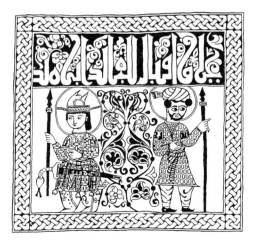

art as developed at Samarra. A textbook case of this influence is provided by the seated cross-legged monarch whose pose – even to his tiny feet – seems to owe much to images of the Buddha. That a secular king should be depicted by Islamic artists in a Far Eastern religious manner in a Christian church at the very centre of the Mediterranean highlights in the most telling way the international quality of medieval Islamic art.

It must be conceded that virtually no echo of this rich cycle of images has been found in Fatimid Egypt proper, with the minor exception of a *hammam* excavated at Fustat, whose painted decoration included a seated youth and affronted birds – scenes roughly comparable with those on the ceiling of the Cappella Palatina. It is true that many single leaves have been found, notably one now in the British Museum showing a fortress being besieged, and a woodblock print depicting a foot soldier; but for the most part these works are of coarse quality (indeed, some are mere scrawls) and suggest that manuscript painting was still relatively underdeveloped at this period. But a few of these leaves, of which the largest group is that in the private Keir Collection in Surrey, England, illustrate not so much an 'Abbasid manner as a familiarity with Byzantine art, which during the Macedonian Renaissance (especially in the tenth century) had developed an extraordinarily fresh and natural reinterpretation of the techniques of Graeco-Roman illusionism by means of modelling and sketchy line.

Too little Fatimid religious architecture is preserved to permit reliable generalizations about it, and the mosques built by the Sunni majority in this period have almost entirely disappeared. But the few surviving major monuments of the dynasty do encourage some interesting speculations. For example, the absence of minarets in the mosques is noteworthy, the major exception being the Hakim mosque, remarkable also for its elaborately articulated façade, in which broad stairways played a significant part, and even more for the enormous size of its courtyard. Perhaps this absence reflects a distaste for the minaret as a culpable innovation, and the converse emphasis on large-scale projecting portals (as at al-Mahdiya) may be linked with a desire to give the call to prayer from them, in a deliberate return to the primordial Islamic practice established by the Prophet himself. On the other hand, a distinctive genre of brick minarets (possibly reflecting Hijazi prototypes) attained popularity in Upper Egypt during this period (e.g. at Luxor and Esna).

It is plain enough from the major differences between the few

51

52

53

72

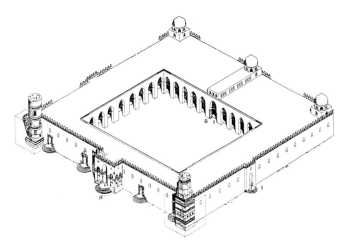

Fatimid mosques which do survive that it is no longer possible to identify the nature of the typical mosque of this period. Some striking innovations may be noted. These include the use of towers as corner salients on the façade of the Hakim mosque – a device which gave them a new and crucial articulating function – and the highlighting of the area in front of the *mihrab* by placing domes at the two corners of the *qibla* wall. Such corner domes serve as pendants to the more familiar dome over the *mihrab* (Azhar and Hakim mosques).   54

53 (*above*) A fortress for the faith. The mosque of al-Hakim, Cairo, 990–1013, develops themes encountered earlier in the mosques of Samarra and of Ibn Tulun, Cairo (*ill.* 28). The degree of emphasis on the main façade is, however, new. Crenellations and towers lend it a military flavour. The triple-arched portal copies palace architecture.

54 (*right*) The world's oldest university. The much rebuilt and constantly enlarged Azhar mosque, Cairo, founded in 970–2 and intended also as a centre of learning and of Isma'ili propaganda. Note such trademarks of Fatimid architecture as radiating roundels and niches, keel-shaped arches and clustered columns.

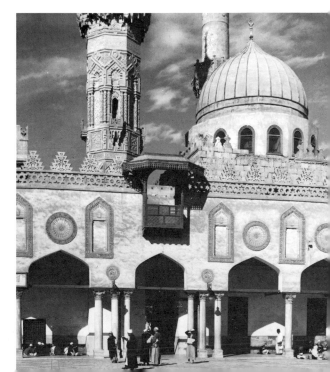

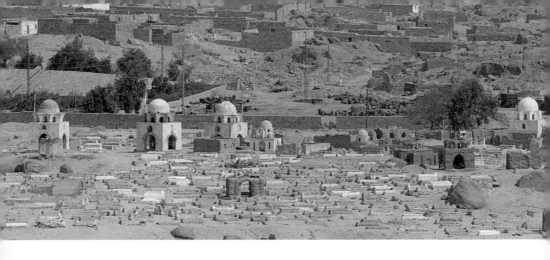

This idea is closely related to the creation of a T-plan in mosque sanctuaries – that is, using a central axial nave which leads up to the *mihrab* at its far end, and similarly picking out the transverse aisle along and immediately in front of the *qibla* – a device which was to have a long history in the Maghrib. Such features show a bold and intriguing readiness to conceive of a mosque in modular terms. Like the triple entrance to the mosque – perhaps a feature which the Fatimids derived from palace architecture – these ideas suggest that the use of the mosque for royal ceremonies, a custom well documented in the literary sources for the Fatimid period, encouraged a fundamental rethinking of its layout. Hence, presumably, the introduction of features already long familiar in palaces.

To judge by surviving public structures, mausolea occupied an especially honoured place in Fatimid architecture. They certainly survive in much greater abundance than any other building type. In Cairo alone, fourteen funerary structures of the period survive, as against five mosques. Of still greater significance numerically and structurally – though not from a religious or political viewpoint – are the fifty-odd mausolea probably of eleventh–twelfth century date at Aswan in Upper Egypt. They form an entire necropolis, a custom of course already established in Egypt for millennia. Since this city was a major departure point for pilgrim caravans, it is likely enough that the original tenants of these mausolea were pilgrims, though some could also have fallen in holy war, since Aswan was on the Nubian border and therefore faced infidel lands. Although – or perhaps because – many of these structures are of mud-brick, they demon-

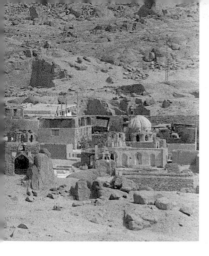

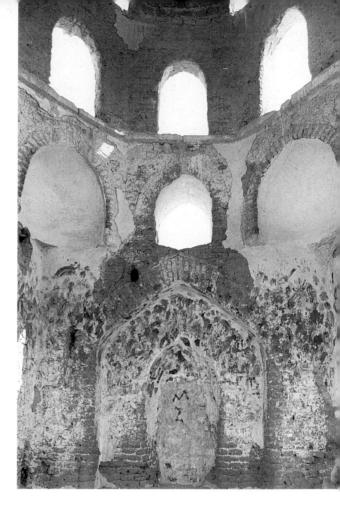

55 (*above*) Tombs for martyrs. 11th-century necropolis at Aswan, Upper Egypt. The Prophet forbade all ostentation in funerary ceremonies; nevertheless, mausolea quickly became fashionable. Among the various justifications devised for them was – as here – the desire to honour *ghazis* or *mujahidin* (warriors for the faith).

56 (*right*) Legal or illegal? Interior of an 11th-century tomb, Aswan. The orthodox ban on mausolea might be circumvented if the burial spot was open to the wind and the rain. Hence the popularity of lavishly fenestrated chambers like this one.

strate a degree of fantasy and playfulness quite unusual in Islamic mausolea, and this was intensified by their plaster rendering, which lent an extra sharpness to mouldings and other details. The contrast between flat and curved planes; between the heavy cubic mass of the lower chamber and the diminutive, almost frolicsome, domed aedicule perched a trifle incongruously upon it; between the pronounced, eccentric rhythms of the transition zones, with their swooping concave volumes, and the austere simplicity of the areas above and below – all this makes these monuments consistently appealing, a satisfying exercise in solid geometry. Their interiors have a curious dimension of surprise: domes spangled with star-shaped openings, the muscular contraction and expansion of their squinch zones, and above all the innate sculptural sense expressed in the strong articulation of the wall surface, scooped out as it were by a giant hand. Such devices ensure continual variation from one mausoleum to the next. Some of the detailing – e.g. the ribbed domes, the busy articulation of the drum, the serried pilasters in the transition zone – recall Coptic or even mid-Byzantine architecture. The chronology of these buildings is now hard to retrieve because the dated tombstones which they once contained have been removed, mainly at the end of the last century, without any record being made of their exact provenance in the necropolis. Aswan provides the earliest example of such clusters of mausolea in the medieval Islamic world but others survive in Cairo, Fez, Rayy (near modern Tehran), Samarqand and Delhi.

Some basic types can be identified. They include 'canopy' tombs, open-plan with an entrance on each side; the same, but with one wall closed to house a *mihrab*; tombs with all four sides closed and a single entrance; tombs with added courtyard or sanctuary; and adjoining tombs which create a continuous vaulted space. All these types are continually overlaid and obscured by variations which, however minor in themselves, still change the essential aspect of these buildings. In both Aswan and Cairo, a type of mausoleum not found in Egypt after the Fatimid period makes its appearance: the *mashhad* (literally 'place of martyrdom'). It comprises a domed square encompassed on three sides by an ambulatory. Important examples of the type are the *mashhad*s of Yahya al-Shabih and Qasim Abu Tayyib. Another type of *mashhad* (such as that of al-Guyushi in Cairo and another in Aswan) comprises a triple-bayed sanctuary with a dome over the central bay, thereby creating a compact cluster of buildings.

The Fatimid emphasis on mausolea was a major innovation in the Arab world and it is surely no coincidence that a similar emphasis can also be detected in contemporary Buyid architecture in Iran. Shi'ism seems to be the connecting thread in this development. The Fatimid caliphs themselves continued the traditional custom of house burial, though in a dynastic tomb situated in the Eastern Palace – later dubbed 'The Saffron Tomb' (*turbat al-za'faran*) because of the custom of anointing it regularly with that perfume. Perhaps this building was intended to rival the 'Abbasid family tomb at Samarra, the Qubbat al-Sulaibiya. The great majority of Fatimid tombs in Cairo, however, which date from the later Fatimid period, were erected to commemorate Shi'ite saints and martyrs, perhaps in an attempt to create a funerary cult that would support the caliphal family, which of course claimed descent from ʿAli. The tombs in the Qarafa cemetery especially became centres for weekend outings, with the faithful spending the night in their vicinity, circumambulating them and hoping for answers to prayers through the intercession of these personages, and, more generally, to profit from the *baraka* or spiritual power associated with these tombs. The forms of such mausolea are very much more modest than those of contemporary funerary structures in the eastern Islamic world. For the most part they comprise small square chambers, largely plain not only externally (except for the occasional fluted dome) but also inside, apart from their monumental *mihrabs*, the latter sometimes disposed in groups of five (Sayyida Ruqayya) or three (Ikhwat Yusuf). Most were dedicated to members of the Prophet's family; several honour martyrs for the Shiʿite cause; and the prominence of women among their tenants is quite remarkable – perhaps a reflection of the key role in popular piety played by women and expressed also in the area of the Qarafa cemetery (that centre of female piety) by the unusually high proportion of tombstones honouring Shiʿite women.

Perhaps the most striking feature of these *mihrabs* is their use of ribs radiating outwards from a central boss – the very image of light. It was a tenet of Ismaʿili belief that the Holy Family existed in the form of light even before the world was created. The Qurʾanic inscriptions in these tombs frequently contain references to the sun, the moon and the stars, and these were interpreted to connote the Shiʿite Holy Family. Any name on the central roundel (significantly termed *shamsa* in Arabic, from the word *shams*, 'sun') would most naturally be interpreted as the source of light, and it is exclusively 'Allah', 'Muhammad' or 'ʿAli'. The latter two names are again found at the centre of a star in the dome of the *mashhad* of al-Guyushi, surrounded by a Qurʾanic quotation which includes the words 'It is He who appointed you viceroys in the earth'. In the highly charged Fatimid context, light had the specific extra connotation of *nass* (the explicit statement whereby legitimacy was conferred on an *imam*, often interpreted as divine light). Hence the repeated literary associations between, for example, Husain – the son of ʿAli – and light. Not for nothing, perhaps, was one of the names for the Hakim mosque 'The Mosque of Lights' (*jamiʿ al-anwar*), just as a contemporary tomb was known as the Shrine of Light. And the Aqmar mosque, whose very name means 'The Moonlit', has its façade festooned with radiating designs, with 'ʿAli' at the centre of the largest, directly over the

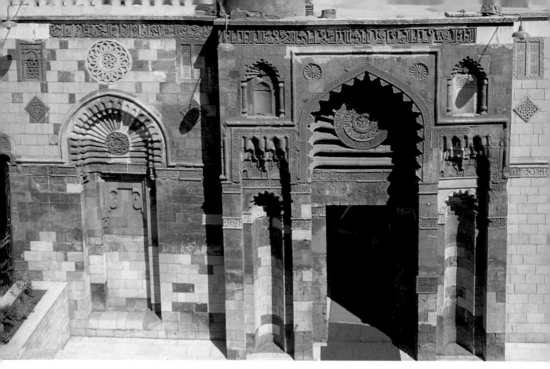

57 A religious and political manifesto. The Aqmar mosque in Cairo was erected in 1125 beside the eastern Fatimid caliphal palace, and was perhaps intended as a court oratory, teaching institution and tomb for al-Husain, the Prophet's grandson. Its inscriptions implore God to give the caliph 'victory over all infidels' (presumably the Crusaders and schismatics) and exalt the family of ʿAli by quoting Qurʾan 33:33.

entrance – presumably a reference to the well-known saying that ʿAli is the Gate of the City of Knowledge; 'let those who want to acquire knowledge approach it by its proper gate'. The entire façade of the 57 Aqmar mosque functions as a gigantic *qibla* articulated by *mihrab*s large and small – an allusion that would have been far clearer in Fatimid times, when the standard *mihrab* had precisely the form of the blind niches on that façade. Indeed, the use of three great *mihrab*s on the original façade (though that façade was *not* orientated to the *qibla*, being skewed in relation to the rest of the mosque) seems to 1 have been a deliberate echo of the layout of the contemporary *kiswa*, the cloth draped over the Kaʿba in Mecca. Pierced window designs, stars and carved representations of lamps are further references to light (and specifically as it is described in *Sura* [Qurʾanic chapter] 24:35) in this iconographically dense façade, in which – as in other Fatimid monuments – numerical symbolism hinging on the numbers 3, 5 and especially 7 (Ismaʿilis being Sevener Shiʿites) is also at work.

78

Fatimid pottery is dominated by lustrewares. Their origin is disputed; some argue that the earlier lustrewares of Samarra provided the direct inspiration, as indeed similarities of graphic style suggest, while others seek its source in glass (see p. 54). But the key point is not the source of the technique but the fact that the importance of Fatimid lustrewares extends far beyond Egypt, since they usher in the first consistent attempt in the medieval Islamic world to make luxury ceramics say something in visual terms. Not that they are the first Islamic wares to carry images – at Samarra and Nishapur, to name only the two most important centres of production, wares in various techniques had already used figural designs. But the number and variety of such themes and motifs expanded dramatically in Fatimid lustreware – although most pieces bore abstract and vegetal designs, half-palmettes being especially popular. Not surprisingly – perhaps because this was indeed a time of experimentation – many of the themes are new to pottery, and some even to Islamic art. A groom leads a giraffe, an elderly man tends a cheetah, men squat on their haunches absorbed in a cockfight, porters carry heavy loads, a lady 58 scrutinizes herself in a mirror while a maidservant hovers nearby, wrestlers strain against each other, men fight with sticks, a Coptic priest swings a censer, falconers or mailed cavaliers ride richly 59, 60 caparisoned horses – there is even an image of Christ in true Byzantine manner. Animals abound: whether commonplace (hares, dogs, ibexes, fish, birds), exotic (lions and elephants) or fantastic (griffins and harpies). Some scenes involve energetic action, such as a dog biting the leg of another animal. A courtly ambience pervades scenes of banquets, dancers, seated drinkers and lutanists (both male and female) who serenade them.

The various figural images can indeed be taken at face value as genre or courtly scenes, but they could equally well (and simultaneously) operate on a deeper level as symbols (e.g. of love or temptation, harmony or fellowship) or as deliberate copies of classical themes – for of course Egypt had been one of the major centres of Hellenistic art, and was a country where the sense of an immemorial past was stronger and more pervasive than elsewhere in the Near East. Moreover, through its Coptic minority – which had preserved much of the Hellenistic heritage – Egypt was more open to these themes than other areas of the Islamic world. A few examples will put these remarks into perspective. Some of the banqueting figures, whose setting could be interpreted as a garden, may refer to Paradise and may derive from classical images of heroization. Several of the

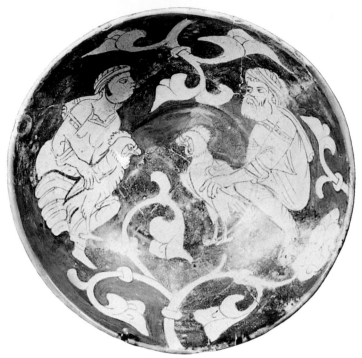

58 Fatimid lustre bowl, 11th–12th century, with cock-fighting scene. The tradition of such images, which typically contrast a bearded older man and a youth, stretched back to ancient Greece and carried associations of warlike spirit, virility and homosexuality. Diam. 23.7 cm (9.3 in).

59 The survival of other faiths. Early 12th-century lustre bowl, signed by the Muslim potter Saʿd, which shows a Coptic priest swinging a censer; a gigantic *ankh* hieroglyph denotes 'life'. Diam. 21.9 cm (8.6 in).

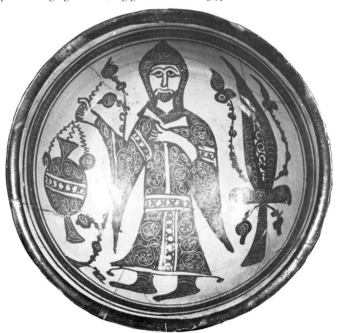

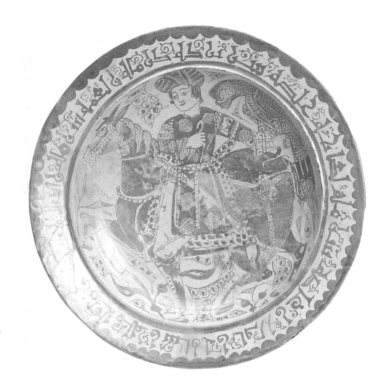

60 'Good health and complete joy to the owner, may he be saved from evil' runs the inscription around this lustre plate depicting a mounted falconer. The iconography is international, but this piece of so-called Fustat ware is inscribed 'well made in Egypt'. H. 7 cm (2.8 in), diam. 38.3 cm (15 in).

animals depicted on Fatimid lustreware have been interpreted as lunar, solar or astrological symbols. Some pieces depict dragons or snakes, perhaps a reference to Jawzahar, the eclipse monster regarded by medieval Muslims as the antagonist of the sun and the moon. A link with the Tree of Life and with water is suggested by trees or fish on some of these pieces, though apotropaic or mystical overtones could also be present. Sometimes, as in the plate depicting a giraffe being led by a groom, a reference to contemporary royal processions may well be intended – a medieval equivalent to the Coronation or other souvenir mug.

Polychrome lustrewares are usually decorated with geometric or vegetal motifs, though a few depict birds and – as noted above – dragons or snakes. Some pieces are entirely covered with cross-banded inscriptions. The considerable differences in style and execution between the major groups of Fatimid lustreware – especially between the monochrome and the polychrome types – drive home the fact that Fatimid Egypt was open to ideas and influences from all over the Mediterranean and beyond, and that one should not therefore expect an integrated style. Fatimid painting tells the same story.

81

It is in the Fatimid period above all that potters' signatures come into their own. Signed wares are admittedly encountered earlier – for example, in 'Abbasid blue-and-white pottery, in glazed relief wares and in yet others found at Madinat al-Zahra in Spain – but they are rare. Over seventy Fatimid pieces are signed, and the names of some twenty-one potters have been recorded. Chief among them is a certain potter called Muslim, whose name appears on a score of surviving pieces. Many of the signatures include the information that the ceramic was made in Misr (probably meaning Cairo, though possibly Egypt). Specialization was well advanced in Fatimid times, as the Geniza records – a cache of medieval Jewish commercial documents – show: thus mention is made of the *qaddar* who produced pots, the *kuzi* who made spoutless water jugs and the *ghaza'iri* who made translucent porcellaneous dishes. Perhaps the painters of ceramics were equally specialized and were distinct from those who produced the pottery shapes themselves. Epigraphic evidence on two lustre pieces indicates that they were made to order – one for a high official, the other conceivably for the caliph himself – and thus prove the existence of high patronage for at least some pottery produced in this period. Frequently these wares carry benedictory inscriptions; forty-six of them are inscribed *sa'd*, 'good luck', though this could also be the name of the potter.

The colours of the monochrome lustrewares vary from golden-yellow through copper to dark brown and the design is usually painted in silhouette, though occasionally it is reserved in white against a lustre ground. The body is coarse and sandy. Shapes vary considerably, though bowls, dishes and cups predominate. Other wares of the period include glazed relief, coloured glazed and incised types – the latter apparently owing something to Chinese celadons. Indeed many lustre pieces derive their forms directly or indirectly from Chinese prototypes. The floruit of Fatimid lustre seems to have been the late tenth and early eleventh centuries, though production continued in Egypt (and possibly Syria) until the fall of the dynasty in 1171. It seems possible that at least some Fatimid lustreware specialists thereupon migrated to Iran, where powerful Shi'ite minorities offered a degree of security conspicuously absent under the aggressive orthodoxy of the Ayyubids.

The presence of many Fatimid ceramics walled as ornaments into the exteriors of churches in Italy (e.g. at Pisa, Rome, Ravenna and Ravallo) and even in France and Greece has been explained as the result of Crusaders bringing back souvenirs from the East. Whether this or just plain trade was the source of such wares, they give a valuable indication of the type of luxury pottery produced in the late Fatimid period. The style of these pieces is so varied that it seems reasonable to look for several quite different sources of inspiration. Sometimes the trick of painting the face, or the exterior of the piece, is so like that of Iraqi lustre that a close connection is incontestable. But other pieces have the vivacity and freedom of Hellenistic art as developed at Alexandria, and yet other images recall Coptic textiles. The figures often have a marked illusionism in the way that their movement is suggested by cross-hatching. But the unpredictable play of light which is so integral to the whole effect of lustre is inimical to such nascent realism, since it abstracts form rather than defining it. Thus line and colour are at war.

Most specialists attribute the great majority of the 180-odd surviving medieval Islamic rock crystal objects to Fatimid Egypt and to the period before c. 1060. The raw material apparently came from the Maghrib and latterly the Red Sea, though the Basra school was supplied from Madagascar, Kashmir and the Maldives, and perhaps these areas also supplied Egypt. Although expertise in hardstone carving was required to work rock crystal satisfactorily, the artists obviously learned much from wheel-cut carving on glass. Al-Maqrizi cites detailed eyewitness accounts describing the rock crystal objects held

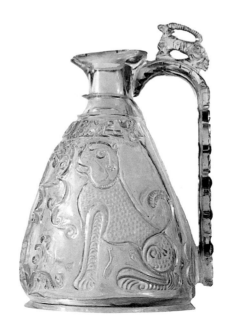

61 Frozen light. Rock crystal ewer naming the Fatimid caliph al-ʿAziz bi'llah (975–96), venerated as a source of divine light. The ibex perched by the rim embodies the conceit that the animal is drinking from the ewer, a theme rooted in pre-Islamic religious rituals and common in metalwork. Rock crystal was believed to be a form of ice, but also to concentrate the sun's rays; the goblets of paradise are from this material (Qur'an 37:46–7). H. 18 cm (7.1 in).

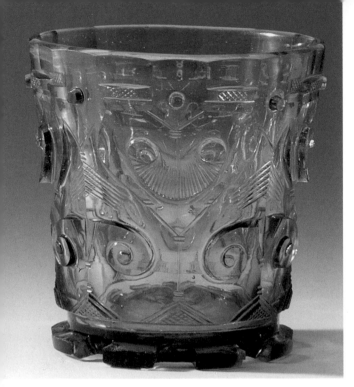

62 Cut-price luxury. Glass beaker with cut relief ornament, resembling precious stone; probably Egypt or Syria, 12th century. Veste Coburg, Germany; formerly owned by Martin Luther. Sixteen such objects, known as Hedwig glasses (from the tradition that St Hedwig changed water into wine in one of them), survive. The thick-walled, smoky topaz glass bears highly abstract motifs ultimately of Samarran origin. H. *c.* 12.7 cm (5 in).

61 in the Fatimid treasuries in the 1060s — even their size and market value were noted, and a group of pieces bearing the name of the caliph al-ʿAziz were singled out for special attention. The total number of rock crystal vessels in this treasury alone was then 1,800. The only three inscribed rock crystals bearing the names of notables were clearly made in Egypt; they mention the caliphs al-ʿAziz and al-Zahir, and al-Hakim's generalissimo, Husain b. Jauhar. The luxury nature of the craft is emphasized by the technique itself; the ewers, for example, were made by patiently hollowing out a solid block of crystal until the walls had been reduced to extreme thinness. The themes of the six closely related ewers which illustrate Fatimid rock crystals at their best are uniformly large palmettes (perhaps intended to represent the Tree of Life) flanked by various animals: lions, ostriches, hawks, moufflons and gazelles. Some of these animals also 62 appear on the heavy monumental 'Hedwig' beakers which mimic in glass the technique of rock crystals. None of these have turned up in the Islamic world, which has suggested to some scholars that they are of European (perhaps South Italian or Sicilian) provenance; but they could also have been made in Egypt or Syria for a European market.

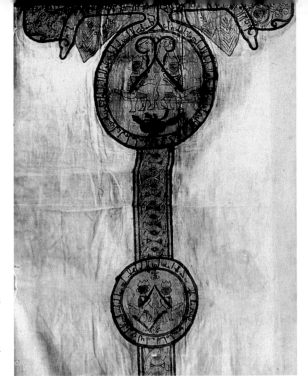

63 From Muslim robe of honour to church treasury. Linen cloth made in Damietta, Egypt, and bearing tapestry ornament depicting birds, addorsed sphinxes and other animals. Known as 'the veil of St Anne', it has inscriptions dated 1096–7 mentioning the Fatimid caliph al-Musta'li bi'llah and his vizier al-Afdal. Apt, Vaucluse, France; probably booty from the First Crusade. Detail of copy made in 1850. 310 × 150 cm (122 × 59 in).

Their presence in church treasuries is an argument in favour of an Islamic origin, for this is where most of the finest medieval Islamic textiles and rock crystals have been preserved, usually because they had fallaciously acquired some sacred Christian association. Many rock crystals were used as containers for relics believed to be drops of Christ's blood or associated with the Last Supper or the Crucifixion. Hence the elaborate European ecclesiastical mountings in which so many of them are set.

The surviving Fatimid textiles do not measure up to those known from literary sources – for example, the hundreds of textiles mentioned by al-Maqrizi with pictures of rulers and other celebrities, all identified by name and accompanied by some commentary. Most of the surviving pieces are *tiraz* products whose sole ornament is their epigraphy. Sometimes they are very close imitations of 'Abbasid textiles from Baghdad – for example, a *tiraz* of al-Mu'izz which copies one of the 'Abbasid caliph al-Muti'. A few are of silk but most are of humbler materials such as linen and cotton. Their epigraphy is far 63 more varied than that of Fatimid inscriptions in other materials; some may ape styles of pen-made writing confined to chancery use.

85

CHAPTER FOUR

The Saljuqs

Arab dominion of the eastern Islamic world came to an end in 945 when the caliphs were forced to surrender their temporal authority to their army commanders, who belonged to the Persian Buyid family. Henceforth the caliphs preserved only the forms and not the substance of power. For the next century, political control of this huge area passed to various dynasties, principally of Persian origin, among which the Buyid family was pre-eminent. One dynasty alone broke this mould: the Ghaznavids, who controlled Afghanistan, much of the Punjab and parts of eastern Iran. They had begun as Turkish military slaves but had assimilated Perso-Islamic ways. This Turkish hegemony became definitive under the Great Saljuqs, whose followers – known as Turcomans – were Turkish nomads and marauders who had recently converted to Islam. The Saljuqs dispossessed the Ghaznavids and Buyids alike, took over Baghdad in 1055 and thereafter began a fundamental reshaping of the body politic.

For the first time since the seventh century, nomads ruled the Middle East – for the Saljuq Turks expanded westwards to the shores of the Mediterranean, controlling Anatolia, Iraq and parts of Syria as well as the Iranian world. From obscure pagan beginnings in their Central Asian homeland on the fringes of the Islamic world they had risen in three generations to become the greatest Muslim power of the day. No contemporary written Turkish sources describe this process, which can therefore be studied only through the medium of much later Arab and Persian historians, whose perception of events is essentially Muslim. It is clear, however, that in their rise to power the Saljuqs had preserved intact their ethnic and tribal identity, and with it their military strength. Henceforth many traditions of steppe society infiltrated the Muslim world. Among these was the principle of clan ownership, with no clearly defined hereditary succession. Territory was often partitioned among a ruler's male relations. Another custom decreed the appointment of a guardian or *atabeg* for a prince in his minority – and such *atabeg*s tended to be military

86

commanders who often usurped power. Turkish traditions like these clashed with Muslim norms and destabilized Islamic society.

Yet this Turkish element was counterbalanced by more ancient ones. Guides to good government ('Mirrors for Princes') were written for the Saljuq rulers, in which the Sasanian tradition of the divine right of kings was modified by the principle that the monarch must obey the law as defined by Muslim jurists. Like the Ghaznavids, the Saljuqs acknowledged the caliph's sphere of influence and generally operated within the existing political framework, for example by having their names mentioned alongside the caliph's in the Friday sermon at Baghdad and on coins. Even their regnal titles stressed the word *din* ('religion'). These various strands are symbolized in the name of the greatest Saljuq ruler, Sultan Malikshah, which blends the contemporary royal titles of Arab, Persian and Turk.

Saljuq administration struck a similar balance between Turkish and Islamic ways. A tripartite system developed in which the Turkish military aristocracy was supported by Persian high officials and a Persian or Arab religious class. Moreover, the revival of orthodoxy which had begun in Baghdad as a politico-religious response to the Shi'ism of the Buyids was consolidated under the Great Saljuqs. Through their high officials the Saljuqs gave vigorous impetus to the building of *madrasas* – colleges where the orthodox Islamic sciences were taught and the administrators of the regime were educated. They favoured Sufism or Islamic mysticism – indeed, some of the sultans and their officials adopted notable Sufis as their private mentors, and encouraged the movement to become part of official orthodox Islam, with organized fraternities. It was under the Saljuqs that the pivotal figure of al-Ghazali, the leading Muslim intellectual and theologian of the Middle Ages, formulated his synthesis of Sufism and Sunnism, thereby introducing a moderate mystical element into orthodoxy. The Saljuqs also took vigorous measures against the extreme Shi'ites. The greatest of Saljuq viziers, Nizam al-Mulk, in his work 'The Book of Government' (*c.* 1090), advised his master the sultan not to employ them, and they were cursed from the pulpits. Shi'ite mosques, *madrasas* and libraries were pillaged. This repression was in part prompted by a powerful resurgence of the extreme branch of the Shi'ites, the Isma'ilis, who terrorized the Middle East by the weapon of assassination – indeed, they are better known in the West as the Assassins.

Yet the apogee of the Great Saljuq state was short-lived. Indeed, after the death of Sultan Muhammad in 1118 the Saljuq empire split; the long reign of Sultan Sanjar (d. 1157) ensured stability in the east, but the western territories were riven with discord. By degrees landed property became so devalued that the entire landowning class, the *dihqan*s – who had survived nearly five centuries of Islamic rule – was wiped out by the early thirteenth century. The bureaucracy was top-heavy; offices were bought and sold, nepotism flourished (the twelve sons of the great vizier Nizam al-Mulk were honoured as if they were religious leaders), and officials shared the fate of their disgraced masters. The fissiparous system of family and clan ownership, the institution of the *atabeg* and the uncertain succession all combined to create periodic crises in the ruling house. A corrupt system of tax-farming led to a loss of central control as the military class gained power at the expense of the state. At a lower level, the nomadic element in Saljuq society was profoundly destructive. The Turcomans were resentful of the 'Persianization' of their chiefs; their prime aim was plunder and they resisted settlement. New waves of nomads, notably the Ghuzz tribes which in the 1150s captured Sultan Sanjar himself and his consort, created further havoc. The last Saljuq sultans followed each other in quick succession and ruled steadily diminishing territories until Tughril II, the last of the line, was killed in battle in 1194.

While remarkably little in the way of the visual arts has survived from pre-Saljuq Iran, under the Saljuqs this situation is dramatically reversed, and for the first time in Islamic Iran the flavour of a period can be captured adequately by studying a mass of its artefacts. This period, like that of the Umayyads, witnessed a prodigious expansion in the forms, techniques and ideas of the visual arts.

The heritage of the Saljuqs – political, religious and cultural – can scarcely be exaggerated. The contrast between the pre-Saljuq and the post-Saljuq periods is striking. The tenth and eleventh centuries had seen minor Persian and Arab dynasties throughout the eastern Islamic world flourish at the expense of the enfeebled caliphate. The unity of the faith had disintegrated, although Arabic was still the predominant language. By the late twelfth century the situation had changed decisively: orthodox Islam was now much stronger, having absorbed some heterodoxies and defeated others. This was principally due to the Turkish dynasties of the Ghaznavids and the Great Saljuqs. The caliph had regained his theoretical power by allying himself with the sultan, and was about to recover actual political strength too. The Turks now dominated the Middle East; certain of the territories which they controlled, such as Anatolia, north-west

Iran and Central Asia, have remained Turkish-speaking ever since. Theirs was in some senses a disruptive influence; they represented a pastoral economy immemorially opposed to agriculture. One contemporary historian remarked wryly that tax-farming was 'the only way to interest Turks in agriculture'. They constituted a recurrent political threat because certain tribes could with impunity flout the authority of the sultan. Plunder was the only aim of many of the tribesmen and this could not always be channelled into holy wars. But the Saljuq leaders quickly adapted themselves to the Persian way of life. Under their aegis Persian became widespread throughout the empire and Iran itself became an artistic centre of the first importance. Above all, the centre of gravity in the Islamic world had shifted from the Arab territories to Anatolia and Iran. The traditional centres of Islamic power in the Middle East – Damascus and Baghdad – had now to some extent been supplanted by such Saljuq capitals as Merv, Nishapur, Rayy and Isfahan – every one of them in the Iranian world. This dominance of eastern Islam, together with the rule of the Shiʿite Fatimids in Egypt and sometimes Syria, made final that break between the eastern and western parts of the Islamic Near East which has endured virtually ever since.

The area within which Great Saljuq art flourished is often loosely taken to be that of modern Iran, but more of it was in fact outside those political boundaries than within them. Modern scholarship has not progressed far enough to identify the full range of local schools inside the Iranian world with confidence, though it is clear that the arts of Syria and Anatolia had their own distinctive character. Similarly, the chronology of 'Saljuq' art is hard to correlate with political events: the rhythms of stylistic development are not those of dynasties. Typically Saljuq work is found in the early eleventh as in the early thirteenth century, and thus outside the time-span of Saljuq political power. And extremely similar work in various fields – notably architecture – was practised under the dynasties that coexisted with or succeeded the Saljuqs proper. Nonetheless, this chapter will confine itself to the output of the Saljuq period in Iran, for that was the centre of Great Saljuq power; and while some Saljuq rulers extended their authority far to the west, and to the north-east, their hold on this territory was more tenuous. Moreover, the visual arts in Syria and Iraq in this period followed their own path, in which local traditions played a major role.

The importance of Saljuq art within the broader context of Islamic art as a whole lies in the way that it established the dominant position of Iran; one may compare the pivotal role of late-medieval Italy in European art. It also determined the future development of art in the Iranian world for centuries. In its own time its impact was felt, either through the agency of the Saljuqs themselves or through their successor states, from Syria to northern India. The period 1000–1220 set benchmarks in various media, from pottery and metalwork to the arts of the book and architecture. However, the overlap between Saljuq art and that of the Buyids, Ghaznavids, Ghurids, Qarakhanids and Khwarizmshahs – to name only some of the major stylistic groupings of the time – is such that these dynastic labels are often unhelpful if not downright misleading. The basic fact to bear in mind is the existence of an artistic koine in the eastern Islamic world between 1000 and 1220. That dialect, moreover, was at its most vigorous in the years of Saljuq decline and after the fall of the dynasty in 1194, and it owed much to the political unity imposed by the Saljuqs on eastern and western Iran. It is to this later period that the major technical advances of Saljuq art can be attributed, though in the fields of architecture and Qur'anic manuscripts consummate masterpieces were produced long before then. Still, the trend is clear.

66   The second half of the twelfth century (the Bobrinski bucket of 1163 in the Hermitage provides a convenient point of departure) saw an unprecedented expansion of figural decoration, whether in the form of narrative scenes (taken for example from the *Shahnama* of Firdausi), pictures of courtiers, animals, zodiacal themes, and images from the princely cycle featuring hunting, banqueting, music-making and the like. Long benedictory inscriptions in Arabic

64   become the norm in the portable arts. Sculpture in stucco, ceramic and metal now takes on a new importance.

The sheer productivity of these centuries in the visual arts represents, in comparison with the output of earlier centuries, a quantum leap forward. With this increased quantity – which is helped by a standardization of shapes – comes an expansion in patronage, which now not only operates at court level but also has a new popular dimension, perhaps an expression of widespread urban wealth deriving from a buoyant economy. This art, then, reveals a cross-section of contemporary society and its tastes: luxury and utility Qur'ans; large royal and small provincial mosques; expensive lustre or *mina'i* (overglaze-painted) pottery and coarse glazed ware reminiscent of folk art; elaborately inlaid metalwork and virtually plain cast pieces. One can identify numerous local schools, for example in architecture and ceramics. A natural by-product of this intense activity was a

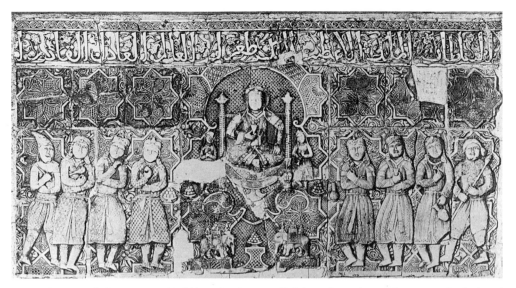

64 Pomp and circumstance, Turkish style. Stucco relief from Rayy; late 12th century. It depicts the enthroned Saljuq sultan Tughril (II?; d. 1194) surrounded by his officers. Directly beneath his feet is written 'the victorious, just king' and in the panel above are his titles, interrupted atypically by the sultan's personal name placed directly over his head.

wide range of technical and stylistic innovations. It must be remembered, however, that the picture is skewed, especially in the fields of pottery and metalwork, by the massive scale of illegal excavations in Iran over the past hundred years. In other countries of the Islamic world most of the comparable material is still in the ground. And the paucity of detailed monographic studies of key objects and buildings means that much basic information is still either unavailable or inadequately contextualized.

Thus the originality of Saljuq art is apt to be exaggerated. In many cases the artists of the Saljuq period (it is misleading to speak of 'the Saljuqs' in this connection) consolidated, and indeed at times perfected, forms and ideas that had long been known. In architecture one may cite the cruciform 4-*iwan* plan, the domed sanctuary pavilion in the mosque, and the tomb tower; in Qur'anic calligraphy, the apotheosis of what has been termed the 'New Style' of Kufic, now integrated with lavish illumination; in metalwork, the technique of inlay using several metals; and in painting, the development of the frontispiece. Above all, there is surprisingly little for which a source right outside the Iranian world can be posited. Although the Saljuqs themselves were Turks, it is hard to point to any specifically Turkish

91

elements in the art of Iran and its eastern provinces in the period under review, with the possible exception of the moon, or Buddha, face in figural depictions. This seems to point to the dominance of Iranian artisans in the visual arts. Parenthetically one may note that the picture in Anatolia, where people of Turkish extraction formed a larger proportion of the population, is distinctively different; there, references to pagan Turkish religious beliefs, funerary customs and royal ceremonial are frequently encountered.

What of patronage? Only two pieces of Saljuq pottery made for persons of high rank, one an *amir*, the other a vizier, are known, and the situation is little better in the case of metalwork. The overwhelmingly rich and varied production in these fields ought presumably, therefore, to be attributed to patronage exercised at a lower level of society, such as merchants, members of the learned class and professional people. Most likely, much of it was made for the market, though this would not exclude its use by those of high rank. Architecture, involving as it did much larger sums of money, is a different story altogether. Inscriptions in mosques and mausolea mention the Saljuq sultans themselves, for example Malikshah and Muhammad, or viziers such as Nizam al-Mulk or Taj al-Mulk. Turkish chieftains are named in the tomb towers of Kharraqan, army commanders at Urmiya, and numerous *amir*s, for example at Maragha, Mihmandust, Qazvin and Abarquh.

Problems of provenance have bedevilled the study of the decorative arts in the Saljuq period. These problems have been exacerbated by the fact that most of the known material has not been scientifically excavated and lacks inscriptions yielding solid information on provenance. Confusing and contradictory information on this topic proliferates. The very few securely provenanced items perforce act as a peg on which to hang all manner of other pieces, and their evidential value is simply not enough to justify this practice. It is now generally accepted that virtually all lustre and *mina'i* wares – the most expensive ceramics of the period – were made in Kashan (though the distinctive heavy red body of lustre tiles found in the Kirman area suggests local production there), and sherding studies suggest that this luxury ware was widely traded. Conversely, many other slightly less luxurious but still fine wares cannot be securely associated with any one city or area, and they might therefore have been produced in several places independently (like the Samanid epigraphic ware of the tenth century, which was produced in both Samarqand and Nishapur, and apparently in Merv too).

65 Ceramic sculpture. Lustre *mihrab* re-used in the Masjid-i Maidan, Kashan. It is dated 1226, inscribed with the names of the Twelve Shi'ite Imams and signed by al-Hasan ibn 'Arabshah. Its many components were separately fired and fitted together. The contrast of buff and blue mimics the palette of contemporary architecture. H. 2.84 m (9.3 ft).

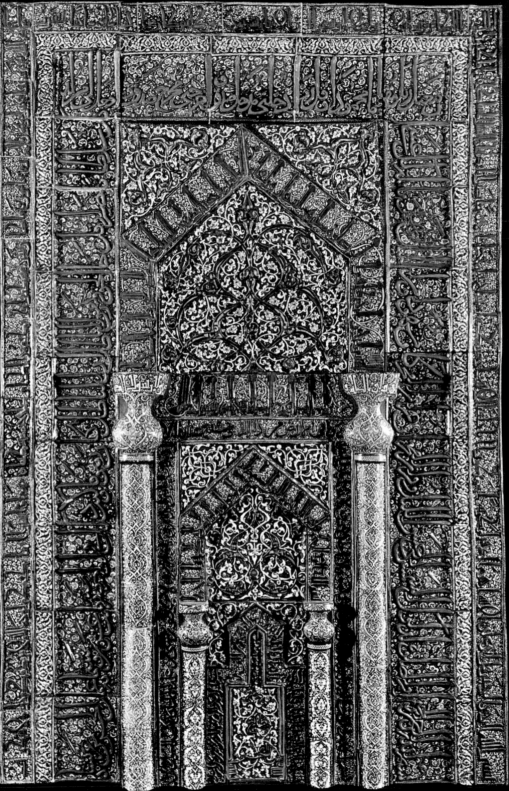

Similarly, the fact that the celebrated Bobrinski bucket and the jug of 1182 now in Tiflis both bear an inscription stating that they were made in Herat indicates that fine inlaid metalwork was produced in that city. The craftsmen's names, which are traditionally supplemented by their place of origin (*nisba*), indicate Khurasani cities – Herat, Merv, Nishapur – and thus confirm the important role of this province in metalwork. But it is not enough to justify the wholesale attribution to Herat of wares that merely share some of the features found on work from that city. This is particularly unlikely for metalwork that is technically simpler than the inlaid pieces, since the demand for such cheaper work must have been too widespread to be catered for by a single production centre. But exactly where these other Iranian workshops were located must be determined by future research. The astonishing range of forms encountered in Saljuq metalwork (including many derived from architectural forms) also points to numerous centres of production. It seems likely that some of the best craftsmen travelled widely to execute commissions, and that fine pieces (e.g. of Kashan tilework) were shipped over long distances. There is evidence too of a division of labour in metalwork

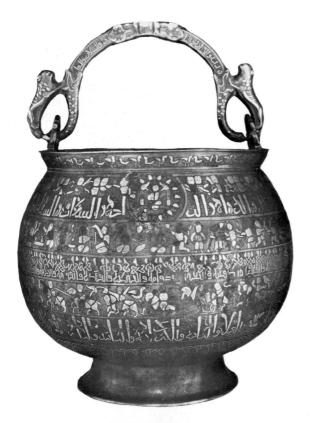

66 The ultimate pilgrimage accessory? The 'Bobrinski bucket', technicolour cast and inlaid bronze; possibly for ritual ablution during the *hajj*. Six long inscriptions mention the makers (caster and decorator, of equal rank); provenance and date (Herat, Muharram 559/December 1163); and the inflated titles of its patron, a pious merchant from far-off Zanjan. Note the human-headed letters (the earliest dated examples known) and the scenes of leisure pursuits. H. 18 cm (7.1 in).

and lustreware that ensured a higher level of quality overall. But the key question remains: scholarship has not yet established whether the pockets of intense activity in a limited geographical area have a wider significance for pan-Iranian production or whether they reflect a well-developed specialization confined to a given area.

Laboratory examination has yet to be used in a systematic way on Saljuq metalwork; the evidence that it would provide on alloys, for instance, could then be correlated with other factors – shape, technique, decoration – to create a more nuanced picture of the various known types. In the current state of knowledge it is safe to say that wares constructed from sheet metal were made of brass while most others were of a four-part alloy; true bronzes are uncommon. A twenty per cent tin bronze was also used but traditional low-tin bronzes are unknown.

The very few pieces of Saljuq metalwork in silver point to a serious shortage of that metal which became more critical as the eleventh century advanced. It was perhaps in part a result of the practice followed by the Viking traders travelling along the great Russian rivers, who hoarded the Islamic silver coins with which they

68

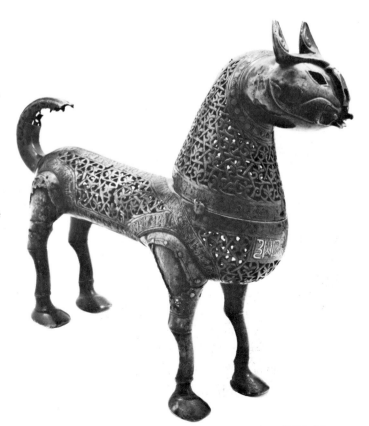

67 Latent iconophobia? Signed open-work zoomorphic incense-burner, bronze inlaid with silver. North-east Iran, 11th century. The litheness and ferocity of this creature are much exaggerated, the body itself dematerialized and reduced to an inscribed and decorated surface. Thus the artist avoids usurping God's prerogative of creating life. Compare Ibn 'Abbas advising a painter: 'You must decapitate animals so that they do not seem to be alive and try to make them look like flowers'. H. 45 cm (17.7 in).

68 (*right*) Luxury tableware. Silver rose-water sprinkler with cap; *repoussé* and chased, with niello decoration and gilding. Rose-water was used to scent the beard before eating, for washing hands, perfuming clothes and carpets and flavouring food. The rose was the favourite Muslim flower and figured largely in Persian love and mystical poetry. H. 24.9 cm (9.8 in), body diam. 12 cm (4.7 in).

69 (*below*) The courtly ethos. Polychrome painted *mina'i* bowl with confronted horsemen and peacocks (symbols of Paradise), a design derived from textiles. Iran, probably early 13th century. The androgynous figures follow contemporary fashion with their Turkish caps and long plaits. The fat palmettes echo Qur'anic illumination. Diam. 21.5 cm (8.5 in).

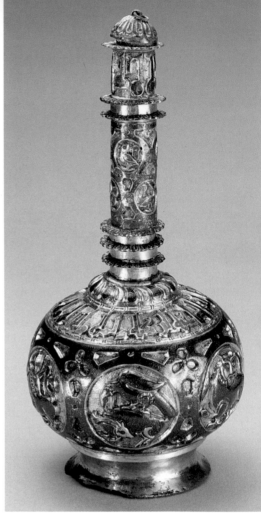

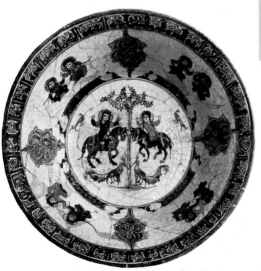

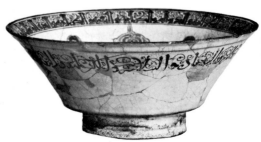

were paid for slaves, furs and amber and who thus took the coins out of circulation. The gradual cessation of the minting of silver coins in the Iranian world and Anatolia in this period, and their replacement by copper *dirham*s, provides incontrovertible evidence of this trend, anecdotal evidence of the survival or use of individual silver objects notwithstanding. Base metal had perforce to fill the gap, but its value was greatly enhanced by the practice of inlaying it with copper, silver, gold and a bituminous black substance, the whole giving an effect of polychrome splendour. Thus fine craftsmanship did duty for precious metal. This technique, with its plethora of detail, lent itself to the creation of elaborate figural scenes; even inscriptions took on human and animal form. These inlaid objects survive in large quantities, probably because their metal content (unlike that of silver and gold objects) was not sufficiently valuable to be worth melting them down, whereas the intrinsic value of their top-quality craftsmanship was obvious.

67

In ceramics, the earliest dated underglaze-painted, lustre and *mina'i* wares are respectively placed by their inscriptions to the years 1166, 1179 and 1180, and therefore all postdate the death of the last Great Saljuq ruler, Sultan Sanjar, in 1157. Conversely, in metalwork there are several dated pieces between 1063 and 1148 – i.e., from in the Saljuq period. The frequency of dated ceramics (and many are signed) argues a higher status for fine pottery than had previously

69

70 A clue to lost Saljuq book painting. Moulded lustre plate made in 1210 by Sayyid Shams al-Din al-Hasani for a military commander. A royal groom sleeps by a pool, oblivious of the monarch's entourage, and dreams of a water-sprite. The fish, water, woman and horse all relate to Sufi mystical metaphors. H. 3.7 cm (1.5 in), diam. 35.2 cm (13.9 in).

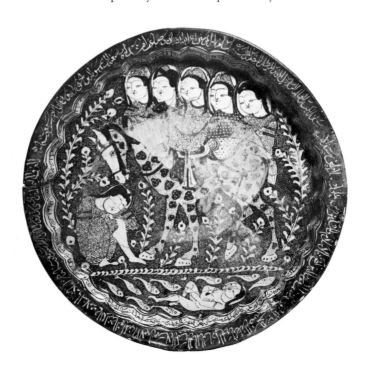

obtained. A new light body known as stone-paste or fritware was devised, though whether this was a Saljuq or a Fatimid invention remains unclear. It was made largely from ground quartz, with small quantities of ground glass and fine clay, presumably an attempt by Islamic potters to imitate the body of Chinese porcelain. (The discovery of Ding and Ch'ing-pei wares at Gulf coast sites provides some of the necessary evidence of trade with China.) Such pieces were mostly moulded. Others belonged to categories known as silhouette and double-shell wares. In these, as in sgraffito wares, much of the decoration was incised with a knife or a pointed object. In the silhouette type the design was often scraped through a black slip under a turquoise glaze. Such incised wares continued a fashion well-established before the Saljuq period. Underglaze painting in blue and black was also popular, as was a type of translucent white ware, often pierced for greater effect. Many of the more expensive wares bear hurried cursive inscriptions of Persian love poetry, mostly indifferent

72, 73

71 (*below left*) A wedding present? Overglaze-painted beaker in *mina'i* or *haft rang* (seven-colour) technique. Iran, early 13th century. The narrative, in strip cartoon format, recounts the love story of Bizhan and Manizha, a highlight of Firdausi's *Shahnama*. This beaker long predates manuscript illustrations of the story, and proves that a well-developed *Shahnama* iconography existed by *c.* 1200. H. 12 cm (4.7 in).

72 (*below right*) The arts were interdependent. Spouted jug, painted black under a transparent turquoise glaze. Kashan, early 13th century. The elaborate perforated shell transfers to the fragile medium of ceramics a technique first developed in metalwork, and better suited to that material.

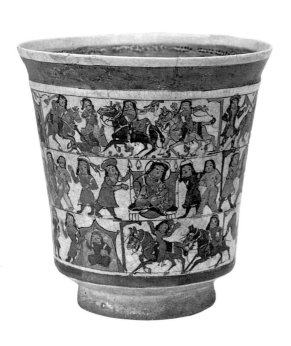

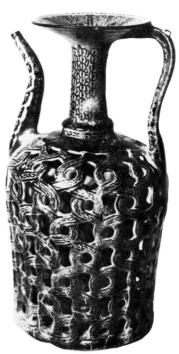

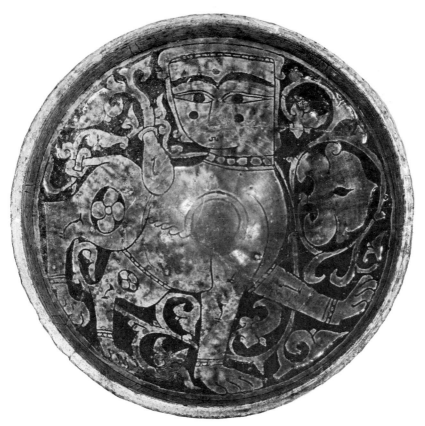

73 The world of magic. Deep green bowl, in *champlevé* technique (i.e. with large areas of slip cut away). Western Iran, 11th century. The sphinx has apotropaic, paradisal and astrological associations, and is also often depicted with the griffin, thereby symbolizing the sun's journey through the heavens. The rosettes echo this theme. The facial features conform to the contemporary ideal of beauty. Diam. 25 cm (9.8 in).

in quality, and praise the maker of the piece. Scientific analysis of pottery has successfully differentiated between the original ceramic and modern repairs to body and decoration alike, a crucial distinction since, apart from a cache of lustre wares found at Gurgan, virtually no medieval pieces have remained intact.

A close connection existed between the most elaborate Saljuq ceramics and book painting, including – in the case of abstract orna- 70, 71 ment – Qur'anic illumination, as shown by figural types, narrative strips and numerous stylistic features, while many details of the shape and decoration of Saljuq ceramics – handles, stepped feet, imitation chains, incising, gilding, fluting – derive from metalwork. Similarly, the ornamental sheen and decorative motifs of Saljuq metalwork reveal close familiarity with manuscript illumination. All this points both to the interdependence of the arts in this period and to the existence of hierarchies within the visual arts, since the cheaper arts copy the more expensive ones – never vice versa.

The recent demonstration that the majority of textiles once thought to be Buyid or Saljuq are in fact of modern manufacture has made it imperative to submit all so-called Saljuq silks to scientific tests, and proper renders premature any art-historical enquiry into them.

The principal centre of book painting in the twelfth and thirteenth centuries was Iraq, which was then under the control of the newly renascent caliphate (see pp. 125–32). But this painting often has marked Iranian features, suggesting the existence of an earlier pan-Saljuq school of painting in which distinctions between Iraq and Iran were perhaps not very significant. The most likely candidate to represent the largely vanished art of Saljuq book painting is the verse romance *Varqa va Gulshah* ('Varqa and Gulshah'), written in Persian by the poet 'Ayyuqi and signed by the painter 'Abd al-Mu'min al-Khuyi. This suggests a provenance in north-west Iran, but Anatolia is a distinct possibility too. The manuscript (in the Topkapi Saray 74 Library in Istanbul) has seventy brightly coloured illustrations in strip format against a plain coloured or patterned ground, with figural types of the kind familiar in *mina'i* pottery. The paintings have a strong narrative drive enriched by a complex iconography in which the animals which figure in many of the pictures take on symbolic meaning, connoting for example watchfulness, fidelity, treachery and courage. A fragment of al-Sufi's *Kitab Suwar al-Kawakib al-Thabita* ('Treatise on the Fixed Stars') in the Bodleian Library, Oxford (Or. 133), undated and unprovenanced but probably of the thirteenth century, might be of Iranian origin. But for all the paucity of the surviving material, the clear dependence of both fine ceramics and fine metalwork on manuscript painting and illumination shows clearly enough the high profile which the arts of the book enjoyed in the Saljuq period.

Several fine Saljuq Qur'ans have survived. They include dated examples in Mashhad (466, i.e. 1073 in the Christian calendar), Tehran (485/1092 and 606–8/1209–11), Philadelphia (559/1164; produced in Hamadan) and London (582/1186), as well as examples which slightly predate the advent of the Saljuqs (London, 427/1036 and Dublin, 428/1037). There are also numerous undated but probably Saljuq examples in Dublin, Paris, Istanbul, Tehran and London, to say nothing of parts of Qur'ans or individual leaves in dozens of collections throughout the world. Saljuq Qur'ans are notable for their magnificent full-page or double-page frontispieces and colophon pages, often of pronounced geometric character, with script in panels taking a prime role. They are known both in *naskhi* 76 and in 'New Style' (or 'East Persian') Kufic. There is a substantial 75 variation in scale – from small one-volume Qur'ans measuring only 12 × 10 cm (4.7 × 4 in) to large ones of 41 × 28 cm (16 × 11 in), and in some the limited amount of text per page resulted in Qur'ans of thirty or sixty parts, large and small, each part with its own frontispiece. The diversity of size and layout extends to the number of lines per page, which varies from two to twenty, and to the scale, quantity and placing of illumination. The task of establishing dates and provenances for this ample material, and devising working categories for it, has only just begun.

In architecture even more than in other fields the dividing line, so far as style is concerned, between what is definably Saljuq and what precedes that period is very hard to draw, though the Mongol invasion and the architectural vacuum that followed mean that there is a distinct break in continuity after *c.* 1220. A few examples will make this clear. The characteristic minarets of Saljuq type – lofty, cylindrical, set on a polygonal plinth and garnished with inscription bands and geometric brick patterning – are known from at least as early as the 1020s (for example at Damghan and Simnan). Of the two standard types of Saljuq mausoleum, the tomb tower perhaps reached its 77 apogee in the Gunbad-i Qabus, dated 1006–7, while the other type, 78 the domed square, had already been brought to a pitch of perfection in the so-called 'Tomb of the Samanids' in Bukhara, datable before 79 943. That building also exhibits a highly developed style of brick and terracotta ornament. Similarly, such standard features of Saljuq architecture as the trilobed squinch and the *pishtaq* or monumental portal are already to be encountered in the tenth century, for example in the mausoleum of Arab-ata at Tim. The same phenomenon can be detected in other art forms, for example in sgraffito pottery or the continuity of ring and dot decoration from pre-Saljuq to Saljuq metalwork; and while the quantity and range of architectural tilework is indisputably a 'Saljuq' phenomenon, its roots in Islamic monuments lie as far back as 'Abbasid Samarra.

The distinctive Saljuq contribution lies rather in the final establishment of several of the classic forms of Iranian architecture

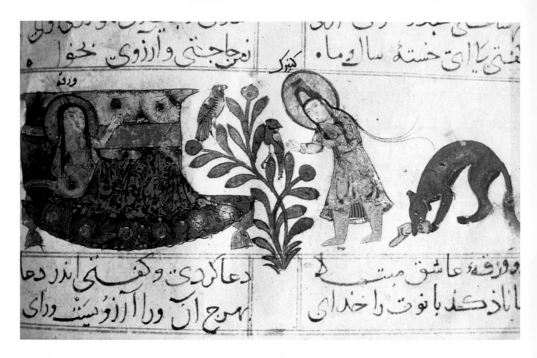

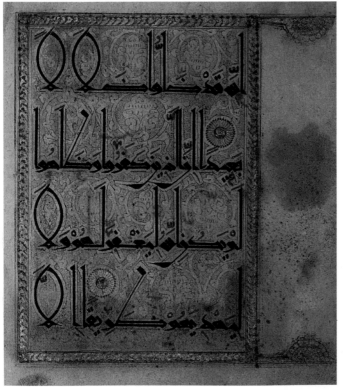

74 (*above*) Animal symbolism. Varqa, recuperating in bed from his travails, asks the maid where his beloved Gulshah is. *Varqa va Gulshah*, perhaps Anatolia, mid-13th century. The dog with his catch is a metaphor for Varqa's persistent and successful search for Gulshah. The narrative moves from left to right.

75 (*left*) Saljuq Kufic Qur'an, 1176. Parchment Qur'ans were typically oblong, paper ones vertical. Note the supralinear and sublinear flourishes which add an expressive dynamism to the calligraphy. In general, red dots add vowelling; in some manuscripts, green dots indicate primary variant readings, while yellow and blue ones represent specific orthographic elements or sounds, or secondary and tertiary variants in the text. 33.5 × 23.8 cm (13.2 × 9.4 in).

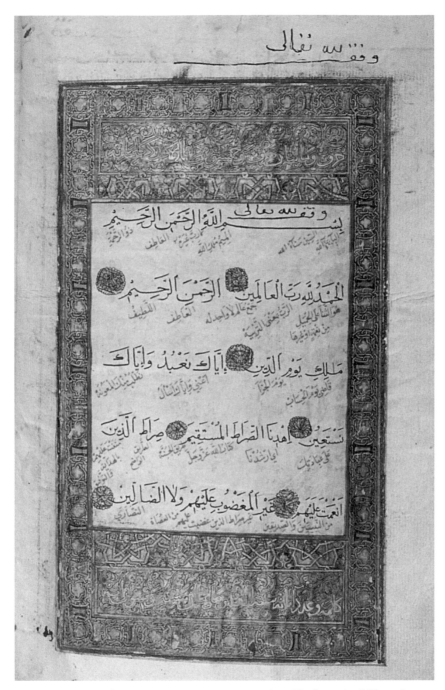

76 Saljuq *naskhi* Qur'an. Copied and illuminated by Mahmud b. al-Husain al-Kirmani, a Shi'ite, in Hamadan in 1164, it also has an 18th-century endowment inscription. Many headings are in Kufic; note the interlinear Arabic commentary. This opening page stands out: it has five lines of text, not the usual seventeen. 42 × 29 cm (16.5 × 11.4 in).

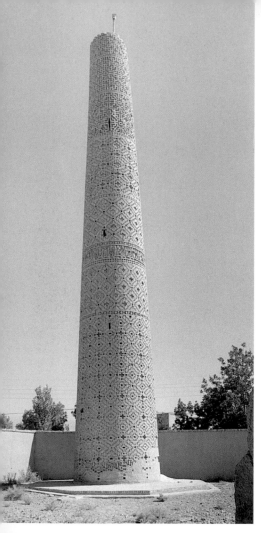

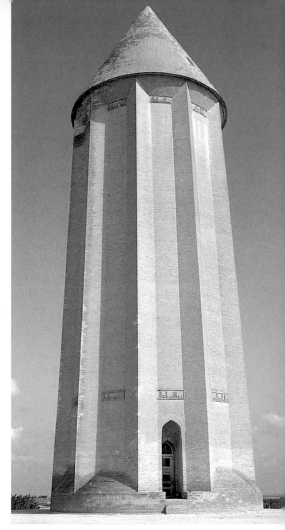

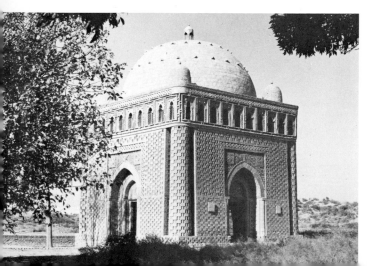

79 (*left*) A fire temple in Islamic dress. Bukhara, 'tomb of the Samanids', before 943. A precocious masterpiece in brick, integrating compact monumentality with refined all-over geometric ornament (derived from basketwork?). The pre-Islamic open-plan domed square is enlivened by engaged columns, gallery and corner domes.

77 (*opposite left*) Damghan, minaret of Tari Khana mosque, built at the order of the chamberlain (*hajib*) Abu Harb Bakhtiyar in 1026. Typically built of baked brick, many such minarets survived the mud-brick mosques which they adjoined. This minaret, now 26 m (85.3 ft) high, probably had an upper gallery for the muezzin.

78 (*opposite right*) Syncretism. Gunbad-i Qabus, 1006–7. This tower crowns an artificial mound and dominates the surrounding countryside; it is 51 m (167.3 ft) high. Ten knife edge flanges girdle the central cylinder in a strikingly modern and minimalist design. The glass coffin was suspended under the roof oriented towards the rising sun, a non-Islamic burial practice with Zoroastrian associations.

80 (*right*) Marital devotion. Mausoleum of the princess Mu'mina Khatun, 'Chastity of Islam and the Muslims', Nakhchivan, 1186, built by her husband, the *amir* Ildegiz; a landmark for the use of glazed ornament in Iranian architecture.

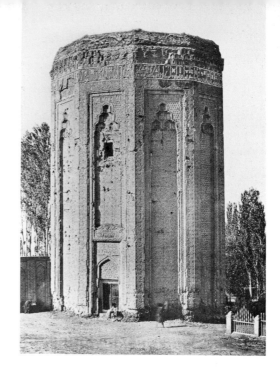

and in the capacity of Saljuq architects to draw out the utmost variety from these types. Mosques with one, two, three or four *iwan*s are known, and the 4-*iwan* plan receives its classic formulation in association with an open courtyard and a monumental domed chamber; a hierarchy of size distinguished major *iwan*s from minor ones. The Friday Mosques of Zavara, Ardistan and above all Isfahan 81 are outstanding examples of this trend. Saljuq domed chambers are characterized by external simplicity, with a frank emphasis on the exterior zone of transition, now reduced to powerful contrasting geometric planes. The interior of the dome chamber is dominated by a highly elaborate transition zone (in the Isfahan area this made a leitmotif of the trilobed arch) whose depth, energy and rhythmical movement has as its foil the austere, low-relief articulation of the lower walls and the inner dome itself. But other Saljuq mosque types, such as the free-standing domed chamber or the arcaded hall, are also known.

In mausolea, the *pishtaq* was developed from a simple salient porch to a great screen which conferred a grandiose façade on the building behind it, as at Tus and Sarakhs. The originally simple formula of the domed square underwent other major changes too, notably in the

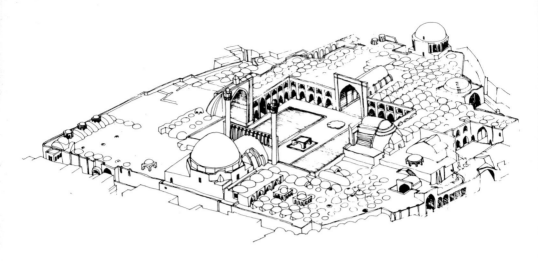

81 (*above and right*) Community centre. Friday Mosque, Isfahan, 10th century onwards. Successive generations embellished, repaired and extended this mosque, which was engulfed in the city's bazaars and served
many functions. The two Saljuq dome chambers mark the principal axis. (*right*) Beneath the myriad small
domes resembling molehills which encircle the courtyard lies an endlessly varied series of vaults, many of
them unique. The best of them date to 10th–12th centuries.

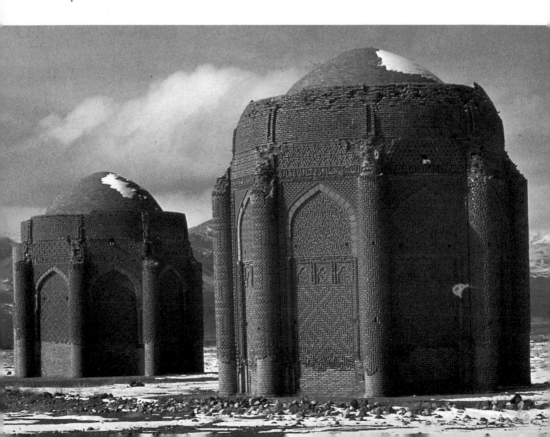

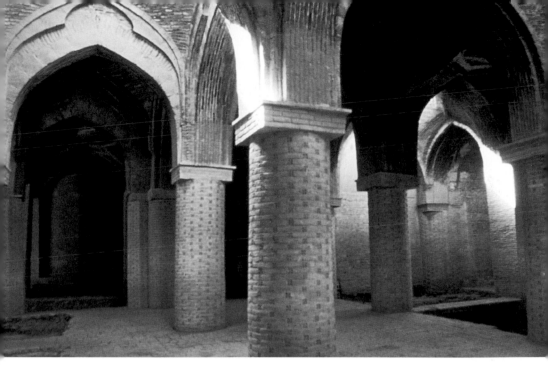

82 (*opposite*) Tents for the afterlife. Tomb
towers built in open country at Kharraqan,
western Iran, by the same architect in 1067
and 1086 for Turkish chieftains. Many details
of structure and ornament evoke the *yurt* or
tent of the Turkic nomads. The later tower,
a *tour de force* of decorative brickwork, has
almost 70 different patterns.

83 (*right*) A lance aimed at the infidel.
Minaret of Jam, Afghanistan, 1190. Built by
Sultan Muhammad of Ghur, hammer of the
Indians and the local pagans, it bears
quotations from the Qur'anic *sura* of Victory
and the whole of the *sura* of Maryam,
traditionally used as an instrument of religious
conversion. Its three tiers rise to a height of
c. 60 m (197 ft).

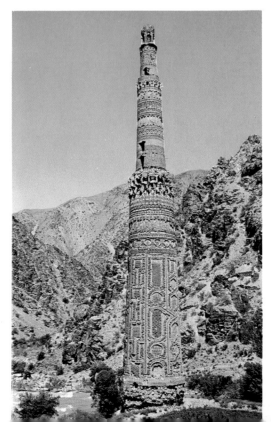

development of a gallery zone (Sangbast), engaged corner columns (Takistan and Hamadan), and double dome (the mausoleum of Sultan Sanjar at Merv). Lofty tomb towers proliferated across northern Iran, many of them built as secular memorials for *amir*s and others of high rank, though some have *mihrab*s and therefore served at least in part a religious purpose. Their form varied: some were square, cylindrical or flanged, but most had 7, 8, 10 or 12 sides, with inner domes crowned by conical or polyhedral roofs. Their form was well suited to the development of brick ornament, for it ensured a constant change of plane and therefore much variety in the play of shadow. Here, too, are found some of the earliest surviving examples of glazed tilework.

The impressive sequence of some forty Saljuq minarets comprises all manner of structural variations, including single or double staircases with or without a central column, flaring corbelled balconies, three-tier elevations, shafts articulated by flanges and engaged columns, and – an innovation destined to have a long history in Iranian architecture – the double minaret flanking a portal, whether this was the entrance to a building or the *qibla iwan*. Many have a symbolic rather than a strictly liturgical role. Minarets also occur as highly visible free-standing monuments unrelated to other buildings, and in such cases seem to have functioned as land-locked lighthouses.

No Saljuq palaces survive in good condition, though excavations have revealed the ground plan of the 4-*iwan* palace at Merv, and the palatial kiosk of Qal'a-yi Dukhtar in Azerbaijan still stands despite its ruined state. But the palaces of Tirmidh, Ghazna and Lashkar-i Bazar, all yielding abundant decoration, belong to much the same cultural sphere even though they are linked to Samanid and Ghaznavid rulers respectively. The same situation applies in the case of the *madrasa*, a particularly serious deficiency given the unambiguous testimony of the literary sources to the effect that such buildings were erected throughout the Saljuq empire. Controversial remains surviving at Khargird, Tabas, Rayy, Samarqand, and near Sayot in Tajikistan (Khwaja Mashhad) permit no clear statement as to the form of the *madrasa* in Saljuq times. The luxuriously embellished and largely ruined Shah-i Mashhad of 1175–76 in Garjistan, identified by its inscription as a *madrasa*, is a Ghurid foundation, while the building at Zuzan, dated 615/1218–19 and also identified epigraphically as a *madrasa*, was erected by a governor of the Khwarizmshahs. Taken together, their awesome scale and magnificence suggest that the

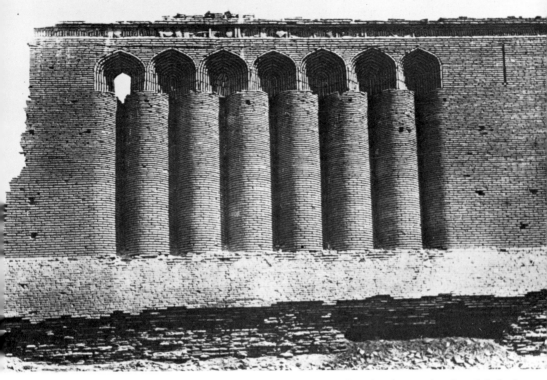

84 Massive monumentality. Central Asian caravansarais of the 11th and 12th centuries, though built for trade, owe much to earlier local fortified manor houses. The Rabat-i Malik of 1078, in Uzbekistan, now mostly destroyed, has a stark power and sense of volume which is strangely modern in feeling.

*madrasa*s of the Iranian world in this period far outshone those from other Islamic territories.

Several caravansarais (lodging places for travellers and their animals) datable to Saljuq times are known; four of them – Ribat-i Malik, Daya Khatun, Ribat-i Mahi and Ribat-i Sharaf – bear lavish decoration. Indeed, Ribat-i Sharaf (probably built 1114–15, repaired 1154–55), with its huge double courtyard plan (repeated at Akcha Qal'a in Turkmenistan) is a museum of contemporary decorative techniques. Such splendour, when linked to its location astride the main road from Merv to Nishapur, makes it plausible that this building served as a royal stopover. Most Saljuq caravansarais, however, are built for use rather than display, with rubble masonry, strong

84

fortifications and minimal comfort. In many of these buildings the prescriptive power of the 4-*iwan* plan made itself felt.

The Great Saljuqs, then, ushered in the last major period of ferment in medieval Islamic art. The innovative power of this era in virtually all media cannot be gainsaid – though too little is known of the immediately preceding centuries to allow the Saljuqs to be hailed as the absolute inventors of a given feature or technique. The role of the Saljuq ruling class was in any case that of a catalyst rather than that of an originator, though influences from steppe society can frequently be detected in Saljuq art, and helped to fashion its distinctive character. That character had a decisive impact on the art not only of Iran but of the numerous Saljuq successor states. These close connections, and thus the full canonical power of Saljuq art, are obscured by the tendency of modern scholars to think in terms of watertight chronological and geographical entities. The key concept here is that the Saljuq synthesis left its mark on all later Islamic medieval art from Egypt eastwards.

85

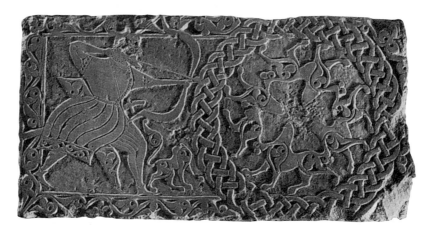

85 The royal hunt of the sun. Stone relief from Daghestan, 12th century. Hunting here takes on cosmic overtones, for the animals forming a wheel design (itself found on ancient Mesopotamian cylinder seals, and especially popular in the Jazira, the Caucasus and north-west Iran at this time) are a solar symbol, representing the full astral cycle across the heavens.

CHAPTER FIVE

The Age of the Atabegs: Syria, Iraq and Anatolia, 1100–1300

Between the eleventh and the early thirteenth centuries Anatolia and the Levant experienced something of a power vacuum. Neither the ailing ʿAbbasid caliphate nor the Fatimids were able to extend their writ to all these areas, some of them remote from their own home base, and even for the Great Saljuqs these regions were peripheral. Thus, while from time to time ʿAbbasid, Fatimid or Saljuq hegemony was recognized in some of these territories during the period under discussion, the norm was for power to be wielded over a limited area by a local warlord. The political orientation of such rulers was decisively to the east, however, the focus of orthodoxy and the Sunni revival, rather than to the Shiʿite state of Fatimid Egypt. They tended, for example, to be more involved in the power politics of Iraq, where the gradually resurgent ʿAbbasid caliphate, shorn of its pan-Islamic power, was attempting to assert itself territorially. This situation became still more pronounced after about 1100, when the power of the Great Saljuqs waned just as the Crusaders arrived in the Near East.

The contemporary power vacuum made it much easier for the Crusaders to establish first a bridgehead and then several fully-fledged independent states. It became the steadfast aim of the more important Great Saljuq successor states in the area of Syria, Anatolia and the Jazira (northern Mesopotamia) – Artuqids, Zangids, Saljuqs of Rum (Anatolia), Ayyubids – to crush the Crusaders, and the gradual build-up of Muslim religious fervour to this end, culminating in full-scale *jihad* (holy war), can be traced throughout the twelfth century. But they were scarcely less keen to fight each other, and the boundaries of their mini-states were in continual flux, especially as they practised the ruinous system of divided inheritance, as had the Great Saljuqs before them. Thus the Rum Saljuq sultan Kilij Arslan partitioned his empire between his eleven sons, bequeathing them a legacy of envy and strife. The situation was complicated still further by the rise to power of still lesser dynasties usually based on a single town, such as, in Anatolia, the Shah-i Arman at Ahlat and the Mengjukids at Divriği. Ethnically, these new rulers were neither Arabs nor Persians but Turks or Kurds, and this added a new element to the political complexion of the time.

De facto power in the Levant, Anatolia and the Jazira was now vested in warlike Turcomans whose tribal and nomadic heritage inevitably placed them at loggerheads with the peasantry and the urban populations whom they ruled. They had entered the Islamic world as the shock troops of the Great Saljuqs, and, proving difficult for the sultans to control, had been despatched to the outskirts of Saljuq territory. They had wrested much of Anatolia from Armenian and Byzantine hands and had also infiltrated the long-Islamized territories of northern Iraq and Syria. In the process, they had encountered not merely urban and rural Muslims but also Christians of various confessional allegiances – Orthodox, Armenian and Jacobite. Similarly, the Ayyubids in the Levant ruled a large population of Christians, mostly oriental but some from western Europe. All this made for a pluralistic, multilingual, multi-ethnic society instinctively hostile to the imposition of orthodoxy. Nevertheless, there are frequent references in the sources to measures taken against the indigenous Christians: for example, destroying churches, refusing permission to have them rebuilt, or converting them to mosques. Much of the interest of the art of the Atabeg polities derives precisely from the varied accommodations which they fashioned with non-Muslim traditions. They frequently employed non-Muslim artists. Equally interesting is the undertow of Persian modes in Anatolia and of Arab ones in Syria and the Jazira, though a Turkish military élite was dominant in all three areas.

The Turcomans' version of Islam seems to have had a distinctive character, involving as it did animistic and folk elements absent from orthodox interpretations of the faith. But this did not prevent rulers of Turkish stock from parading themselves as paragons of orthodoxy. The political gains of such a stance in the long-drawn-out wars against the Crusaders were obvious. In the case of the later Zangids and early Ayyubids, moreover – especially Nur al-Din and Saladin – the personal piety of certain rulers is harder to doubt and must have imparted an extra charge of energy to their prosecution of *jihad* and their hostility to the Isma'ilis. The titulature of these rulers reflected precisely these concerns. Many of these rulers also treated members of the *'ulama* (religious classes) with special and public marks of distinction. They were also great builders of religious foundations.

Others lavished honour on Sufis and founded special establishments (*khanqahs*) for them.

It is extraordinarily difficult to define a significant degree of homogeneity – politically, ethnically or culturally – in these areas during the twelfth and thirteenth centuries, even though they were contiguous geographically and experienced similar forms of government. In some ways the period constitutes an interlude sandwiched between epochs that were dominated by more powerful dynasties. Moreover, in the visual arts the inherited tradition differed markedly from one region to the next, and this alone effectively forbade the creation of a single style. But the vigour of contemporary art gives no clue to the uncertain political complexion of the times; as so often, the rhythms of art and politics do not synchronize. Not surprisingly, Ayyubid art continues Fatimid modes, Nurid art in northern Iraq is clearly a province of the Saljuq art of Greater Iran, while the Saljuqs of Rum owed much to Armenian architecture. Hence the difficulty of understanding the place of each of these very different styles within the composite picture of contemporary art. Accordingly, to lump them together in a single chapter may smack of manipulating historical realities. What do Ayyubid Syria and Saljuq Anatolia have in common? Perhaps what most links them is the fact that all of them could be described as Saljuq successor states – and that not only because they followed the Saljuqs chronologically but also because they maintained similar traditions of Sunni orthodoxy and governmental practice, and were shot through with Turkish customs and habits of thought.

Saljuq Anatolia was the most long-lived of these polities. Culturally speaking, it was in many respects a province of Iran. This situation had its roots in political realities, for the area was originally overrun by Turcomans from Iran, and the ruling dynasty from 1186 was related by blood to the Great Saljuqs of Iran. Soon after the line of the Great Saljuqs had been extinguished, the Mongol invasion of Iran brought in its train not only unprecedented carnage but also a new state, major upheavals in religious practice, and new cultural priorities. These factors caused a stream of Iranian refugees to seek asylum in the safer, more familiar and congenial atmosphere of Saljuq Anatolia. Persian poets, mystics and men of letters like Rumi and Nasir al-Din Tusi received a warm welcome in court circles, where the language of cultural interchange was Persian, where viziers of Persian origin (like the Pervane, Burujirdi and the Juvaini brothers) wielded power and the court chroniclers (like Ibn Bibi and

Aqsarayi) wrote in Persian. It was the same story in the visual arts. Persian architects and tileworkers left their names and those of their home towns on Anatolian buildings from Konya to Divriği. Much Anatolian luxury pottery favoured and continued the themes and techniques of Saljuq Iran (as at Qubadabad), as did the local metal-work (e.g. the basin known as the Nisan Tasi). Even Anatolian mau-solea replicated, though on a smaller scale and in stone rather than in brick, the forms of Iranian Saljuq tomb towers.

A Saljuq Anatolian provenance has been proposed for the earliest surviving illustrated Persian manuscript, the romantic epic *Varqa va Gulshah* (see p. 100). By far the closest parallels to the style and format of its cartoon-strip pictures are provided by the so-called 'small *Shahnama*s' ('Books of Kings'), whose provenance has long been disputed. This is because they do not fit easily into the evolu-tion of book painting in Iran proper during the fourteenth century, in which the influence of ideas derived from China is ubiquitous. True, these *Shahnama*s contain occasional references to Mongol costume and armour, but that is entirely appropriate in view of the imposition of Mongol rule in Anatolia after the battle of Köse Dagh in 1243. Given the close kinship of the figural types of the small *Shahnama*s with those of lustre and *mina'i* pottery, given too the Iranophile and Iranophone nature of the court culture of the Rum Saljuqs, and finally given the remarkable fondness for archaic *Shahnama* names evinced by successive Rum Saljuq rulers – Kaikhusrau, Kaika'us, Kaiqubad – it does seem at least tenable to see these small *Shahnama*s as a kind of refugee art and thus to consider as a possible provenance later thirteenth-century Anatolia, with its per-vasive fashion for all things Iranian, even though – or perhaps because – the area was a Mongol protectorate. The choice of text would then evince a staunch patriotic commitment to the home country – temporarily down, but emphatically not out. That said, equally strong arguments could also be marshalled for a provenance in Iran itself.

The absence of a major Islamic power in the region of Syria, Anatolia and the Jazira meant that each dynasty tended to establish its own court, and of course these local 'courts', if that is the right word, varied in size and sophistication. It was the Saljuqs of Rum whose lifestyle was the most ambitious and lavish of all; they were at pains to model their court ceremonies on those of the Great Saljuqs, and their chronicler Ibn Bibi provides detailed descriptions of the protocol followed at public audiences, banqueting, the hunt and

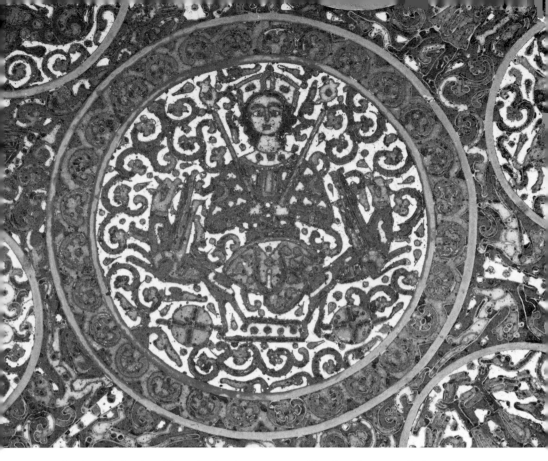

86 The classical afterglow. Alexander the Great – a powerful and mythic totem for East and West alike – ascending to heaven. Detail of bronze plate inlaid with 7-colour cloisonné enamel bearing the name of the Turkish Artuqid prince Da'ud (reigned 1114–42). This object is thoroughly international. It bears inscriptions in Arabic and Persian; its technique is Byzantine; and its iconography has Byzantine, Georgian and Islamic connections.

other activities. Whether it is strictly accurate to speak in terms of an Artuqid court, on the other hand, is another matter. These rulers were campaigning for most of the year and were therefore constantly on the move, and – unlike the situation under the Great Saljuqs – they did not have an established bureaucracy to back up political and military control with administrative authority. They had their palatial residences in their citadels – examples have survived in Mardin, Mosul, Diyarbakr, Aleppo and smaller castles like Sahyun – and they would at times commission works of art such as doors and automata, illustrated manuscripts and enamelled metalwork. It is even possible that by the end of the twelfth century palace workshops were maintained on a regular basis.

But by far the major expression of royal patronage was religious architecture. In this respect the ruling class was conforming to an ancient Islamic ideal which dictated that the ruler should build widely for the public good. Thus it was standard practice for *amir*s to build *madrasa*s, usually with their own tombs attached, as soon as they had the means to do so – and it was this custom above all, more than any government-sponsored building programme, that ensured the rapid spread of these institutions of learning throughout the Near East in the twelfth and thirteenth centuries. Large cities like
87 Damascus and Aleppo had scores of such monuments, while in Saljuq Anatolia the tally ran to several hundred in the thirteenth century alone. Indeed, it is here that the early architectural history of the *madrasa* institution can best be traced. The function did not require any particular form. Domed *madrasa*s focused on a single large chamber with adjoining cells and occasionally a courtyard may perhaps have catered for a reduced clientele of students, while the more ambitious 2-*iwan* or 4-*iwan madrasa*s, which were often graced
88 with imposing 2-minaret façades (as at Kayseri, Sivas or Erzurum) could house substantially larger numbers. In some larger cities competition between viziers seems to have generated increasingly elaborate buildings.

Mausolea proliferated even more, becoming the favoured means of conspicuous consumption in architecture. In Syria the standard form was a domed square, relatively plain inside and out, with the all-important identification of the tenant, complete with genealogy and titulature, on a panel over the door. Much of the appeal of such buildings lies in their stonework. Egypt preferred something bigger and grander, with a much more elaborate zone of transition incorporating multiple tiers of squinches, as in the tomb of al-Shafi'i. In northern Iraq rather squat square tombs with pyramidal roofs and façades in decorated and glazed brick were the rule (for example those of Imam 'Awn al-Din and Imam Yahya b. al-Qasim). Further south the *muqarnas* dome reigned supreme, with a sculpted many-tiered sugarloaf on the exterior matched by an inner dome like a fitfully illuminated honeycomb (as in the tombs of Sitt Zubaida and 'Umar al-Suhrawardi in Baghdad); the fashion spread briefly to Damascus (as can be seen in the funerary *madrasa* and *maristan* of Nur al-Din). But it was in Anatolia that the mausoleum genre was

88 (*opposite*) College for the religious élite. Erzurum, Çifte Minare Medrese, before 1242. This, the largest *madrasa* in medieval Anatolia, accommodated perhaps a hundred students. A mausoleum was added *c.* 1284, perhaps by Padishah Khatun, the wife of two Mongol khans. The building is of local volcanic stone, except for the two Iranian-style fluted brick towers with glazed ornament.

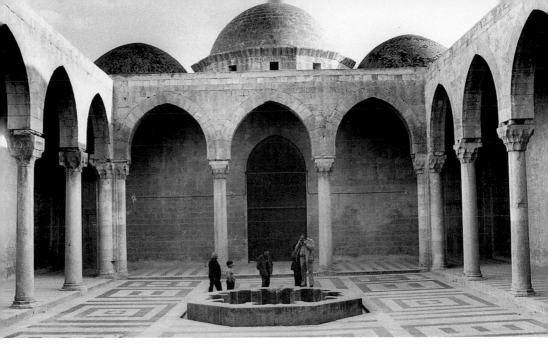

87 (*above*) The teaching of the law. Al-Firdaus Friday Mosque and *madrasa*, Aleppo, 1235–6. Built by Daifa Khatun, the wife of the local ruler, Sultan al-Malik al-Zahir – it was a time of lavish female patronage of religious buildings – it illustrates a newly fashionable type, the funerary complex. The marble floor with geometric designs is a local speciality.

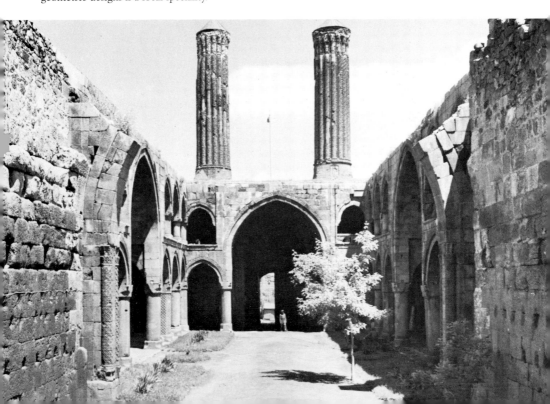

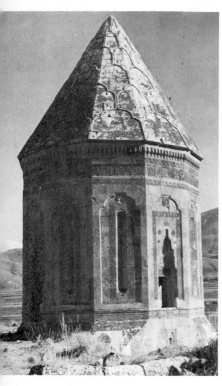
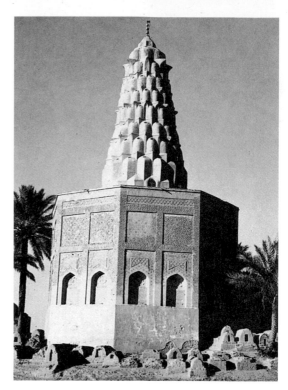

89, 90 The pervasive Middle Eastern fashion for mausolea dates from the 11th century onwards and took many forms. At Gevas (*left*) in eastern Turkey the tomb tower of Halima Khatun, 1335, has clear Armenian connections in material and design; the mausoleum of Sitt Zubaida (*right*), built *c.* 1200, has a standard Iranian lower half, decorated with geometric brickwork, but is crowned by a conical *muqarnas* dome whose external form has ancient Mesopotamian associations.

explored with the greatest energy and ingenuity. The preferred type
89 was the tomb tower, as it had been in Iran for the preceding two centuries: a circular or polygonal lower chamber (often with an
90 underground crypt for the body) crowned by a conical or polyhedral roof. Yet now, probably under the impetus of ideas drawn from Armenian church architecture, the articulation of the façade by medallions, animal sculpture, blind arcading and multiple mouldings – all executed in stone – transformed the Iranian model. Brick mausolea of authentic Iranian type were common in eastern Anatolia, while to the west and south forms cognate with the Syrian tradition flourished. Iranian modes, expressed in cylindrical brick minarets (Raqqa and Qal'at Ja'bar) and decorative brickwork (Raqqa Gate) were also briefly fashionable in the later twelfth century in eastern

91 (*opposite*) The mosque as dynastic memorial. Congregational mosque of 'Ala al-Din, built intermittently between 1155 and 1220, in Konya, the Rum Saljuq capital. Its hypostyle or Arab plan, with re-used columns, includes a dome chamber in the Damascus manner, and two royal mausolea. It shows the use of carpets not only for the comfort of the worshippers but also to inject colour into the interior.

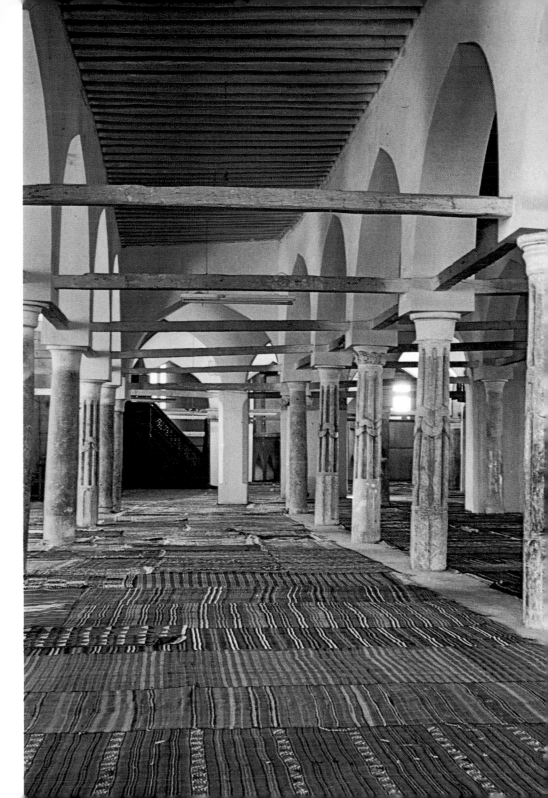

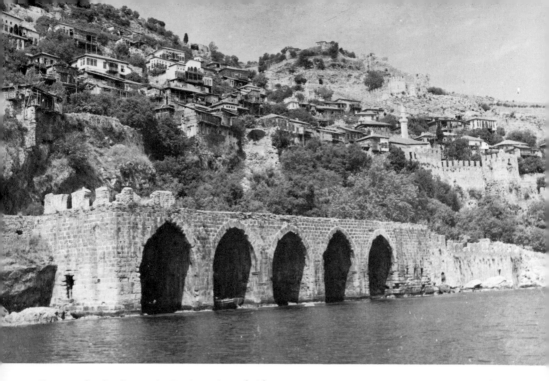

92 Entrepot for the slave trade. Dock at Alanya/ʿAlaʾiyya, a city founded in 1228 by the Saljuq sultan ʿAla al-Din Kaiqubad and exceptionally named after him. It was a summer resort and a fortified seaport of strategic importance, with an artificial harbour. In this rare example of Islamic naval architecture, with five brick-vaulted galleries some 40 m (131 ft) deep, large ships could be built safely and secretly.

Syria, while Damascus and Aleppo saw a brief classical revival which manifested itself in astonishingly accurate renditions of classical mouldings, capitals and the like.

More than any other contemporary dynasty, the Saljuqs of Rum concentrated their patronage of the arts into the medium of architecture. And it was not only in the genre of mausolea that they combined their own ideas with others taken from Syria and Iran to fashion a new style. The architecture of the mosque, for example, experienced an absolute transformation. The gable type popularized by the Damascus mosque, the ancient Arabian hypostyle, the Iranian 4-*iwan* schema – all found a place in the Anatolian world, but all were subtly changed by a new emphasis on an integrated domed space. It may well be that the germ of Ottoman religious architecture is to be sought here. As in the case of *madrasa*s and mausolea, the sheer number of mosques is as remarkable as their variety. The cumulative impression is unmistakable: there was no building tradi-

91

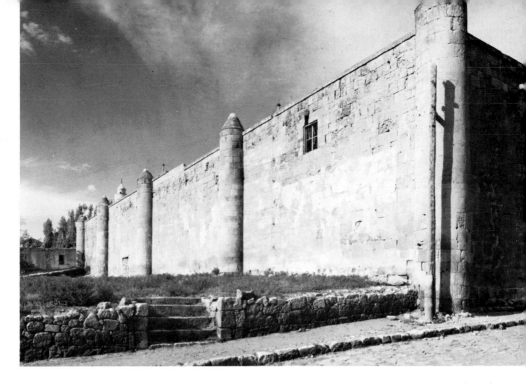

93 Castles of commerce. Caravansarai at Tercan, eastern Anatolia, early 13th century. The plan is that of a *madrasa* with two *iwan*s (bays) in its living accommodation, but it has additional lateral halls, which served as stables. Such buildings, usually financed by the state, punctuated the major overland routes at intervals of a day's journey.

tion in the entire Near East to rival that of the Saljuqs of Rum in the thirteenth century. This was partly due to the geographical position of their territories, which made them open to ideas from east, west and south; but a consistent commitment to architecture by the ruling élite made it possible for local schools to flourish mightily, so that even minor Anatolian towns can often boast major monuments in this period – most of them constructed in finely dressed stone.

The consistent state involvement in architecture is seen to best advantage in the network of *khan*s or caravansarais which criss- 93 crossed the country. Many of them have fortifications on a scale better befitting a castle than a stopover for the caravan trade. They could often hold scores of travellers and hundreds of animals. Ornate and stately portals give on to an open, arcaded courtyard, frequently furnished with a central raised kiosk to serve as a mosque. Cells for travellers lie behind the arcades. On the axis of the entrance there may be a lofty three-aisled extension of ecclesiastical aspect. This

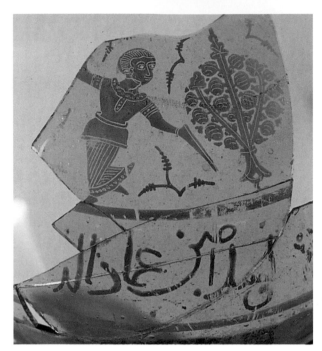

94 (*left*) The click of castanets. Dancer on a gilded glass (wine?) bowl with the title of the Atabeg Zangi (reigned 1127–46). Clichés of Islamic (and Byzantine) images of dancers include the raised right foot indicating a dance step, the three-quarter depiction of the head, the frontal torso, and the tree. Dancers, like musicians, were regarded as children of Venus and thus under the influence of that planet.

95 (*opposite*) The Turkish image of power. Group of cross-and-star tiles, palace of Qubadabad, 13th century. The disposition of tiles and the firing technique are Iranian, but the iconography draws on pre-Islamic Turkish sources (e.g. tombstones) from Inner Asia. The cobalt used for the blue colour was worth its weight in gold and was doled out carefully to selected potters from the royal treasury.

space was used for stables. Chains of Saljuq caravansarais serviced particular trade routes. Thus the slave trade from the Black Sea ports used a north–south artery departing from Sinop and terminating at Alanya, where the ample docking facilities helped in the trans-shipment of the slaves to Mamluk Egypt. Yet other routes hooked up with the long-haul traffic from Iran and points east, and also with Syria and Iraq. About a hundred of these caravansarais have survived, perhaps a quarter of the total originally built – telling testimony to the administrative efficiency of the Rum Saljuq state.

This Saljuq architecture, built for the most part of well-dressed stone and sometimes employing ornamental marble inlays which suggest Syrian workmanship, has a wonderfully varied decorative repertoire. The traditionally Muslim predilection for geometric and vegetal themes is enriched by Armenian interpretations of such motifs – for in the largely Christian hinterland of eastern Anatolia, Armenian architecture was in full flower. Figural carving abounds, in flat defiance of standard Muslim practice, and is found on religious and secular monuments alike. Its themes sometimes reflect Armenian influence, but the dominant impression is of a pagan Turkish

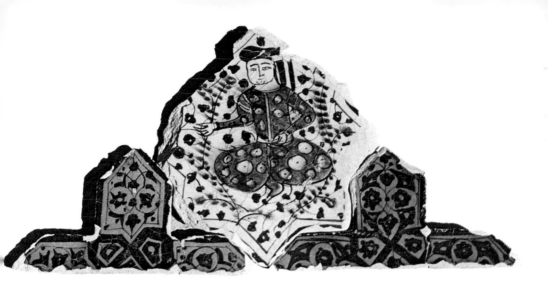

thought-world rather than an Islamic one, especially in the images of lions, eagles and bulls. But elements from the ancient Near East (solar images, fish motifs, the lion/bull combat) and the East Asian animal calendar also appear, as do the astrological and planetary images so popular throughout the Middle East in this period. Glazed and plain brick ornament of Iranian type, often executed by Iranians, was also popular; in fact glazed tilework, perhaps developed with the help of Iranian craftsmen fleeing from the Mongols, reaches a level of design and technique unequalled in Iran for another century or so. Figural tiles – *mina'i*, lustre and above all underglaze-painted in blue 95 and white – were used lavishly in the Saljuq royal palaces at Konya, Qubadiye and Qubadabad.

Iraqi architecture of this period is uneven in quality, though its decoration – whether in carved stucco, terracotta or polychrome inlaid marble – is often splendid. In the area of Mosul there flourished, from the later twelfth century onwards, a school of figural carving which decorated *khan*s (Sinjar), palaces (Sinjar and Mosul), mausolea (Mosul), bridges (Jazirat ibn ʿUmar) and city gates at Mosul and ʿAmadiya. Sometimes the themes are ceremonial – at Sinjar, for 96 example, tiers of the ruler's *mamluk*s, each bearing an emblem of office, flank a throne niche – but animal themes dominate, including griffins, lions, serpents and dragons, all of which seem to have served an apotropaic function, as on the appropriately named Talisman Gate 97 at Baghdad. Similar designs, augmented by heraldic and astrological motifs that often refer in punning fashion to the ruler himself, appear

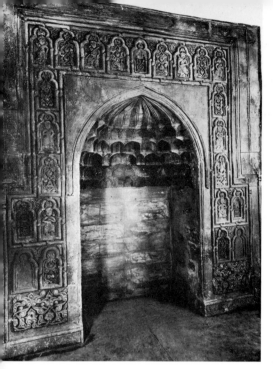

96 (*left*) The sultan's slaves. Royal niche from Sinjar, northern Iraq, before 1240. A small baldachin above the apex of the arch marks the axis of sovereignty; in the remaining niches plant motifs alternate with images of beardless figures in military dress holding emblems of office. These are specially selected slaves destined for high office.

97 (*below*) Sympathetic magic. Apotropaic relief at the apex of the now destroyed Talisman Gate, Baghdad, 1221–2. Like its accompanying magic-saturated inscription, it underlines the role of the caliph al-Nasir as sole divinely appointed head of the Muslim community; it symbolizes his victory over two internal enemies: the Grand Master of the Assassins and the Khwarizmshah Muhammad, both of whom died around this time.

98 (*right*) The language of power. Mustansiriya *madrasa*, Baghdad. Inscription dated 630/1232–3 commemorating the building of the 'noble *madrasa* for the students of wisdom, which brings happiness to (all) creation and (is) an illuminated path in the eye of God' by the ruling caliph and calling down God's blessings on him. The text is replete with Qur'anic echoes.

on Atabegid coins. The same visual language is to be found in contemporary Syriac churches in the Mosul area (Mar Behnam and Mar Shem'un), and in the Yazidi shrine at 'Ain Sifni nearby.

The Friday Mosque of Nur al-Din at Mosul, completed in 1172, is notable for a major dome over the *mihrab* surrounded by a battery of vaults in the sanctuary. Several contemporary *madrasa*s are known in Mosul and Wasit, but these pale before two masterpieces of the 98 genre in Baghdad: the Sharabiya and the Mustansiriya of 1232. The latter was built by the eponymous reigning caliph on a massive scale as an instrument of politico-religious propaganda, as shown by its

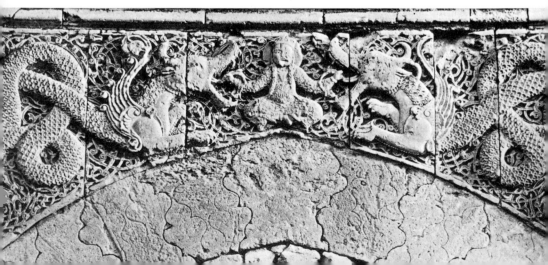

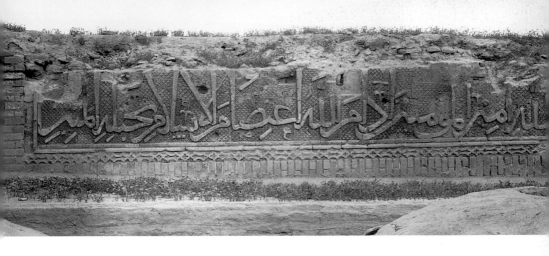

huge external riverside inscription extolling the caliph in letters
almost a metre high. It was designed to serve all four major schools
of Islamic law – a major innovation which turned it into a symbol of
Muslim unity and resurgent caliphal power. No standard plan was
followed in these structures, though all those in central Iraq are on
two floors and feature monumental portals and rooms opening off a
central courtyard, itself often furnished with *iwan*s. The Sharabiya
(formerly known as the ʿAbbasid palace) is notable for its narrow
corridors crowned by multiple tiers of steeply stilted *muqarnas* vaulting arranged in diminishing perspective towards a distant vanishing
point. These vaults exploit illusionistic devices in an entirely novel
way. They are covered in lacy terracotta carving of remarkable precision and intricacy whose closest parallels lie, intriguingly enough, in
Central Asia.

The thirteenth century witnessed the first golden age of Islamic
book painting, most of it produced in Syria and Iraq, where the
major centres were Mosul and Baghdad. The reasons for this sudden
flowering are obscure. That it soon spread very widely – to Iran,
Egypt, even Spain – is beyond doubt. To be sure, earlier Islamic
painting on paper exists, but the rubbish-heaps of Fustat have yielded
only individual sheets with illustrations of mostly indifferent quality,
while high-grade illumination was confined to Qurʾans. Literary
references prove conclusively that illustrated manuscripts were produced at the ʿAbbasid and Samanid courts, and that examples of
Sasanian book painting were carefully preserved in southern Iran in
the tenth century. Moreover, astronomical texts had been illustrated
for centuries – the earliest surviving version of al-Sufi's 'Treatise on

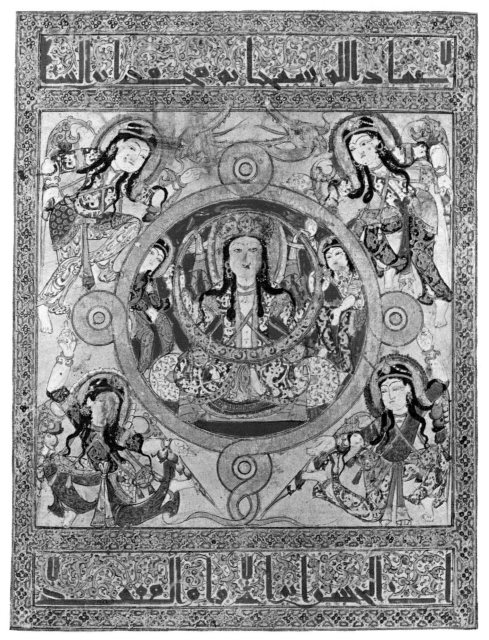

99 The old gods die hard. Apotropaic frontispiece to *The Treatise on Snakebite*, 1199. This book was written during an eclipse, which was perhaps thought to make its recipes for snakebite more efficacious. In popular belief, eclipses happened when the monster Jawzahr swallowed the sun or moon; hence the personification of the moon (of Babylonian origin) is within the serpents' stomachs. Note the echoes of Buddhist iconography. 21 × 14 cm (8.3 × 5.5 in).

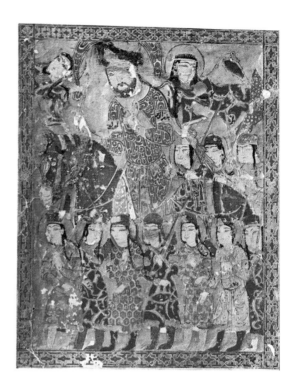

100 Mark of ownership. Frontispiece to a book from a 20-volume set of the *Kitab al-Aghani* ('Book of Songs') made for the *amir* of Mosul, Badr al-Din Lu'lu', 1217–19. The patron, whose name appears on his armbands, is resplendent in *moiré* silk and sable-fur hat and, in an unusual adaptation of standard enthronement iconography, towers over his ant-like courtiers. Flying angels (or Victories) hold an honorific canopy over his head. Echoes of Byzantine art abound.

the Fixed Stars' was produced at Baghdad in 1009. No claim can therefore be entertained for the chronological primacy of thirteenth-century painting. But it does seem likely that book illustration was only sparsely practised in earlier centuries in the Islamic world, and that this was at least in part due to the severely practical and didactic function to which it was confined. The notion that illustrations to a text could be fun seems to have dawned on Islamic artists only during the thirteenth century.

Since few of the extant illustrated manuscripts are dated, and far fewer still are provenanced, the detailed history of this school of painting has occasioned lively debate. The current scholarly consensus favours Iraq as the principal centre of production, with ateliers at Mosul and Baghdad, and a secondary Syrian school based at Damascus. Production seems to have tailed off dramatically after the sack of Baghdad by the Mongols in 1258.

The debut of this vigorous and inventive school of painting is decidedly low-key. Byzantine influences are dominant both in the choice of texts, the subject-matter of which is largely botanical and pharmaceutical, and in the didactic and diagrammatic style favoured for the illustrations. In this tradition, which continued that of the classical world, the picture was the handmaiden of the text, although in some cases – such as the very popular *Automata* manuscripts, of which fifteen copies are known – the pictures were needed to make sense of the text. There was no question of giving them an elaborate background or frame – indeed, the plain colour of the paper serves as the background – or of allotting a full page to an illustration.

One important exception to this rule, however, must be noted. In accordance with classical and Byzantine precedent, the frontispiece used a full-page painting to honour either the author or the patron of the manuscript – or even both. This practice had classical roots, themselves reworked in the Byzantine evangelist portraits which may have been the immediate source of the Islamic version. Hence the omission of the author's muse; hence, too, the gold background and the white highlights on the drapery. The Islamic contribution is at first limited to details of costume and architecture. By degrees the range of options widened to include visual references to the content of the work (Paris *Kitab al-Diryaq*, 'Treatise on Snakebite', 1199; *Rasa'il Ikhwan al-Safa*, 'The Epistles of the Sincere Brethren', 1287; *Mukhtar al-Hikam wa Mahasin al-Kalim*, 'Choicest Maxims and Best Sayings') or to the activities of court life (Vienna *Kitab al-Diryaq*; *Kitab al-Aghani*, 'Book of Songs').

Byzantine influence makes itself felt even in the layout of some of these frontispieces, which mimic the division of space used in ivory polyptychs. Lavish application of blue and gold, imitating Byzantine enamelwork and chrysography, to say nothing of iconographic motifs such as angels or victories and the symbolic use of drapery, lend some of these frontispieces an unmistakably Byzantine flavour. So too do drapery conventions and details of costume. Nor is this surprising, given that the Islamic paintings associated with northern Mesopotamia were produced in a predominantly Christian milieu, and that Jacobite painting had a strong impact on them. Where the manuscript was rounded off with a finispiece, the design would be identical to that of the frontispiece (*Kitab al-Diryaq*, 1199; *Mukhtar al-Hikam wa Mahasin al-Kalim*), perhaps following the example of Qur'anic design. The layout of all these frontispieces quickly became the vehicle for quite complex messages which had to do with subjects as diverse as talismanic protection, the royal lifestyle or scholarly activity, whether co-operative or confrontational. Yet for all their Byzantine flavour, these paintings also looked to the East. Some facial types, for example, with their slant eyes and heavy jowls, are familiar from Saljuq lustre pottery, while other figures are best paralleled in *mina'i* work.

Alongside the practical treatises, which maintained their popularity throughout the thirteenth century and even later to some extent, and which gave Arab painting such a potentially wide range, contemporary taste also favoured works of literature or *belles-lettres* whose entertainment value was paramount. Two works in particular enjoyed widespread popularity: the *Maqamat* ('Assemblies') of al-Hariri (d. 1120) of which more than a dozen illustrated thirteenth-century versions survive, and the collection of animal fables known as *Kalila wa Dimna* ('Kalila and Dimna'). The text of the *Maqamat* consists of fifty episodes in the career of a con-man, one Abu Zaid, whose trickeries depend on his surpassing mastery of the Arabic language. Al-Hariri was a wordsmith who fashioned each *maqama* so as to exploit the full resources of the language. Virtuoso linguistic display is thus the keynote of the text, which is peppered with quotations, allusions, puns and obscure vocabulary. It is essentially a thesaurus of curious and recondite terms in which action, narrative and drama are of distinctly secondary importance, and so it gave minimum encouragement to the artist. In a sense, text and image are at cross purposes. But the picaresque framework presented illustrators with the chance to produce some remarkably varied settings, often with a strongly realistic flavour but occasionally of a fantastic nature too, such as the images illustrating the adventures of Abu Zaid in the Eastern Isles.

The crowning masterpiece of the school is the *Maqamat* copied and illustrated by Yahya b. Mahmud al-Wasiti in 1237, now in Paris. 101 Its illustrations throb with vitality. Husbands and wives bicker, plaintiffs harangue judges, drunkards carouse in taverns to the strumming of lutes. The artist favours scenes of intrigue, fraud, disputa- 102 tion: he loves to group his many figures in tight bunches and is at his best in depicting processions. He relies on precise draughtsmanship and bright colour rather than on modelling or an elaborate landscape. The action is always crammed into the frontal plane while the background is the neutral colour of the paper itself. Architectural settings are rendered with a notable precision although without any attempt at perspective. Indeed, laborious spatial devices are consistently avoided. A few fleshy plants do duty for a landscape and the sky is rarely indicated. The scene shifts from the slave market to a village, from a Bedouin encampment to formal parades or pilgrims departing for Mecca.

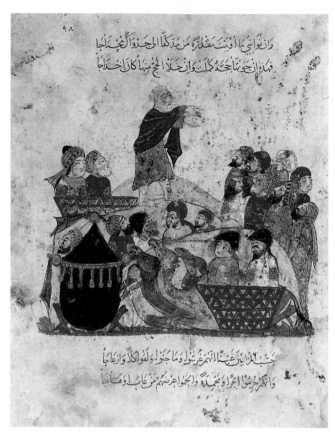

وَاِنْ نَوَانِي مَا اَقْتَنَتْ مَا قَفِزْ مِنْ مَدِّكَهَا الجِدُ وَالنَّغْنَجَا
فَمْلِهِ اِنْ رَجَحَ بِنَاجِحَةٍ مَلَّكَ وَاِنْ جَلَا الحَجَّ بِنَا كَانَ اِخْلَاجَا

١٠١ Grandiloquence rewarded.
This is the message of the
Maqamat, whether the speaker
performs in a secular context or
in a religious one (as here, in a
Baghdadi manuscript of 1237).
Here, however, the usual
oratorical posturings of the
disreputable hero, Abu Zaid,
atypically serve piety rather
than self-interest. Spotlighted
on a hill, he harangues an
audience of pilgrims, which (in
satirical vein?) even includes
camels. Much depends on
gesture and the glance in the
eye; context is deftly delineated
by a few well-worn landscape
props. Note the *mahmal* or
palanquin, typically used by
noble ladies for the Pilgrimage
to Mecca.

Such illustrations do not depend on any earlier pictorial tradition,
and among the many hundred *Maqamat* pictures of this period no
consistent iconographic cycle can be recognized. All this suggests
that the artists held up a mirror to daily life and found out of their
own resources an appropriate visual equivalent for what they saw —
though they might have been inspired, for example in their choice of
the silhouette mode, by the contemporary shadow theatre. But older
Near Eastern traditions also make themselves felt in the strong
outline drawing, the exaggeratedly large eyes and the interest in
surface patterning which here expresses itself in the technique of
rendering drapery in convoluted scrolling folds. Given the atrocious
difficulty of the text (couched in rhyming prose) one may wonder
whether the flood of illustrations (about a hundred in some manuscripts), which resulted in a picture for every two or three pages on

103

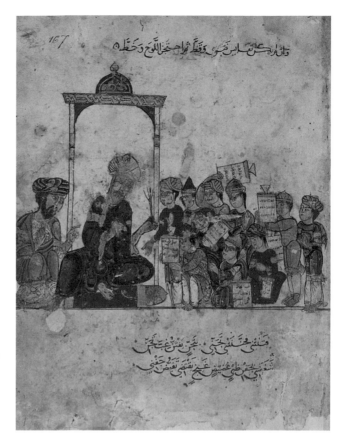

102 Literacy begins early. This *Maqamat* image (possibly Damascus; the tablet held by the boy in front states that the manuscript was executed in 1222–3) shows Abu Zaid in the guise of a schoolteacher. He holds a split cane, the traditional instrument of correction. Undeterred, his motley class crowds around him, with most of the boys holding a *tabula ansata* (the form of which replicates the writing slate of classical times) covered with Kufic writing, not the cursive script one would expect. The teacher's authority is suggested by his greater size, his stately turban and the honorific arch underneath he alone sits.

average, was the result of a specific trend in patronage. Clearly it was fashionable to possess a copy of this most popular of contemporary texts in the field of light literature; and those patrons whose literary accomplishments were too slight to profit from the text itself could nevertheless derive enjoyment from the pictures. These, then, are some of the earliest coffee-table books.

Much the same could be said of the illustrated versions of the *Kalila wa Dimna*, a text of Sanskrit origin which had already been translated frequently into the languages of Europe and western Asia. Here the purpose of the text is only incidentally entertainment. Its real purpose is to provide a 'Mirror for Princes' through the medium of animal stories whose anthropomorphic quality is only thinly disguised. As with the *Maqamat*, then, the attractiveness of such manuscripts was two-fold. Ancient Indian, 'Abbasid, Samanid and south

131

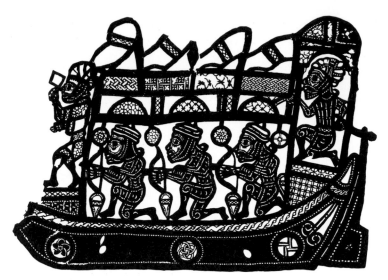

103 Popular culture. Egyptian river boat of painted leather, Mamluk Egypt, 15th century. Prop for a shadow play; the style recalls *Maqamat* paintings. The articulated figures were backlit against a white wall. The contemporary historian Ibn Khaldun noted of the Turks that they place their archers 'into three lines, one placed behind the other. They . . . shoot from a squatting or kneeling position.'

Italian illustrated cycles of these stories either survive or are recorded in literary sources and it is therefore no surprise that in the Syrian and Iraqi versions, too, specific iconographic cycles can be recognized. Bright colours, strong, dramatic profile poses, simple symmetrical compositions – all combine to push the narrative along. Later Mesopotamian painting petered out in a stale imitation of the style in vogue *c.* 1240, though court painting in the Persian manner was occasionally practised in Baghdad.

Speculation has abounded as to the patrons who called this school of painting into being. The short and unhelpful answer is that none of these manuscripts specifically names the patron who ordered it, though the ruler who figures in the frontispieces of the surviving volumes of a luxury *Kitab al-Aghani* ('Book of Songs') wears *tiraz* bands with the name of Badr al-Din Lu'lu'. The popular nature of the most frequently illustrated texts perhaps encourages the notion that they were produced either directly for members of a well-to-do middle class – that very class whose life is mirrored so accurately in the *Maqamat* manuscripts – or that they were intended for sale in the open market, in the certain knowledge that a steady demand for such

132

works existed. Such bourgeois patronage would contrast sharply with the courtly milieu in which almost all the best Persian painting was to be produced (see pp. 205–12).

In no area of the visual arts is the flux of cultures represented in the Jazira and neighbouring areas in the twelfth–thirteenth centuries more apparent than in coinage. Here a decisive break was made with the long-established Muslim tradition that coins should bear inscriptions only, and not images. The Artuqid and Zangid rulers minted literally scores of different figural types drawn from a bewildering farrago of sources. This phenomenon remains basically unexplained. The aberrant issues were confined to large copper coins and were thus intended for local circulation; gold and silver denominations (the latter comparatively rare) would have travelled further afield and thus perhaps remained strictly orthodox in design and content.

Since the copper coins were of substantial size (up to 36 mm [1.4 in] in diameter), they could accommodate quite elaborate designs. Their reverses customarily bore confidently executed Arabic inscriptions. Figural themes include more or less maladroit copies of the busts of dozens of specific Greek, Seleucid, Byzantine, Sasanian and contemporary Turkish rulers, standing or enthroned figures of Christ or the Virgin, and planetary and astrological images such as Libra, Virgo, Jupiter in Sagittarius, Mars in Aries, figures seated on a lion   104 (Mars in Leo?) or a serpent (the constellation Serpens?), the lion and the sun, and a seated figure holding a crescent, a representation of the moon. Such images referring to the heavenly bodies are common in the other arts of the Jazira and were accessible not just to Muslims but also to people of other faiths. This pervasive fascination, bordering on obsession, with astrological imagery may well reflect, as

104 Malignant planets. Artuqid coin, Mardin, 1199–1200, depicting Mars. Detailed familiarity with astrological concepts was expected of a man of culture and is a stock-in-trade of medieval Islamic literature, especially Persian poetry. Reporting on the arrival of the Crusaders on the Levantine coast in 1096, al-ʿAzimi adds laconically 'Saturn was in Virgo': in other words, disaster was imminent.

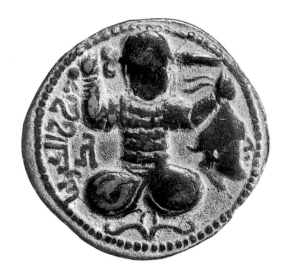

recent research suggests, the abnormal frequency of eclipses and other celestial phenomena in this area and period, which must have struck dread into the hearts of those who experienced them. Other themes include horsemen; double-headed eagles; angels and Victories; and affronted or addorsed heads, sometimes crowned with eagles. On occasion Roman and Byzantine models turn up on the same coin, or a borrowed type is altered for no clear reason – thus Heraclius has his beard shaved off. Some of the prototypes were well over a millennium old, which argues some antiquarian interest on the part of the mint-master; others were recent Byzantine issues. They share an indifference to the accurate rendering of the model; hence their frequently grotesque proportions. Other designs may have been copied from seals or other small objects, and would thus have had to be reworked for use on a coin.

What characterizes this body of coins above all is the random, jackdaw interest in the *disjecta membra* of the past – a past which had been inherited by virtue of conquest. Sometimes the design refers in punning fashion to the ruler himself. In that sense these coins could be interpreted as a formal *prise de possession*. And ancient non-Islamic coins provided a ready-made numismatic source for royal iconography – so perhaps the Turcoman rulers adopted these ancient imperial busts as self-portraits. The Christian themes of so many of these coins can be explained by the fact that the population in these territories was largely Christian and had long been accustomed to exclusively Christian copper coinage. As with funerary and architectural sculpture of figural type, the lesson of these coins is that in a Turkish context the hand of Islamic orthodoxy lay rather lightly, and that artists were accustomed to look very far afield for inspiration.

Medieval twelfth- and thirteenth-century Syrian ceramic wares include fine specimens of lustre and of underglaze, the latter typically in turquoise and black. Tell Minis has yielded the most distinctive group, and several glazed apothecaries' jars can be associated with Damascus, but the exact localization of the numerous so-called 'Raqqa' wares, with their trademark silhouette style, is still disputed. Unglazed barbotine ware in this period, seen to best advantage in the *habb* or storage jar, often draws on a remarkably tenacious repertoire of pre-Islamic mystical and apotropaic images. Syria also produced quantities of glazed three-dimensional ceramic sculpture in this period – animals, horsemen and even nursing women.

Metalwork reached new heights of technical sophistication in the thirteenth century. It is now generally agreed that some of the artists

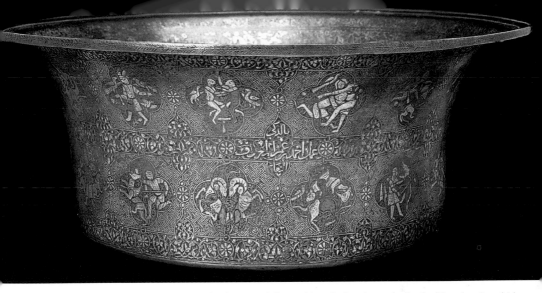

105 *Joie de vivre*. Brass basin, inlaid with silver, used for washing the hands; made for the libertine Ayyubid sultan al-Malik al-ʿAdil; datable 1238–40 and signed by Ahmad al-Dhaki al-Mausili. The upper images, reading left to right, depict a striding falconer, dancing monkeys, acrobatic dancers (one a nude female, unique in Islamic metalwork); man killing lion; below, man spearing winged quadruped, two moufflons affronted, bull attacked by winged lion; man fighting bear. H. 19 cm (7.5 in), diam. 47.2 cm (18.6 in).

who fled westward from Khurasan during the Mongol invasions settled in Iraq and that they included metalworkers. The principal centre of production was Mosul in northern Iraq, but the industry also flourished at Damascus and Siirt (Isʿird) in eastern Anatolia. Mosul was famed throughout Muslim lands for its inlay work in red copper, silver and even gold, though the technique had been employed in the Iranian world since the first half of the twelfth century, as had many of the favoured Mosul themes. The names of several craftsmen have survived in a sequence of some thirty signed or dated pieces which can be attributed to the city and which extend over the entire thirteenth century. Foremost among them was one Ahmad al-Dhaki who flourished in the 1220s. A hallmark of Mosul work is the intricate background of interlocking T-shapes, while animated scripts in both Kufic and *naskhi* scripts proliferated in narrow bands which compartmentalized the densely worked surface. Other bands were crammed with figural cycles depicting scenes from court life – music, banqueting, the hunt, mounted combats, enthronements; or similar motifs occupied lobed medallions set against geometrical ornament or interlace, as in the Blacas ewer in London.

105

Bowls, vases, ewers and candlesticks predominated in Mosul metal-work. The coming of the Mongols enfeebled and eventually killed the industry in its home city; but local craftsmen took their skills elsewhere, notably to Damascus and Cairo, to such effect that it is sometimes hard to distinguish between authentic Mosul production and that of these other centres.

One short-lived specialization associated especially with Damascus is represented by a group of eighteen surviving inlaid brasses of extremely elaborate workmanship depicting New Testament narra-tive scenes alongside the standard cycle of princely amusements. This suggests less the activity of Crusader patrons (though that is also pos-sible) than a new readiness to make such decoration reflect the con-temporary culture in all its diversity – a culture in which native Christians had acclimatized themselves and in which refugees from the East were arriving in ever greater numbers. Such mixtures of Muslim and Christian images are also known in Armenia and Sicily, areas where Muslim and Christian lived in close proximity. Certainly many Latin Christians developed, like the Normans of Sicily before them, a taste for the luxuries of local life; as a certain Foucher remarked, 'We who are occidentals have now become orientals'. It would be wrong to interpret such 'Christian' metalwork as intended purely for Christian patrons, partly because of the strong Islamic tenor ensured by their Arabic inscriptions and by scenes from the Islamic princely cycle, and partly because of the very way that the Christian themes are treated. They contain numerous iconographic solecisms and their layout, with its frequent emphasis on single or paired figures in arcades, suggests that visual symmetry counted for more than meaning. Thus the Christian themes were rendered more decorative and less meaningful and their iconographic charge was defused. The absence of images of the Crucifixion and the Resurrection is a pointer in the same direction. These key events were not part of Muslim belief and their absence helped to make such objects acceptable to the Muslim majority. This metalwork may even have connoted the subject status of the Christians under Muslim rule, as the details of hierarchical placing suggest. Such works of art had something to say to Crusaders, local Christians and Muslims alike; and, although three of the most splendid were clearly made for Ayyubid rulers or dignitaries, the majority were perhaps produced not to order but for the market.

Damascus, along with Aleppo, was also a major centre for the rela-tively new and technically demanding craft of enamelled glassware.

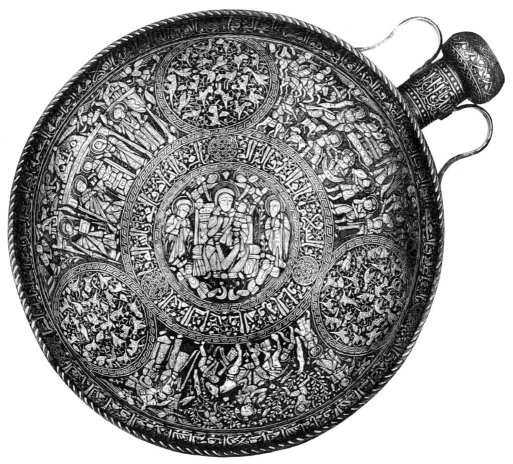

106 Pluralism. Brass hanging canteen inlaid with silver and black organic material. The form derives from pilgrim flasks; its design features units of three. Muslim ornament and inscriptions alternate with Christian themes: the central Madonna and Child, and the Nativity, Presentation and Entry into Jerusalem in the outer zone. Their iconography reflects Christian Syriac manuscript illustration. Diam. 36.9 cm (14.5 in).

Here too, alongside the inscribed mosque lamps produced in large quantities for the Muslim market, beakers and goblets – and occa- 94 sionally larger pieces like the Cavour vase, midnight blue in hue, and the Corning Museum candlestick – found their way into European ownership. Their decoration of hunting and battle scenes, sometimes enlivened by topographical themes, all executed in a style akin to the Iranian *mina'i* wares, ensured them an international success.

CHAPTER SIX

The Mamluks

In a narrow political sense the Mamluk dynasty began in 1250 as a direct continuation of Ayyubid rule in Egypt and the Levant, with the significant difference that power now passed into the hands of the slave soldiers employed by the Ayyubid sultans (the Arabic word *mamluk* means 'owned'). Yet while the notion of loyalty to one's master rather than to one's family was theoretically fundamental to Mamluk society, the reality often contradicted this, and occasional short-lived family dynasties wielded power in the Mamluk state. Court life revolved around the sovereign, who – like his officers – had begun his career as the military slave of some powerful *amir*. Fresh supplies of such slaves were procured at regular intervals, mostly from the Eurasian steppe via the great markets at the Black Sea ports. The majority of these slaves were ethnic Turks. Thus for two and a half centuries the central Arab lands of Egypt and the Levant were under non-Arab control.

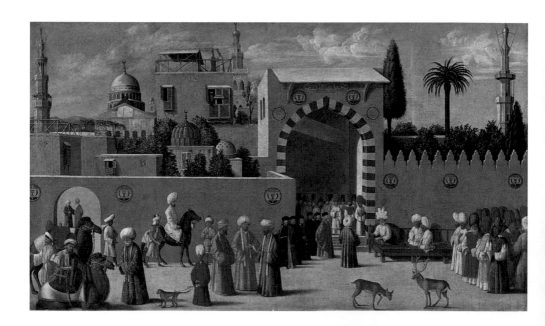

107 (*opposite*) Nascent orientalism?
Anonymous Venetian '*Reception of
the Ambassadors*', after 1488, set in
Damascus. This symbol of East-West
interface is crammed with accurate
architectural, heraldic and sartorial
detail; the lure of exoticism makes
itself felt in the emphasis on
extravagant headgear (note the sultan's
spoked turban) and on non-European
animals like the monkey, camels and
gazelles.

108 (*right*) 'Seek the bounty of your
Lord by trading' (Qur'an 2:199) – the
Prophet Muhammad was himself a
merchant. Lithograph by David
Roberts, 1849. Bazaar of the silk
merchants in Cairo, sandwiched
beween the towering funerary
complex of Sultan Qansuh al-Ghuri,
c. 1504. High windows leave ample
room for stalls below. Such
foundations, deliberately over-
endowed for investment purposes
(see *ill.* 111), effectively legalized
self-interest.

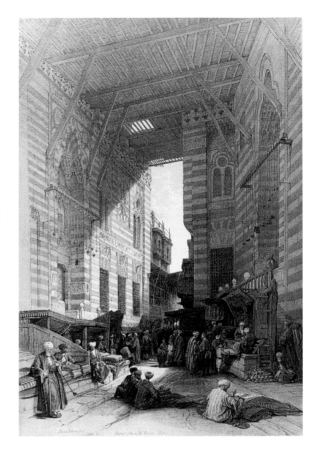

On the broader political scene the Mamluks achieved spectacular
successes. Above all, it was they who turned back the seemingly irre-
sistible tide of Mongol conquest and decisively prevented a Mongol
takeover of the entire Near East. Beginning with the first major
defeat inflicted on the Mongols by an Islamic army – at 'Ain Jalut
(Goliath's Spring) in 1260 – they maintained a steady and successful
defence for more than half a century against repeated Mongol incur-
sions in Syria and the Hijaz. At the same time they flushed out the
Crusaders and the Armenians of Cilicia from their remaining strongholds and thereby established a grip on the Levant which was not to
be broken until the Ottoman conquest in 1517. Thus they were able
to present themselves to the rest of the Muslim world as the successors of Saladin and the upholders of Islamic orthodoxy. In the process,
they confirmed and extended the Egyptian dominance of the Near

East begun in the Fatimid period. In the field of art and architecture, this entrenched primacy of Egypt was such as to inhibit the development of separate, individual styles in the Levant, and to eclipse Iraq. Indeed, when the Mongol invasions created a widespread refugee problem, Cairo was the obvious haven for the displaced craftsmen from Iraq and Iran. Hence, it seems, the sudden flowering of metalwork in Egypt and the introduction of glazed tilework, high drums and ribbed domes into Cairene architecture. Only in the far west of the Islamic world, sundered from Egypt by thousands of miles of sea and sand, did an Arab art independent of Egypt continue to flourish.

The key to Mamluk art is the city of Cairo. This was quite simply the greatest Islamic metropolis of the Middle Ages, and reduced to provincial status even such renowned cities as Damascus, Jerusalem and Aleppo. It had inherited not only the prestige of Baghdad, but also – because it now housed the ʿAbbasid caliph, even though he was no more than a puppet – the religio-political authority that was inseparably linked to the institution of the caliphate. In that respect Mamluk Cairo was able to play the central role for orthodox Muslims which had been denied to it as the capital of the Shiʿite Fatimids. Cairo was better placed geographically than was Baghdad to be the pivot of the Arab world, but by the same token it was of course further removed from the Iranian sphere and the lands still further east. Nevertheless, its favoured location meant that its horizons opened on to the Mediterranean and thus the Christian cultures to the north, as well as on to the Red Sea and so the trade with India and South-East Asia. Mamluk trading interests embraced the Italian city-states, notably Florence; southern Russia and the Eurasian steppe, the source of the slaves on which the Mamluk élite depended; and the trade in spices and other luxuries with India and points east. For all these products Cairo was the natural mart. This far-flung international trade helped to make Cairo the most cosmopolitan Muslim city of its time. As such it provided the perfect setting for the tales of the *Thousand and One Nights*, a text which took shape in the Mamluk period, although its milieu purports to be that of early ʿAbbasid Baghdad. It says much for the glamour of late medieval Cairo that it could take on the mantle of the most prestigious of Islamic cities.

That glamour was in large measure created and sustained by the public pomp and circumstance which distinguished the Mamluk court. An anonymous Venetian artist working in the late fifteenth century captured the pageantry of a Mamluk procession in a painting

(now in the Louvre) entitled *The Reception of the Ambassadors*. 107
Gorgeous turbans, heraldic blazons, festive hangings and stately
steeds all play their part in a carefully stage-managed spectacle. That
same theatricality permeates Mamluk architecture, which of course
provided the setting for so much of public life. The emphasis on
façades is especially telling in this respect. Paradoxically, the sheer
quantity of surviving Mamluk buildings seems to have deterred
scholars (with the exception of Meinecke) from tackling the architecture of this period as a whole. Individual monuments have
attracted close study, but a few detailed monographs are a poor
exchange for a full general survey. The last two centuries of Mamluk 116
rule in particular – in other words, most of the period in question –
have been especially neglected. This means that no general picture
has yet emerged of how Mamluk architecture changed in the course
of almost three centuries.

One major factor in these changes was the sheer density of urban
development in medieval Cairo. Given that space was at a premium
(and this was equally true in, say, Jerusalem), architects not only had
to think in terms of gap sites, with all the shifts and compromises
which that entailed, but also were almost forced to develop their
buildings vertically rather than horizontally. The canyons of modern
Manhattan were foreshadowed in the great thoroughfares of
medieval Cairo, especially in Bain al-Qasrain, effectively an extensive
open-air gallery where the buildings of one royal patron after
another vied for space. The resultant emphasis on façades often conflicts with the basic need for a *qibla* orientation. Solutions to this
problem became a deliberate aim pursued with increasing sophistication in a wide range of buildings; and often the aim is to ensure not
that the building should proclaim its Mecca orientation from afar but
rather that the façade should blend smoothly into context, leaving
accurate *qibla* orientation for the interior alone, safely out of sight.

The same emphasis on outward appearance dictates that minarets
are subtly designed so as to yield their best only at roof level and
above. Open loggias or belvederes break out at second-storey level.
In dome chambers, bull's-eye windows – single, double or in groups
– lighten the zone below the cupola; powerfully sculptural roll
mouldings accentuate the chamfer that marks the external zone of
transition. Narrow portals streak upwards to explode – as in the
Sultan Hasan *madrasa* – some 25 m (80 ft) up in a vault of sunburst
design. Domes are set on high drums and develop a vocabulary all of
their own, full of architectural fantasy: a high stilt, rippling ribs like

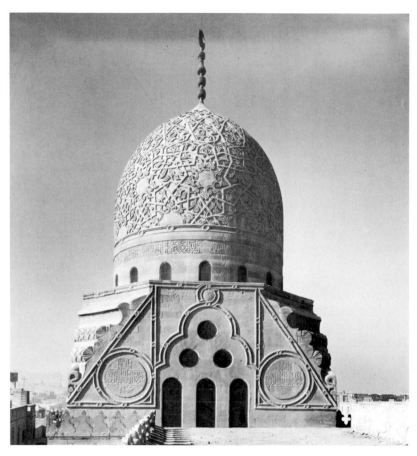

109 The Mamluks were military men. Small wonder that their domes resemble carved helmets. The larger dome (1474) in Sultan Qa'itbay's funerary complex, Cairo, fittingly symbolizes his wealth and status. Its interlocking networks of stellar and arabesque design synchronize to perfection: a fugue in three dimensions.

organ pipes, networks of arabesques or of geometric designs. They became a natural focus of attention and the architects consistently exploited the fact that they were visible from all sides. Lower walls are kept deliberately plain so that they function visually as sheer cliffs. If they are given articulation, the effect is again to emphasize their height – whether by minor salients, pilasters or mouldings.

Although the almost continuous building boom, and its concentration on three or four building types, imposed a certain sameness on the architectural forms themselves, the architects had plenty of room for manoeuvre in the choice, the type and the placing of ornament. Certain architectural features in particular became the focus for decoration. Flat lintels with shallow relieving arches above proved consistently popular, with the individual stones or voussoirs of either lintel or arch, and occasionally both, taking ever more complex and baroque forms. Eventually these interlocking voussoirs were executed in marble of different colours. The motif of the radiating shell niche, originally a Fatimid device, was definitively removed from its earlier preferred context of the *mihrab*, though the keel arch continued in use for some time. Instead, during the Bahri period (1250–1382) the shell motif was widely employed all over the exterior of a building and now developed into a multi-framed flattened *muqarnas* composition.

Fenestration takes on a new importance. Mamluk architects favoured long narrow windows with gridded screens to provide external articulation and also to reduce and modulate the play of light within. Windows animated, for example, the base of a dome and the zone of transition. In a single building – such as the funerary *khanqah* of Baibars al-Gashankir – they can vary continuously

110 'The best protection for the community's money is the community itself' said the Prophet. Hence the small domed treasuries in some mosques, as here in the Great Mosque at Hama, Syria, originally a church (8th–14th centuries). This example – probably Umayyad – employs re-used Byzantine columns. The square minaret derives from local pre-Islamic Christian bell-towers.

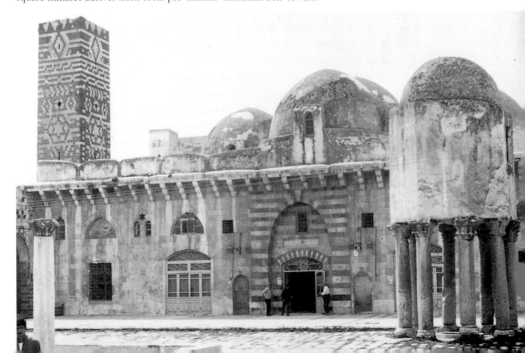

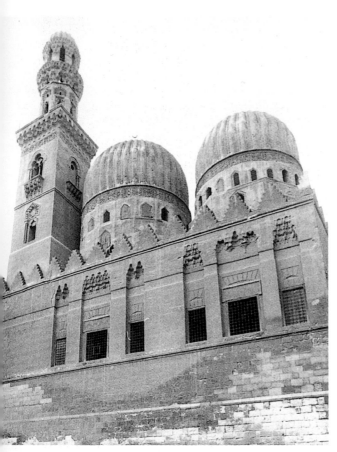

111 (*left*) The sultan's turrets. Funerary *madrasa* of Salar and Sanjar al-Jauli, Cairo, 1303–4. The funerary complex, a charitable endowment, served to keep wealth in the family; thus relatives filled key posts and shared in surplus revenues. The Mamluk obsession with rank and status resulted in domed private mausolea hijacking the public *madrasa*s which were ostensibly the purpose of such foundations.

112 (*opposite above*) Luxury flats for medieval merchants. The *wakala* or *khan* of the Mamluk sultan Qansuh al-Ghuri, Cairo, 1504–5. Its revenues serviced his funerary *madrasa* next door. The lower two stories served as warehouses and workshops, with a gallery for easy circulation; the upper part consisted of apartments for rent, each on three floors.

113 (*opposite below*) Antiquarianism with an agenda. Mausoleum of Sultan Qala'un, Cairo, 1284–5. This interior, opulent even by Mamluk standards, echoes the polychromy and varied media and textures of the Umayyad monuments of Damascus and Jerusalem, and quotes from them the octagonal plan, vine scroll band and arcaded *mihrab*. Is Qala'un claiming something of their sanctity and thereby legitimizing his dynasty?

in both scale and shape. Some of their forms – such as the double lancet window with a crowning oculus – may evolve from contemporary European styles. Aside from their function of providing light and ventilation, they operate as black voids in a blank external wall, and thus animate otherwise dead space. This contrast between a plain expanse and some form of articulation is a favoured device of Mamluk architects. It can best be appreciated in the densely carved openwork medallions which so frequently garnish Mamluk façades, such as that of the funerary *madrasa* of Sunqur Sa'di. New forms of window grille, using the time-honoured vegetal and geometric modes, made their appearance (as in the mosque of Baibars or the Qala'un complex), often framed by inscription bands. Similar epigraphic friezes girdle the bases of domes and even of columns.

113

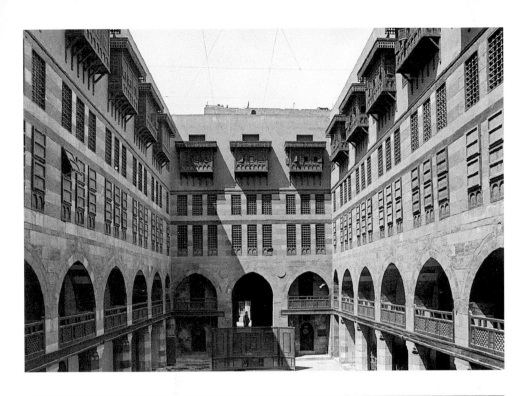

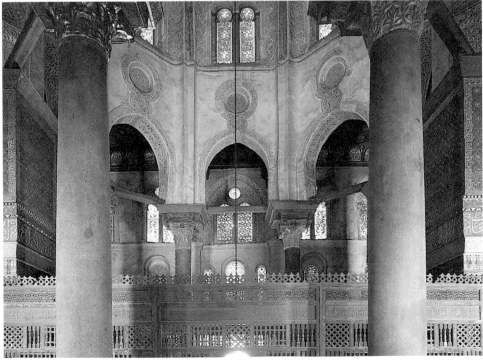

In the Burji period (1382–1517), however, it became common practice to employ the wall as a neutral surface for panels of elaborate ornament like pictures in a gallery. Since much of the colour in Mamluk interiors was provided by polychrome marble inlay, and not principally by more perishable materials, its effect can be measured to this day. Integral to the overall impact was the use of *ablaq* (literally 'piebald'): marble used in bands of contrasting colours, for example horizontally along a wall or vertically in the soffits or undersides of an arch. It was handled with consummate virtuosity in *mihrab*s to produce explosive radiating designs, and was ideally suited to parade the complexities of interlocking voussoirs. Fresco, mosaic, enamel and stained glass widened still further the range of colour and texture.

Mamluk architectural decoration is distinguished not merely by its strong sense of colour but also by its pervasive sculptural quality. This finds expression, for example, in multiple mouldings with intricate and profuse detailing, but most of all in the enthusiastic application of honeycomb *muqarnas* vaulting to surfaces suitable and not so suitable: portal domes, niche hoods, squinches, *mihrab*s, and tier upon tier of cornices on minarets. Whereas in other Islamic traditions, for

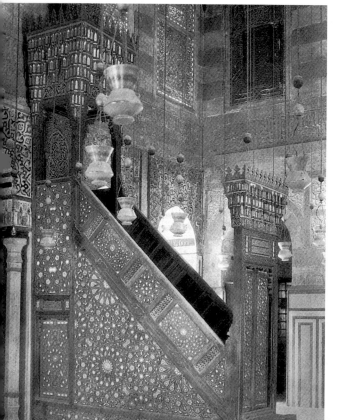

114 A mosque in miniature. *Minbar* in the mosque of Qijmas al-Ishaqi, Cairo, 1479–81. The doors serve as entrance portal, the steps as the principal *qibla* axis, the arch at the top a miniature *mihrab* surmounted by an elaborate *muqarnas* domical construction. The imagery of light, suggesting spiritual illumination, is pervasive – ivory, gilding, stellar and sunburst designs, and lamps galore.

115 'Thieves stealing from thieves' was how the 15th-century historian al-Maqrizi described contemporary Cairene patrons of architecture; the dearth of fine materials forced them to ransack earlier buildings. Here, the salient façade of the *madrasa*, mosque, mausoleum and *khanqah* of Sultan Barquq, 1386, employs two-tone marble veneer and a bronze oculus grille.

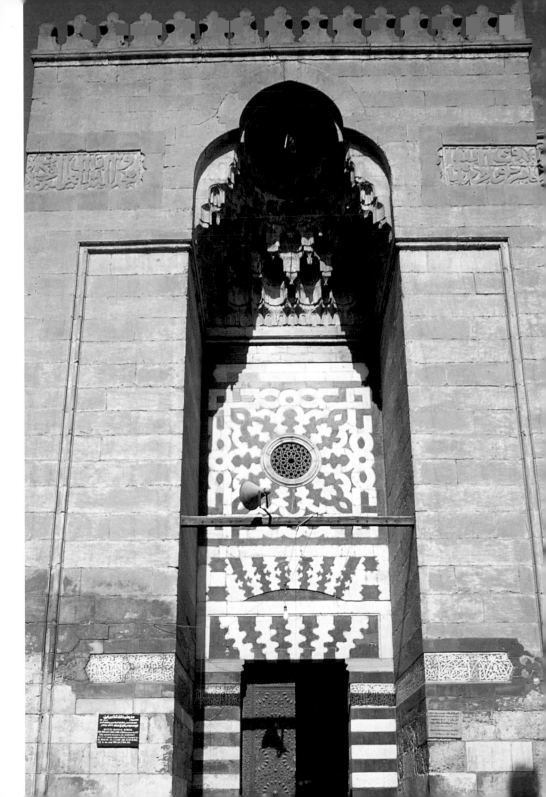

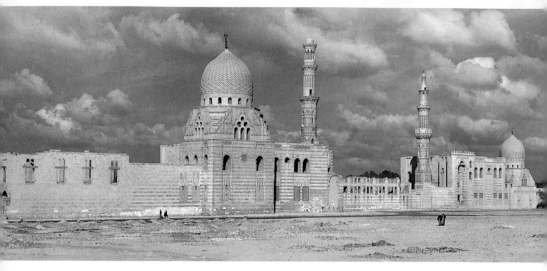

116 In the shadow of the pyramids. The Egyptian obsession with death resurfaces in new guise under the Mamluks. The funerary complex (mosque, mausoleum, *madrasa*, *khanqah*) of Sultan Inal, 1451–6, in the so-called City of the Dead in Cairo, flouts the Prophet's insistence on modest burial.

example in Iranian tilework or Iraqi carved terracotta, the applied ornament within the individual *muqarnas* cells is of major visual importance, in Mamluk buildings their sculptural role, intensified by stark contrasts of light and shade, is paramount.

The presence of so many major buildings in such a small space is not confined to Bain al-Qasrain. It is repeated in the area of the Eastern Cemetery and, on a lesser scale, in other parts of Cairo. More to the point, perhaps, it recurs in Tripoli, Damascus, Jerusalem and Aleppo. The sheer quantity of Mamluk architecture tells its own story. Buildings tend to make their impact *en masse* rather than individually. Each draws on its neighbours – in fact they frequently blend into each other. Altogether more than a thousand buildings of Mamluk date survive in the Near East, and they pose insistently the question 'why?' For all that such buildings perform a notional function – prayer, burial, teaching, accommodation – the fact that time and again they cluster close together in areas where they can be assured of the greatest public exposure (notably the area of the Haram al-Sharif and its surrounding streets in Jerusalem) betrays quite another motivation. This building activity was fundamentally competitive. Of course it also had an economic function, in that it allowed an *amir* to sink his money in an enterprise whose charitable status protected it from confiscation or a later takeover, but which

148

could nevertheless benefit his descendants as well as serving the wider public. Above all, though, the building of such monuments was expected of a member of the Mamluk élite once he had reached a certain position. By so doing he joined the club. And he was also playing his part in ensuring that the dominance of the Mamluk élite was well understood by the average citizen.

Hence, perhaps, the emphasis in Mamluk architecture on those individual elements of the design that have the most direct impact: domes, portals and minarets. Again and again it is these elements that dictate the entire aspect of a building, as if the rest of the monument were of merely secondary importance. This may help to explain the modular nature of so much Mamluk architecture and why the more interesting monuments are those specifically designed for an unusual, often prestigious site or purpose, or those in which the architect has had to grapple with an unfavourable setting – say a gap site – or has tried to accommodate in one structure the divergent axes of the street and the *qibla*.

The obsession with hierarchy and status was carried further in Mamluk society than anywhere in the medieval Islamic world. Presumably it had much to do with the thorough militarization of the ruling élite. Whatever the reason for it, the result was to permeate the art of the period with references to official rank. At one level this was achieved by epigraphy. Mamluk calligraphers found an ideal objective correlative to the class-conscious and rank-dominated court in the mannered script which they developed for official inscriptions. Form matches content to perfection. The inscriptions which unfold so majestically and rhetorically across the surfaces of hundreds of metal bowls and dishes, ceramic vessels, glass lamps and, of course, buildings, often list a lengthy protocol of titles held by even quite minor officials. Their impact is intentionally cumulative, and this again is as true visually as it is of their meaning. Formality and discipline are of the essence, and are indeed taken to extremes. These inscriptions seem so designed that their massed uprights stand at attention like soldiers on parade – no mean feat when one considers the uneven distribution of vertical letters in a given piece of Arabic prose. It is a tribute to the flexibility and resource of the Arabic alphabet that it can express such rhythmic power. The effect could be likened to a drum roll or a fanfare of trumpets. Moreover, the nouns and epithets which constitute these titles are carefully balanced not just for their meaning but also for rhyme and rhythm, assonance and alliteration. A typical sequence might read – and it helps to utter the words in Arabic, so as to transmit at least some flavour of their grandiloquence: *'izz li-maulana al-sultan al-Malik al-Nasir, al-'alim, al-'amil, al-mujahid, al-murabit, al-muthaghir, Nasir al-Dunya wa'l-Din* ('Glory to our Lord the Sultan, the victorious king, the learned, the diligent, the holy warrior, the warrior on the frontier, the guardian of the frontiers, the protector of the world and of the faith'). Such inscriptions are of course intended not merely to

inform. They boast. They assert ownership. They advertise power, and often – if the object they decorate has a religious purpose – piety as well. And they naturally function as ornament too. Not surprisingly, such inscriptions were widely copied – in Nasrid Spain, in Central Asia, southern Iran and even Sultanate India.

Rank was expressed in Mamluk times not only by inscriptions – as had long been standard practice in the Islamic world – but also by a new device: the blazon. Like the distinctively-styled official Mamluk epigraphy, the blazon functioned as a logo of possession and identification, and was almost as pervasive. Indeed, within half a century of the appearance of the first such blazon in Egypt, its standard form – a circular medallion with a thick horizontal strip at the centre – had already been adapted to carry epigraphic messages. The commonest of these was 'Glory to our Lord the Sultan', but it soon became common practice to fit into this same format an abbreviated version of the sultan's titles or a reference to him by name. Thus was developed the epigraphic blazon, perhaps the single most defining characteristic of Mamluk art.

The blazon, then, functioned as a kind of livery and was encountered very widely in the Mamluk domains, and even beyond. Thus the Mamluk *amir* Qarasunqur, who suffered political disgrace and had to seek asylum in Iran, nevertheless saw to it that his mausoleum in Maragha bore the emblem of his long-defunct rank as polomaster. Not all of the symbols employed have been fully explained, but there is general agreement on the meaning of most of them – not, as it happens, because of detailed explanations in literary sources, but because a given blazon is often accompanied by an inscription identifying the official in question. The remarkably rich and detailed historical sources covering the Mamluk period make it possible to put together quite a full biography of many high officials, and both to trace and to date the various promotions of their careers. Coins are a very useful check to such sources, since they are strictly contemporary documents, and many of them bear blazons.

Considerations of ready legibility, easy reproduction and symbolic expressiveness ensured that the designs of these blazons were kept simple. It is instructive to note that these blazons postdate the first European coats of arms, which the Muslims may well have encountered as early as the First Crusade (1095 onwards). By the early twelfth century European powers were using as emblems the lion, the fleur-de-lys and the eagle. Certain similarities of design, such as the round or shield-shaped cartouche which enclosed the emblem proper and made it a blazon, and the division of the field into separate segments, seem to support such a connection, as does the use of certain animals, for example the lion that was the personal totem of Sultan Baibars, or the double-headed eagle associated with Nasir al-Din Muhammad. Similarly, a rosette was used for two centuries as the dynastic emblem of the Rasulids in the Yemen. A high-stemmed cup indicated the butler, a napkin the *jamdar* or master of the wardrobe, paired polo sticks the polo-master, a bow the *bunduqdar* or bowman, a sword the *silahdar* or sword-bearer, a fesse (a plain three-fielded shield) the courier, a crescent or horseshoe the stable-master, a ewer the quartermaster, a round table the royal taster and a pen-box the secretary. Other devices included the mace, the banner and the drum, all connoting specific offices.

These logos are almost exclusively the preserve of the nobility; the sultan himself used an inscribed roundel or shield as his emblem. However, neat as these definitions seem, they should not be taken at face value, for the evidence of Mamluk copper coins and ceramics demonstrates beyond question how indiscriminately these images were employed — whether as emblems of authority (e.g. the eagle with wings displayed), as specific blazons, or as mere decorative motifs. The random way in which they are combined points to the same conclusion. A similar debasement can be traced in this period in the use of titles, so much so that the lengthier and more high-sounding the title is, the lowlier the rank of the person who claims it. What is new in these devices is that blazons were used as emblems and identification tags of official rank — the office rather than the man. As such it was appropriate for that blazon to be used for everybody and everything within the household of the *amir* in question. Hence the sheer ubiquity of blazons in Mamluk art — and their effect was no doubt intensified by the importance allotted to colour in their design (indeed, the Arabic term for blazon is *rank*, meaning 'colour'). Sometimes the enclosing shield is subdivided and holds several emblems, thus functioning as a composite blazon. Sometimes such blazons were used collectively by all the slaves or *mamluks* of a sultan. These various distinctions all reveal a society obsessively concerned with rank and status.

Aside from architecture the major art form in the Mamluk period was unquestionably metalwork. Many hundreds of pieces are known; probably the social system of the Mamluk military élite, which favoured a complete service of objects as part of the appropriate ambience of an *amir*, offered a powerful impetus for their production, and ensured a steady demand. Hence, no doubt, the predominance of pieces bearing lengthy official titulatures. The sudden efflorescence of elaborately executed metalwork in a region which appears earlier to have lagged well behind the best work of the age, as exemplified principally by the schools of Herat and Mosul, suggests that strong influences from abroad revolutionized the local situation. To what extent this change was wrought through imported techniques or through an influx of large numbers of actual craftsmen from Iraq and Iran is a matter of some dispute.

When Mamluk metalwork is considered as a whole, the immediate impression is one of mass production, and thus inevitably of a decline in quality in comparison with earlier metalwork in the eastern Islamic world. This impression is based on a series of interconnected changes, embracing shape, material and technique, as well as the sheer quantity of surviving pieces. In comparison with twelfth-century metalwork, the range of shapes is now drastically reduced. This is not to deny that a wide variety of forms can be found in Mamluk metalwork, but the overwhelming majority of pieces falls into a few well-defined categories: lamps, basins, candlesticks, dishes. It now became common practice for the more popular pieces to be cast. The material changed too. From the thirteenth century, brass began to replace bronze. In itself, this might not be regarded as a significant innovation, but a concomitant veering of fashion away from inlay work resulted in a much reduced chromatic range. In place of multicoloured inlay work, metalworkers turned to engraving and thus produced monochrome metalwork.

It seems probable that short cuts were taken in technical matters too. The preference for huge inscriptions as the principal decorative accent, their relatively uniform style, and the fact that most of them comprise formulaic sequences, probably encouraged the use of templates, whether in thin metal, paper, leather or other materials. Thus quite elaborate objects could be executed in a relatively short time. But it was also inevitable that the metalworking industry would succumb to staleness and repetition, especially at the lower end of the market. Here thin-walled single-metal wares prevailed, their vegetal or geometric engraved ornament of somewhat restricted type setting off the dominant inscription band. Sometimes this ornament adopted Far Eastern motifs like the lotus or the peony, a reminder that the Mamluk domains provided a ready haven for refugees from the East. But these were little more than cosmetic changes; they did not herald a thorough sinicization of Mamluk decorative vocabulary.

The best Mamluk metalwork is of course an entirely different matter and is a worthy continuation of the Mosul school. Such pieces as the incense-burner of Muhammad b. Qala'un, the pen-box of Mahmud b. Sunqur, the mirror made for Amir Altunbugha, and above all the three works signed by or attributed to the craftsman Muhammad b. al-Zain – notably the Baptistère de St Louis – invite comparison with the very best of Islamic metalwork. Such pieces, made for sultans or high *amirs*, display dazzling technical skill, frequently innovative shapes and above all a capacity to cram the worked surface with all manner of designs. In the works of Muhammad b. al-Zain, the technique of inlay is pushed further than ever before and placed at the service of a wonderfully fluid and ingenious pictorial composition. Hunters, grooms, animals and vegetal scrolls intermingle and overlap with no sense of strain. Surfaces are carefully differentiated by modelling and hatching – birds' feathers, animal fur, the scroll-folds of a tunic. Preternaturally elongated salukis, leopards and other animals prowl along narrow borders. Facial features are rendered in sufficient detail to allow ethnic distinctions to be made, and figures adopt a variety of poses: they turn to speak to each other, bend their backs to shoulder a burden, look up or down – and all this in the context of music-making, banqueting or taking part in a ceremonial procession.

In such pieces, metalwork begins to take on the lineaments of painting. The purpose of the design is apparently to capture the spirit of court life rather than to tell a particular story; as such, it replaces the benedictory inscriptions so often contained within similar bands. Whether a deliberate pun is intended – whether the serried upright figures acting out their privileged lifestyle are intended to evoke the rhythmical sequence of upright letters in inscriptions referring to that same lifestyle – must remain a matter of speculation. It is perhaps more likely that the manipulation of epigraphy to create a succession of tightly massed uprights deliberately conjured up the image of a protective hedge surrounding the property of an *amir* or a sultan, for all the world like a verbal bodyguard. Earlier animated inscriptions

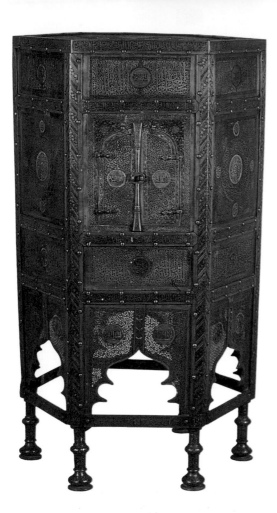

117 (*left*) Epigraphic overload. Brass
hexagonal table inlaid with silver, dated
1328 and made (presumably in Cairo) by
Muhammad al-Sankari (?). As full of
official inscriptions as *ill*. 118 is empty of
them, it is a *tour de force* of epigraphy, with
the words 'Glory to our Lord the Sultan,
al-Malik al-Nasir Muhammad' repeated
no less than 54 times.

118 (*below*) The supreme masterpiece of
Islamic metalwork? Syrian?, *c*. 1300; brass
inlaid with silver and gold. Proudly signed
six times by its maker Muhammad b. al-
Zain, the 'Baptistère de St Louis' was
employed until 1856 to baptize infants of
the French royal family. With remarkable
narrative flair, the roundels show rulers
hunting or fighting, while flanking panels
show the aftermath of each activity. Soon
inscriptions replaced these witty and lively
figural scenes.

119 (*opposite*) The ruler as cosmocrator.
Bronze mirror with gold and silver inlay
made by Muhammad al-Waziri for 'Ala'
al-Din Altunbugha (d. 1342), viceroy of
Syria and cup-bearer to Sultan Nasir al-
Din Muhammad. It symbolizes the
universe – note the planetary and zodiacal
signs – ruled over by the sultan, whose
central epigraphic 'image' and radiating
inscription have solar associations, like the
rosettes and outermost rays.

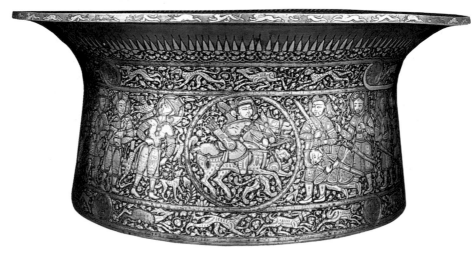

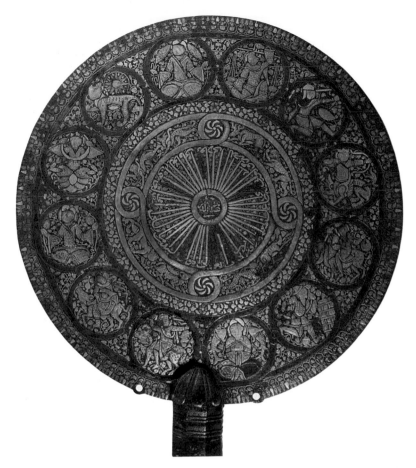

indicate that the visual connections between animal or human bodies
and the letters of the alphabet had been thoroughly exploited a full
century earlier. Such puns would not be the only imaginative use of
inscriptions in this period. In later Mamluk times, for example, the
severity of the tightly-packed *thulth* inscriptions was offset and lightened by changes in the upper epigraphic storey, for example by
devising pincer-shaped terminations for the shafts, or intercalating a
second inscription half-way up the forest of shafts. The radiating
inscriptions found on some of the best Mamluk metalwork irre-
sistibly evoke the image of the sun, an idea driven home by the use
of gold inlay for the letters. And the phrase 'Glory to our Lord the
Sultan' at the centre of the sunburst harnesses such solar imagery to
the glorification of the ruler.

155

Yet other pieces employ a well-worn visual vocabulary of solar, lunar, astral, planetary and astrological images of talismanic intent. The lavish use of gold and silver inlay not only renders such pieces more precious but is also singularly appropriate for such themes. It is characteristic of these more ambitious pieces that they operate on several different levels both visually and intellectually, with for example both large and small inscriptions on the same piece, or major and minor themes.

The Mamluk metalworking industry by no means followed a consistent development. On the contrary, it had its full share of ups and downs. One may cite the sudden fall in the production of brasses between c. 1380 and c. 1450, or conversely the lavish output under Sultan Qa'itbay (1468–96). Economic factors may have played a significant role here – shortages of the more expensive metals, a ruthless quarrying of precious materials from earlier buildings, a new ingenuity in making a little metal go a long way (for example, designing doors so that they contain roundels and other isolated elements in expensive metals which are attached to cheaper materials). The increasing scarcity of copper and silver meant that objects and accoutrements in these metals (and of course gold) disappeared almost entirely, and the metalworking industry also suffered extensively as a result of continuous inflation which peaked between c. 1394 and c. 1416; its effects were exacerbated by armed conflicts between rival Mamluk groups, famines, plagues and disastrous fires, and by the Mamluk government's insatiable demand for silver and copper to mint the coins needed to buy new *mamluks* when war was decimating their supplies of manpower.

Mamluk glass is closely related to contemporary metalwork in the vocabulary of its decoration: it favours the same heraldic motifs and epigraphic style. At the top end of the market, namely enamelled glass, most of the known production was of mosque lamps – with the odd exceptions provided by beakers, perfume bottles, bowls or candlestick bases. Here Qur'anic inscriptions – especially 9:18, 'Only they shall enter God's sanctuaries who observe the poor due', the verse which occurs more frequently than any other in Islamic architecture – supplement the usual parade of titles. Once again, piety and propaganda converge; for when lit, these lamps would have blazoned forth not only the word of God but also the names and titles of the great and the good. In this medium too, patronage was effectively confined to the ranks of sultans and amirs. In form and technique Mamluk glass follows traditions established in the Ayyubid period. A

120

particular speciality was dark blue or purple glass with trailing designs in brilliant white.

Easily the largest body of late medieval Islamic textiles are those from Mamluk Egypt. This need not necessarily reflect the actual rate of production – for example, the historian Abu'l-Fida mentions that Abu Saʿid, the Mongol ruler of Iran, sent the Mamluk sultan al-Nasir Muhammad seven hundred precious textiles in 1323, which argues a well-established luxury textile industry in Iran at that time, as indeed contemporary literary sources confirm. The Mamluk textile industry was under constant pressure from abroad. Until the late fourteenth century, it dominated the Mediterranean market, but a mere fifty years later, undercut by the products of Spanish, Italian and Chinese weavers, it had suffered irreversible decline. Yet the fact that these weavers copied Mamluk textiles so closely is a measure of the high international status of the Mamluk textile industry. In Europe, for instance, textiles with Arabic inscriptions – no matter what those inscriptions actually said – were honorific objects. As such they are frequently encountered in early Renaissance paintings; thus the robe of the Virgin Mary or the haloes of saints bear official Arabic titulature. This is also why so many of the finest Mamluk textiles have been preserved in Western cathedral treasuries, and were used for the shrouds of European monarchs and for ecclesiastical vestments. Europe also provided a ready market for Mamluk damasks, probably made (as the name indicates) at Damascus. Such terms as fustian, cashmere, mohair, organdy, taffeta, tabby and muslin also point to the Islamic (sometimes Mamluk) origins of these fabrics.

The single overriding problem in the study of Mamluk textiles is that of determining whether a given piece was actually made in the Mamluk domains, and if so whether at Cairo or at other major centres of production such as Asyut, Alexandria or Damascus. Yuan textiles made for the Mamluk market have irreproachably accurate and appropriate Arabic inscriptions but may reveal their Chinese origin by motifs like *chi'lins*, dragons, phoenixes and turtles. Otherwise they can be recognized as Chinese only by their different style and technique. They may even be signed by craftsmen (such as a certain ʿAbd al-ʿAziz) with Muslim names. Fine textiles were widely used as a mark of rank or office – for example, a different textile was hung behind the seat of each member of the council of state – and were often used to drape objects in other materials, and to decorate or partition architecture and its spaces. Promotion within the Mamluk hierarchy was often rewarded by the gift of a set of

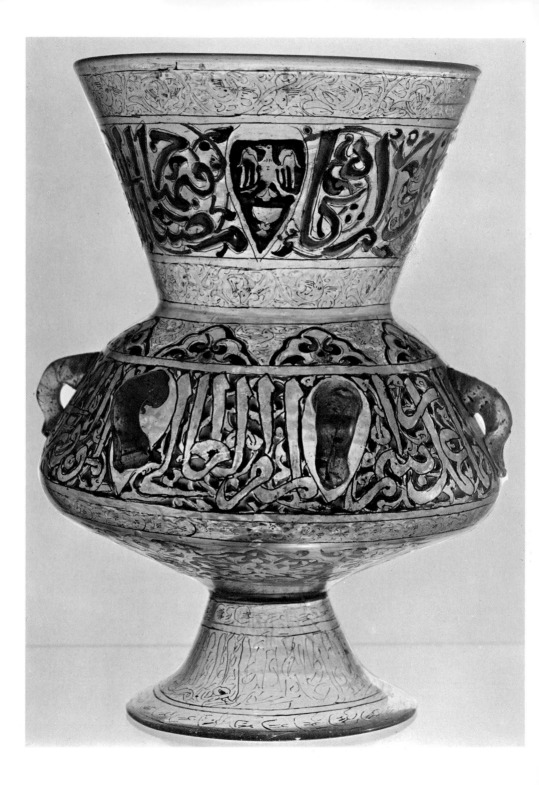

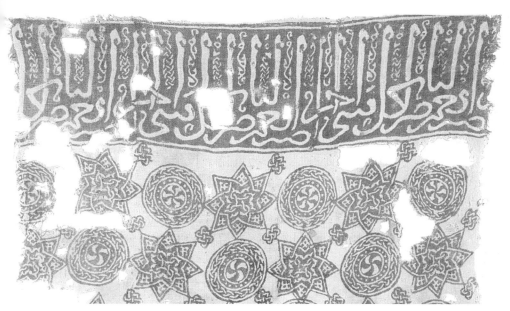

121 'Patience is the blessing of al-Nasir; everything has its appointed end' proclaims this block-printed linen. Egypt, 14th century. Its decorative repertoire of epigraphy, whirling rosettes and stars is all derived from more prestigious metalwork.

garments, and elaborate ceremonies involving a complete change of wardrobe, literally from head to toe (for both silk caps and silk slippers with royal titles have survived), marked the beginning of spring and of autumn.

The range of patterns and motifs was very wide, but certain types recur with such frequency that they can be taken as a trademark of the period – for example, ogival or otherwise curvilinear lattice designs, sometimes made up of inscriptions, multicoloured sequences of narrow horizontal bands or vertical stripes containing inscriptions, floral motifs, or roundels with animals and repeated tear-shaped blossoms often alternating with lotuses, peonies or other Far Eastern flowers. Blazons are often separately sewn on to otherwise finished textiles. A remarkably high number of of fine Mamluk textiles bear inscriptions mentioning sultans or *amirs*, often woven separately in thin strips and then applied to garments such as sashes or turbans. The migration of courtly themes to humbler milieux is illustrated by the popularity of block-printed linens and cottons (a technique   121 perhaps borrowed from India) decorated with the *thulth* inscriptions that were so popular elsewhere in Mamluk art. For the most part

120 (*opposite*) 'His Light is as a niche wherein is a lamp' (Qur'an 24:35) reads the inscription on the neck of this glass lamp with enamelled decoration made for Saif al-Din Tuquztimur al-Hamawi (d. 1345), an officer of Sultan Muhammad b. Qala'un. His blazon – an eagle over a cup – identifies him as the cup-bearer.

these inscriptions refer to rulers or high officials, or are benedictory, but sometimes they spell out proverbs ('Patience is blessed with success and everything is rewarded') or apostrophize the viewer ('To whoever looks, I am the moon'). Similar sentiments are encountered in contemporary Nasrid textiles in Spain. Indeed, it seems very possible that textiles were the source for certain design conventions found in other media, such as the division of the field into bands as found in metalwork, glass and ceramics. The repeat textile patterns found on metal animal sculpture such as the Pisa Griffin exemplify this. Here, then, is further evidence for the primacy of the textile industry in medieval Islamic art.

Finally, Mamluk Egypt is famed for a unique type of rug whose production can be documented only for the very end of the period and may have been introduced by refugees from the Qaraqoyyunlu court in Iran after 1467. Their colouring of crimson, lime green and pale blue is unmistakable, as are their designs, usually dominated by a central radiating stellar form within an octagon, with further octagons wheeling around the periphery. The kinship of such compositions with the astral character of the frontispieces to Mamluk Qurʾans or mosque doors leaps to the eye. The borders are usually taken up by linked circular or oval cartouches, a disposition familiar in Iranian Qurʾans. Two of the known Mamluk carpets bear blazons, but none are inscribed, a minor curiosity given the dominance of epigraphy in Mamluk art generally. Their manufacture continued long after the Ottoman conquest.

Mamluk pottery has remarkably little in common with its Fatimid predecessors. Lustre becomes much rarer, though there was a strong demand for it in western Europe until production ceased around 1400. Instead, contemporary fashion favoured underglaze wares of predominantly blue and white tonality, broadly derived from Chinese

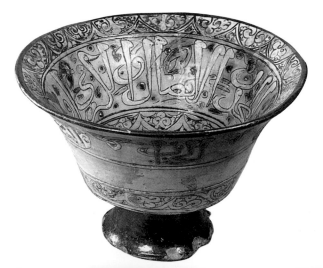

122 Even domestic pottery reflected the obsession with status. This coarse, heavy red-bodied ware was covered with white engobe, incised with bold, somewhat playful *thulth* inscriptions, painted in coloured slips and finally glazed – here, in yellow. An Egyptian speciality, it copied metalwork shapes and often bore amiral blazons and titles.

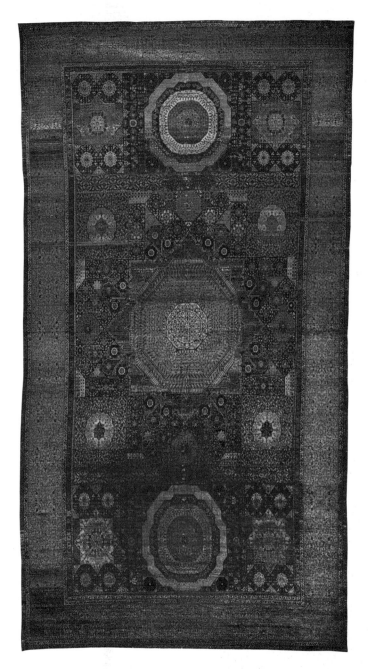

123 The firmament on the floor. Mamluk carpet, late 15th century. The lustrous silk and sheep's wool material, the dominant intense red palette and the radiating solar and stellar designs – which find parallels in Mamluk marble floors, Qur'ans and stone carving, and also Buddhist mandalas – characterize Mamluk carpets generally. 5.42 × 2.80 m (17.8 × 9.2 ft).

porcelain, as in the many Burji Mamluk hexagonal tiles also made in Syria. Frequently the wares are divided into radiating segments, while vertically striped or multifoil designs are also common. Creatures borrowed from the Chinese repertory, such as geese and ducks, also make their appearance, and Yuan celadons were widely copied in the Bahri period. The impact of Chinese Ming ceramics waxed ever stronger in the later Mamluk period. A popular category of glazed yellow and brown sgraffito wares, presumably mimicking the more

prestigious metalwork of the time, was mass-produced for the amiral market and displayed blazons and inscriptions giving official titles. These seem to have been made in sets. The Fatimid penchant for signing ceramics continued apace; some thirty signatures have been found on Mamluk wares. Damascus, it seems, bade fair to rival Cairo as a centre of production, especially for underglaze wares. The workshops there, to judge by style and the references to Tabrizi craftsmen, seem to have derived inspiration from Iran, as did the masters responsible for the tilework in early Ottoman Bursa at the same time. In no medium of Mamluk art is the evidence for the strength and consistency of the trade links with the Far East clearer than it is in ceramics.

The art of the book in Mamluk times presents a fascinating paradox. Secular book illustration languished. No single text captured the imagination of contemporary patrons in the way that the *Maqamat* had done in thirteenth-century Iraq (see pp. 129–31) or that the poems of Firdausi and Nizami were to do in Iran (see p. 224). Mamluk painting by and large is the neglected handmaiden of the didactic text which it accompanies, whether that text is concerned with military exercises (*furusiya*), animal lore or automata. Admittedly, some *Maqamat* texts were illustrated in Mamluk times, but they are clearly at the tail end of the artistic ferment which had earlier generated the Iraqi school of painting, and the same goes for

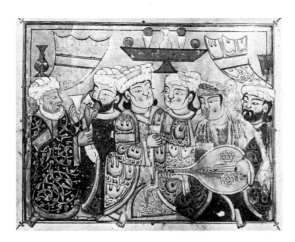

124 (*left*) Wine, women and song, Islamic style. Tavern scene (defying the Islamic prohibition of alcohol) from the *Maqamat* of al-Hariri, 1334 (f.42a), probably made in Egypt. The facial types reflect the fashion for Far Eastern ideals of beauty.

125 (*opposite*) Aristocratic leisure. Frontispiece to the *Maqamat* of al-Hariri, 1337. Produced for one Nasir al-Din Taranta'i, probably in Egypt, its iconography is of Persian derivation (compare the 1307 *Kalila wa Dimna* double frontispiece), and implies a (lost) facing page with an enthroned monarch. Note the tamed cheetah leaping from the hunter's horse before chasing the prey. Female musicians perform below.

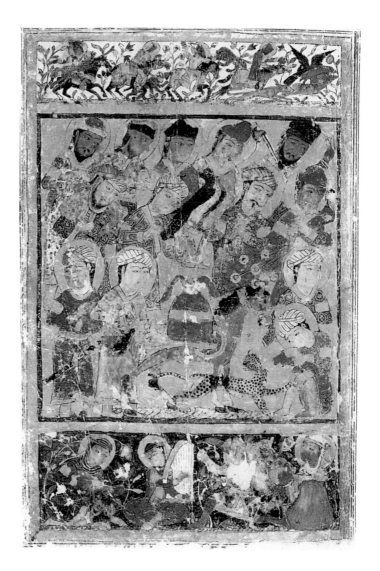

illustrated versions of the *Kalila wa Dimna*. A peculiar stiffness invests
Mamluk figural painting and even the depiction of animals betrays a
quality of rote not entirely disguised by bright, cheerful colours. In
secular painting, then, the Mamluk realms can fairly be described as
a backwater; this work significantly lacks that Far Eastern element
which energizes later Mamluk pottery and metalwork and which
was of course so consistent an inspiration for Iranian painters.

Yet side by side with this uninspired, run-of-the-mill work was produced the most consistently superlative sequence of illuminated Qur'ans in the history of Islamic art. This contrast speaks volumes about the nature of patronage in the Mamluk period. The manuscripts containing secular paintings are for the most part anonymous. The Qur'ans, on the other hand, very frequently bear the names of sultans and high *amirs*. Like so much of Mamluk art, then, this patronage had a public dimension – for such Qur'ans were commonly donated to mosques where they could be displayed. Indeed, such was their size – often more than a metre in height – that they could only be read when displayed on a lectern. It was customary, moreover, for a patron to endow a religious foundation with an appropriately splendid Qur'an, and given the building boom in Mamluk times this ensured a steady demand for such luxury copies of the sacred text. Like so much Mamluk architecture, they served to proclaim the patron's piety. Some sultans gained still further renown by copying out the Qur'an in their own hand. While most Qur'ans were transcribed in a single volume or in two-volume sets, it was common practice at this time for the text of the grandest Qur'ans to

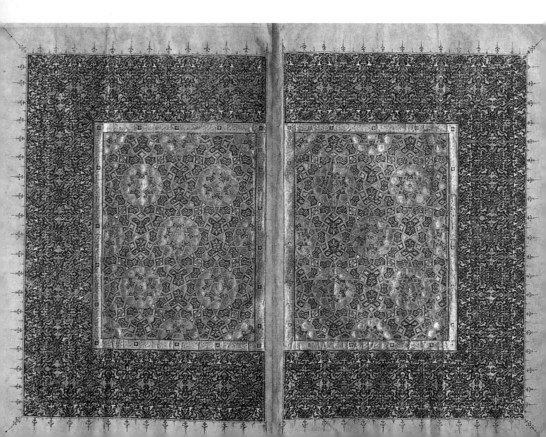

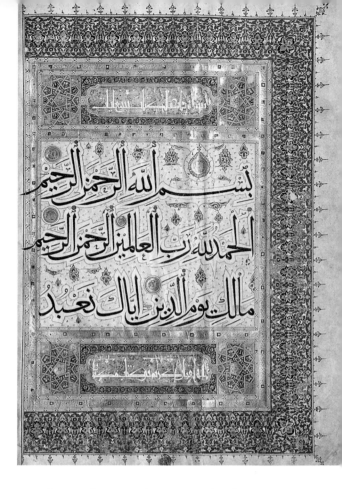

126 (*opposite*) Sultan 'Sha'ban . . . has bequeathed all this Noble Qur'an as a legal true bequest to find favour with his Lord' reads the colophon to this single-volume Qur'an. Illuminated by Ibrahim al-Amidi, Cairo, 1372. Subtly distorted axes ensure that this portion of an apparently infinite pattern fits harmoniously into the available space. The overall effect recalls contemporary enamelled glassware.

127 (*right*) The Opening. In the 1372 Qur'an, the first double-page spread of text incorporates all of *Sura* 1, the *Fatiha*, written roughly twice as large as the rest of the text. There are three lines to the page, in black *muhaqqaq jali* script outlined in razor sharpness with gold, and gold roundels as verse dividers.

be transcribed in thirty volumes; often each page of text contained no more than three lines. These would be enclosed by cloud-like forms which themselves were sandwiched between vegetal scrolls; and this entire field would then be enclosed by a continuous braided gold band, with Kufic captions in elaborate cartouches at the top and bottom of the page. Additional roundels or extra borders animated the outer edge. All this elaborate ornament would be laid upon an otherwise empty page; indeed, sometimes more than sixty per cent of a given page would be empty. Thus the ornament, with its preponderance of gold and blue, would gain maximum éclat from the dull ivory of its setting.

These Qur'ans, however, also epitomize the art of the period in their formality and conservatism, and in the way that they echo other crafts and techniques. Their great frontispieces and finispieces, for example, are less carpet pages than great doors which swing open to reveal the sacred text and which solemnly close the book. Their design is often essentially identical to that of mosque doors in metalwork or inlaid wood. But the predominant theme of these pages is almost always a geometric framework of centrifugal designs which explode with astonishing energy from the central figure. It is hard not to read such designs as references to the heavenly bodies, especially in view of the prevalence of gold and lapis lazuli, and the sacred nature of the text. That text itself frequently employs a stately *thulth* or *muhaqqaq* script developed in a manner akin to the inscriptions on metalwork, while Far Eastern flower motifs proliferate, as they do on fourteenth-century Mamluk metalwork. Occasionally the colours mimic the tones and the effect of contemporary enamelled glass.

Since such steady, long-term patronage was available from the highest in the land, it is not surprising that several schools developed and that the careers of certain craftsmen, such as Sandal, can be traced in detail. The first such school was that created by the patronage of Sultan Nasir al-Din Muhammad, who ruled intermittently from 1293 to 1341. Seven calligraphers signed major Qur'ans produced between 1304 and 1372, and the signatures of three illuminators are known from the same period. This suggests the prestige attached to working on Qur'ans and incidentally indicates that the calligraphers enjoyed a higher status than the illuminators. Some of these artists also turned occasionally to the illumination of Coptic Gospel books, which are thoroughly in the Mamluk idiom. By degrees a standard format evolved, with a frontispiece comprising a double-page spread followed by a double page of illumination preceding the text itself. The same arrangement operated in reverse at the end of the volume.

Sometimes a patron would donate several Qur'ans to a single foundation; thus in 1425 Sultan Barsbay endowed his *madrasa* with single-volume, double-volume and thirty-volume Qur'ans. Just as generations of Mamluk *amirs* vied with each other to erect buildings, so too did the competitive spirit – a reflection on the artistic plane of the endless and ruthless jockeying for power in court life – extend to the production and embellishment of Qur'ans. And this same emulation may itself account for the co-existence of several different styles of illumination.

CHAPTER SEVEN

The Muslim West

The art of the Muslim world west of Egypt (the Maghrib) was conditioned to a remarkable extent by its geography. Sundered from the rest of the Islamic world by the extensive deserts of Libya and western Egypt, its maritime communications with the East frequently threatened by hostile Christian powers, the Maghrib was compelled as early as the eighth century to turn its focus inwards. This process was sealed after 1050 with the invasion of the Banu Hilal and other nomadic Bedouin tribes who, travelling westwards from Egypt, overran the eastern Maghrib like locusts. Their flocks devastated good agricultural land, bringing in their wake economic ruin and permanently destroying the ecological balance of the whole territory. Sedentary life contracted; towns and villages, deprived of their agricultural hinterland, decayed. The break between eastern and western Islam proved irreparable. Not surprisingly, this physical isolation entailed a gradual but destructive intellectual and cultural isolation. In most fields of Islamic learning, Maghribi scholars were either unproductive or lagged far behind their colleagues to the east. It is true that many of them travelled eastwards in search of knowledge; but this was one-way traffic. By the later Middle Ages, an occasional luminary like the philosopher-historian Ibn Khaldun stands out by his very rarity.

For some three centuries Muslim Spain, whose history begins with the Arab invasion in 711, constituted an honourable exception to this trend. Yet the gradual erosion of its territory as a result of unremitting pressure from the Christians to the north put an increasingly forseeable term to this intellectual flowering. Even so, certain cities of Muslim Spain, notably Cordoba and Toledo, were important centres of scholarship in the secular sciences, such as medicine, astronomy and mathematics. In Toledo, after the Christian reconquest and under the rule of Alfonso VI (from 1085) and some of his successors, these works were translated into Latin and thence made their way throughout Europe. Thus Muslim Spain served as the conduit for international scholarship to travel from east to west.

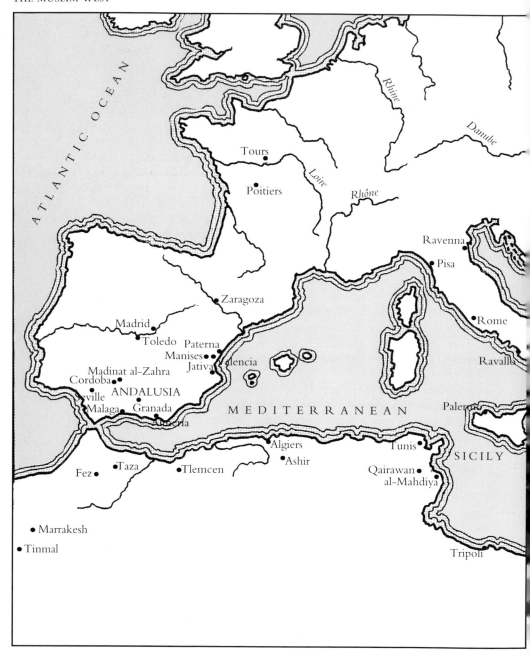

But for good reason the Muslims of Spain could not match the self-confidence of their co-religionists to the east. They lacked the lands and the wealth, and – less tangibly – the security that came from being surrounded by a vast and successful community of the faithful. It is no accident that Spain is more richly endowed in medieval Islamic castles and fortified settlements – from cities to villages – than any territory of comparable size in the Muslim world. For most of its existence – an existence eked out to the threshold of the modern age, for Granada fell in 1492, the year that Columbus discovered America – Muslim Spain had a beleaguered mentality, especially after the fall of the Umayyad caliphate of Cordoba in 1031 and the consequent proliferation of some forty minor dynasties (the so-called *taifas*). Even at the height of its power it was still only a small principality sandwiched between the aggressively encroaching Christian presence to the north and the Berber-dominated territory to the south, whose restrictive cultural and religious orthodoxies were in many ways profoundly at variance with those of Andalusia. In this relationship, North Africa, for all its vastly greater physical extent, was undoubtedly the junior partner in most respects, continually looking northwards for inspiration. This is not to deny that the lands now subsumed in the modern states of Morocco, Algeria and Tunisia did indeed produce great empires, notably those of the Almoravids (1054–1147) and the Almohads (1130–1269), which even ruled briefly in southern Spain. But these states were short-lived and the activity of their rulers as patrons of art was limited to religious architecture. This lack of a dynamic or even useful hinterland threw Muslim Spain back on its own resources. Small wonder that it looked ever more obsessively back to a golden past.

For indeed the art of the Muslim West cannot be understood without reference to the Umayyads of Syria. The tantalizing memory of that dynasty, of its fabulous wealth and power, is the constant subtext of the art of the Muslim West, particularly of Spain, and of the rest of its culture too. The sole Umayyad prince to escape the massacre of his ruling house by the 'Abbasids in 750 had, after many adventures, made his way to Spain, where he had set about recreating the lost glories of Umayyad Syria in an alien land. Hence, for example, the deliberate rejection of that imperial 'Abbasid art whose various manifestations infiltrated the rest of the Islamic world, surfacing as far west as Qairawan in Tunisia. Conceivably this rejection brought in its train a corresponding reluctance to develop such major 'Abbasid art forms as pottery, metalwork and the arts of the book –

fields which (illuminated Qur'ans apart) are represented in only marginal form in the Muslim West. Or one could attribute this reluctance to the fact that the Umayyads of Syria did not seriously practise these arts. Yet another possibility would be to see the key factor as religious, specifically the dominance of the ultra-conservative Maliki *madhhab*, a school of Islamic law whose strong puritanical streak made it hostile to the arts in general. None of these explanations is entirely satisfactory, though the fact that they can all be entertained might suggest that all these factors played their part. But the absence of several key art forms practised enthusiastically by Muslims further east had the effect of concentrating attention on those fields of artistic endeavour that did enjoy popularity, such as textiles and ivories. In such cases it is Muslim Spain, not North Africa, that produced work of quality. Similarly, in architecture, the absence of building types which were commonplace further east, notably mausolea and *khan*s (the latter absent perhaps because most land-based trade was with the sub-Saharan regions, and followed routes for which *khan*s were impracticable) would have freed the energies of the medieval Maghribi builder (and the resources of patrons and communities) mainly for religious architecture. Yet cumulatively these various lacunae would have resulted in an environment in which the visual arts could not have had the same impact as they had in the Muslim East. In some respects, one might even say, the Maghrib might have struck a visitor from the East as provincial.

The well-nigh crippling mental dependence of the art of Umayyad Spain on that of Umayyad Syria ruled out the constant replenishment of traditional forms by others from outside that magic circle. Thus there is no parallel in the western Islamic world for the major change of direction between, say, Saljuq and Ottoman architecture in Anatolia (in which Byzantium was the alien factor) or the Chinese element in the painting and minor arts of the medieval Mashriq — the eastern Islamic lands — or the constant and fruitful interplay between the various media in Iranian art. It is true that Islamic ideas and motifs transformed certain aspects of medieval and even later art in Spain and the Spanish dominions overseas, but there was no comparably strong reciprocal current of Christian influence in the medieval art of western Islam. Tradition exerted a vice-like grip on the visual arts which, despite their distinctive character and some significant innovations, favoured the imitation of earlier modes, expressed for example in a preference for archaizing compositions made up of confronted or addorsed figures or animals.

The high-water mark of western Islamic art is synonymous with Cordoba, already an ancient city when it was selected as the Umayyad capital in 756. Andalusia was quickly colonized by Syrian refugees who brought their dialect, their tribal rivalries, their place names and even their plants with them. It was therefore natural that the memory of the Umayyad architecture of Syria should also be kept alive. This memory expressed itself in various ways. Tradition asserts that the Great Mosque of Cordoba, like its predecessor in Damascus, was built on the site of a Christian church bought and then demolished by the Muslims. For centuries, the model of the Damascus mosque was copied more faithfully in the Maghrib than anywhere else in the Muslim world. It was the Muslim West and no other area that adopted as canonical the lofty square minaret traditionally associated with Syria. The Cordoba mosque used a vocabulary of horseshoe-shaped arches and two-tiered arcades first found at Damascus, and there too Byzantine craftsmen were called in to execute mosaic decoration.

128 Christian vandals. The Great Mosque, Cordoba. The minaret, like the Giralda in Seville, bears an elaborate Christian Baroque superstructure. But it was the intrusive chapel inserted into the heart of the structure in 1523 (for triumphalist motives?) that really disfigured the mosque – Gothic verticality versus Islamic horizontality – and called down the wrath of the Emperor Charles V upon the local clergy.

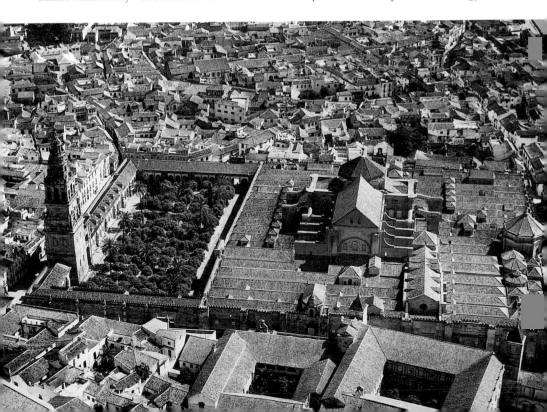

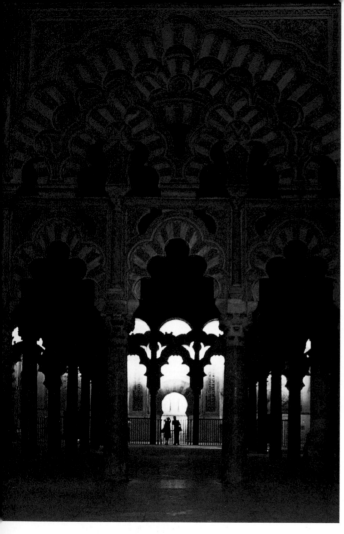

129, 130, 131 Royal precinct. Great Mosque, Cordoba: *maqsura*, 961–5. White columns and arches, like the 356 oil lamps, would only partially have reduced the claustrophobic gloom in the vast low sanctuary, often uncomfortably close and warm. Amidst this relative darkness the lavishly fenestrated and vaulted royal enclosure around the *mihrab* stood out. Light flickered off its golden mosaics, a metaphor of spiritual illumination to which the caliph, as the prayer leader according to Islamic law, subtly staked his own claim as he stood framed in the rayed *mihrab* on Fridays. The *mihrab* was the work of a craftsman specially brought – with his materials – from Constantinople, a tribute to the pan-Mediterranean culture of the time.

Yet these Syrian echoes (which could be multiplied) do not give the measure of Islamic art in Spain – often termed Moorish or Hispano-Moresque. The Great Mosque of Cordoba in particular developed over the centuries its own distinctive architectural and decorative vocabulary. In the course of four expansions in less than three centuries – a vivid illustration of the additive nature of the mosque in general – it grew to become one of the largest mosques of all. This gigantic size seems to have encouraged its architects to explore subtleties of lighting, repetition and rhythm to a degree rare

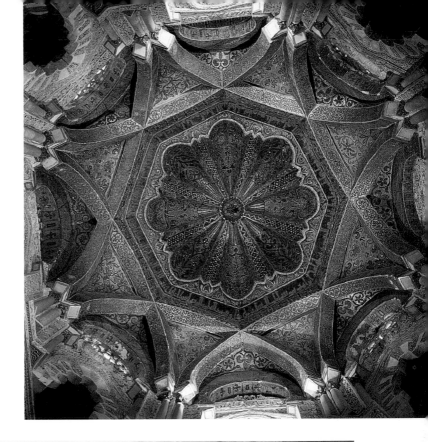

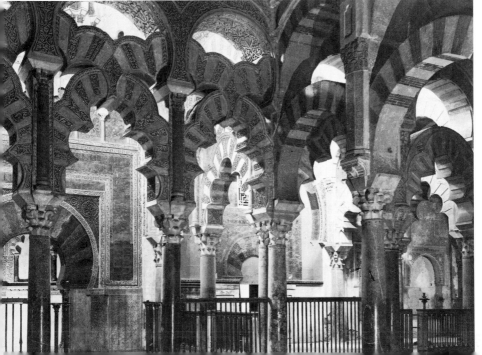

in mosque architecture. They repeatedly employed the vanishing point to suggest infinity, and a concentration of ornament to exalt the area around the *mihrab*. Yet all these visual effects were, so to speak, incidental to a major structural innovation called forth by the need to roof a vast area even though only short columns were available. Extra height was imperative and was secured by building broad block-like piers resting on these columns and braced by strainer arches. These arches were illusionistically lightened by the use of alternating red and white voussoirs, but the contrast between airy, freely circulating space in the lower elevation and a relatively dense thicket above was unmistakable. In the area around the *mihrab*, as rebuilt from 961 onwards, the notion of a forest – an analogy already suggested by the files of living trees planted in the courtyard, which would have merged smoothly with the sanctuary arcades – is intensified. A royal enclosure defined by a network of interlacing multifoil arches with arabesque decoration creates a blooming petrified garden in which honorific and paradisal undertones mingle – and from which the congregation at large was excluded. A remarkable sequence of ribbed domes of great variety and complexity (technologically far beyond anything known in the rest of Europe at this time) provides a fitting culmination for these splendours, and indeed intensifies their impact by a nexus of interrelated solar and celestial references. This area of the mosque abutted directly on the royal palace and provided a fitting environment for a monarchy which had only recently (928) claimed the numinous title of caliph. The princes of Cordoba thus challenged the ʿAbbasids as the divinely-ordained rulers of the Muslim world, and their mosque was part of that challenge.

So too, perhaps, is the palace-city of Madinat al-Zahra outside Cordoba – for it is highly likely that rumours of the fabled luxury of Samarra soon filtered back to Spain and lost nothing in the telling. Its marvels included ponds of quicksilver and jasper floors, while the statue of a Roman Venus over the main entrance was a reminder of the Mediterranean heritage of Islam. Most of this material was looted within a century of the city's foundation, but excavations have revealed audience halls with columns of many colours and, above all, abundant carved stucco decoration with arabesque ornament so delicate that it is almost finicky. This is the authentic idiom of the Mshatta façade (see p. 33), but somewhat reduced in scale so that it belongs with the minor arts rather than with architecture. Indeed, the striking absence of major buildings at Madinat al-Zahra tells its own story. Many of the standard hallmarks of royal pomp are duly there – the ceremonial triple-arched portal, the lavish use of water, the use of axial emphasis to exalt the monarch – but the vital dimension of scale was missing. Madinat al-Zahra was large enough in all conscience, but it was apparently innocent of any integrated overall plan. Its buildings ramble, and none of them is of substantial size. The will to power expressed so unmistakably in the architecture of Samarra is just not there. Here if anywhere in the Islamic world was a pleasure capital.

And this is entirely appropriate, for Cordoba in its prime had no peer in Europe for the amenities of civilized life. Its houses were bountifully supplied with hot and cold running water, its streets were lit at night, its royal library – if one may trust the chroniclers – had 400,000 volumes at a time when the major libraries in western Europe scarcely reached a thousand. In this metropolis, moreover, Muslim, Christian and Jew lived together with a degree of harmony rare in the Middle Ages, while Berbers, negroes and Slavs formed the caliphal bodyguard. Cordoba owed much of its sophistication to this multicultural and multi-confessional environment.

Yet the rapturous reception accorded to a flashy visitor from Baghdad, the singer Ziryab, who quickly became the *arbiter elegantiarum* on matters of taste, costume and etiquette, suggests that many Cordobans were uneasily aware of their isolation from the rest of the Islamic world. Indeed, there survives a medieval Spanish silk whose inscription fraudulently claims that it was made in Baghdad. A similar dependence on the art of Iraq can be detected in the only known illustrated manuscript of non-scientific character from Muslim Spain, *Hadith Bayad wa Riyad* ('The Story of Bayad and Riyad'), a tale of courtly love. The manuscript is generally attributed to the thirteenth 132 century. The poses and gestures of its figures, often in silhouette, have a studied intensity which seems to owe something to the art of mime, as do contemporary illustrated *Maqamat* ('Assemblies') manuscripts from Iraq. Both schools also share a love for the antithetical placing of figures in the interests of dramatic storytelling. Yet both the courtly atmosphere of the Spanish manuscript – so at variance with the robust, rapacious, street-wise world of the *Maqamat* paintings – and its ambience of gardens, waterwheels, polylobed arches, square towers and luxury pavilions faithfully evoke the spirit of medieval Andalusia, the land of the lute and the lyric, rather than Iraq. The prominence given to women here, which reflects their roles as scribes, musicians, librarians and poets in Muslim Spain, is also foreign to the male-dominated society pictured in the *Maqamat*.

175

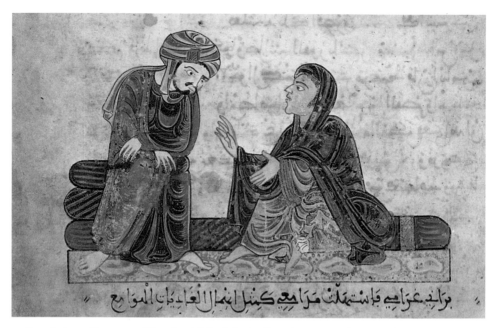

Courtly love. The story of Bayad and Riyad. Spain (?), 13th century. This type of romance originates in the ʿUdhri poetry of ancient Arabia: idealized, melancholic and unfulfilled. Here the machinating go-between tries to inject some backbone into the lovelorn youth.

A distinctive style of Qurʾanic illumination developed in the Maghrib and Muslim Spain. The books are small, usually about 20 cm (8 in) square. The script itself was decidedly different from all the styles that prevailed further east, for instance in the forms of certain letters, the placing of some diacritical marks and the preference for the horizontal rather than the diagonal in vocalization. But the prime trademark of this style was the extravagant looping of terminal flourishes, creating a tangled thicket of lines. *Sura* or chapter headings are in archaic Kufic which is unmistakably of Syrian Umayyad origin, even though this was many centuries out of date. The letters are usually in gold and are set within ornamental panels. This was a profoundly conservative style and it continued with relatively little change almost until modern times. Equally conservative was the preference for vellum right up to the fourteenth century, at a time when the rest of the Islamic world had long switched to paper for illuminated Qurʾans. As with Qurʾans from Egypt and points east, there are examples of pages with only four lines of text, and the

133

words so widely spaced that there is room for no more than a dozen of them; equally, there are very closely written Qur'ans with over twenty lines per page. Extreme elongation (*mashq*) is used here, as in Qur'ans produced elsewhere in the Muslim world, for visual, rhythmic and perhaps spiritual effect. Little progress has been made with the identification of the individual schools in this tradition. One major centre for this art, however, was Valencia in the later twelfth and early thirteenth centuries, where the craftsmen specialized in full-page square polygonal designs of dynamic, indeed explosive, character, cunningly interspersed with inscriptions. These compositions, placed at the beginning of a volume and mirrored in the binding itself, may have had apotropaic intent.

In the minor arts, the glory of the Cordoban caliphate is its ivory carving. The intense if short-lived concentration on working this costly material finds a parallel in the rock crystals made for the contemporary Fatimid court in Egypt. As befits the nature of ivory, the objects themselves are small, principally caskets, cosmetic cases, 134, 135 pyxides and the like, which held perfumes, unguents or jewels. Their inscriptions mention high-ranking personages of the court such as the princess Subh, the prince al-Mughira or the chief of police, Ziyad b. Aflah. Recent research has revealed that many such items were intended as presents to ladies who had given birth to an heir-apparent, and thus their splendour had a major political dimension. Cross-references with architecture may sometimes be detected, as in

133 Leaf from multi-volume Qur'an in gold on vellum. Probably Spain, 11th century. The reed pen is cut to produce letters of even thickness, unlike the dramatic alternations of thick and thin found in eastern Kufic hands. Maghribi scribes were taught, says Ibn Khaldun, by writing complete words, not individual letters. 27 × 22 cm (10.6 × 8.7 in).

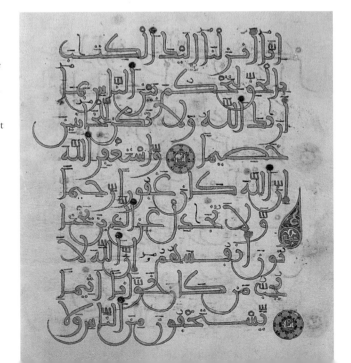

cylindrical boxes with domical lids, and even the celestial associations of such forms can be exploited, for example by depicting on the lid eagles whose outstretched wings bear a rayed solar rosette. On the bodies of such objects, affronted creatures such as camels, deer, goats, and more often those of royal symbolism – usually griffins, elephants, lions, peacocks and eagles – parade against a backcloth of densely carved arabesque which again has close affinities with Umayyad work in Syria. Many of these animals may have been intended as references to the royal game park. The grander dimensions thus implied lend an impressive monumentality to these little objects. Other images include ruler figures seated in majesty on elephants, hunting, jousting or banqueting scenes, musicians and wrestlers – in other words, images derived from the princely cycle first established in Islamic art by the Umayyads of Syria (see p. 32). The amount of detail crammed into such a diminutive space is quite remarkable. This intricate carving, formerly embellished by bright colours, is especially appropriate for such precious material and subtly underlines the association with jewelry.

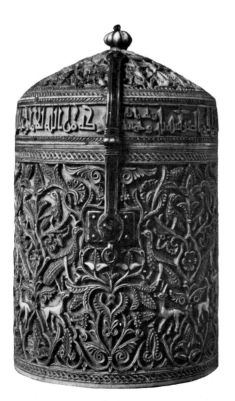

134 (*left*) 'I am a receptacle for musk, camphor and ambergris'. Ivory pyxis made, as the inscription states, for Princess Subh ('Dawn'), Basque mother of two sons of the caliph al-Hakam II, 353/964. Archaizing Syrian elements include the epigraphic style and the lavish use of the drill.

135 (*below*) The ceremonial hunt. Ivory casket dated 1004–5, made for 'Abd al-Malik, son of the regent al-Mansur, and wishing him 'respite from the appointed time of death': detail of hunter attacked by lions. It contains an unparalleled series of 13 craftsmen's signatures (here 'the work of Khair').

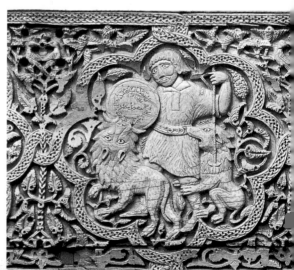

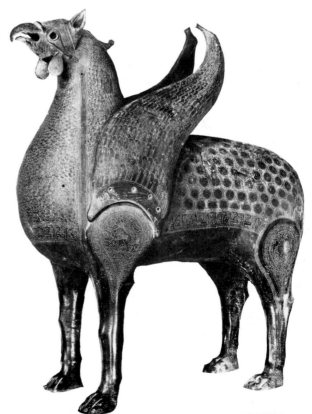

136 (*above*) Worn by St Thomas-à-
Becket? Made in 1116 in Almeria,
the centre of the Spanish textile
industry, this is the earliest Islamic
embroidery inscribed with both date
and provenance. It was refashioned
into a chasuble and, tradition says,
owned by the saint, a sharp dresser.
Its light-blue silk is embroidered in
gold thread with some 40 roundels
depicting animals, birds, mythical
creatures and courtly scenes.

137 (*right*) Talisman. The Pisa
Griffin. Probably Spanish, 11th
century; the largest Islamic bronze
figure, though much smaller than
some classical, ancient Near Eastern,
medieval Italian or Chinese bronzes.
Essentially a fantasy assembled from
bits and pieces of many creatures, its
exaggeration betrays very little
feeling for sculpture. Perhaps one of
a pair, displayed with apotropaic
intent on a pedestal by a fountain or
gateway. H. 107 cm (42.1 in), l. 87
cm (34.3 in).

Most of these scenes are enclosed within heavily outlined pearled roundels or rosettes which are joined by knots. This is clearly a borrowing from textiles, and indeed such textiles survive in abundance from slightly later periods. *Tiraz* factories operated in Seville and Cordoba; later, Almeria and Malaga became celebrated for their silks, and indeed at Malaga mulberry groves provided the raw material on the spot. Fabulous beasts such as griffins, double-headed eagles, basilisks, harpies and sphinxes, plus exotic creatures like lions, ante-

136 lopes, and birds galore – strutting peacocks, eagles and ducks – formed the repertoire for such silks. Their rarity or other-worldliness made them apt ideological symbols of majesty. Many themes, however, expressed the theme of royal power more explicitly, whether by inscriptions which gave royal titles or by symbols such as the lion-strangler or the eagle seizing its prey. Some of these themes

137 turn up in the stone sculptures of the Cordoban caliphate, for example in the troughs now at Jativa, Granada and Marrakesh. Others turn up in metalwork. The bronze griffin in Pisa, triumphantly displayed for centuries on the façade of the town's cathedral, was probably captured as booty in one of several campaigns against the Muslims around the turn of the eleventh century. At 1.07 m (3.5 ft) in height, it is the largest piece of animal sculpture in Islamic metalwork, and represents a formidable technical achievement. Yet its hybrid form and overall patterning, both markedly anti-naturalistic, betray the residual unease which Muslim artists felt for representational sculpture. It may originally have guarded, perhaps as one of a pair, the entrance to a palace or throne room. Its back bears textile patterning which, like the style of its epigraphy, suggests a Spanish source.

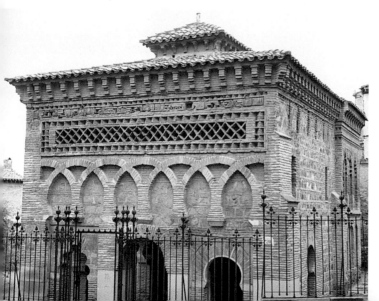

138 Intercontinental connections. Toledo, Mosque of Bab Mardum, 999–1000. Executed in humble brick and rubble, and later re-used as a Christian church, it illustrates a type of nine-bayed mosque, probably derived from a Baghdadi prototype, that had spread throughout much of the Islamic world by this time. Here interlaced and horseshoe arches lend it Spanish character.

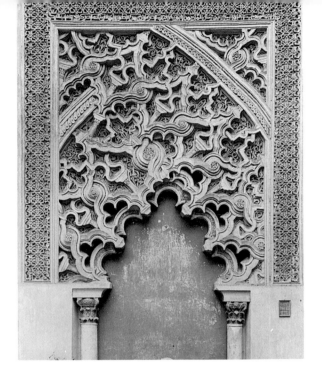

139 Islamic rococo. Aljaferia, Zaragoza; southern portico, after 1050. This palace of the Banu Hud dynasty, completed in 1080, now houses the autonomous Aragonese parliament. Note the tiny columns, stripped of structural function, marooned in a thicket of interlace ornament. Partly mathematical theorem, partly geometry as contemplation, this is made deliberately hard to read because only a small section of a much larger design is shown.

The authority and prestige of the art of Cordoba was such that it imposed itself on the various lesser Muslim principalities of Iberia, and continued to do so long after the fall of the Cordoban caliphate, when the whole country became split into numerous warring states. Thus the mosque of Bab Mardum at Toledo, dated 999, is in some 138 respects a miniaturized version of the Great Mosque at Cordoba, complete with a façade of interlaced arches (presumably a toned-down version of the sanctuary façade at Cordoba) and a set of nine patterned ribbed vaults, each one different. Interlaced arches are again a leitmotif at the palace of the Banu Hud at Zaragoza, known as Aljaferia (1080), but they are now carried to dizzy heights of 139 complexity, especially in the area of the audience hall and the oratory. The latter building, a kind of pocket Venus in architectural and decorative terms, is a lineal descendant of the *mihrab* bay at Cordoba. As for the palace itself, which acquires extra importance because it documents the art of a period from which very few significant remains survive in Spain, and thus provides a link between Madinat al-Zahra and the Alhambra, it demonstrates yet again how thoroughly Islamic Spain was in the thrall of Umayyad Syria. The multi-bastioned exterior with its single centrally-placed monumental

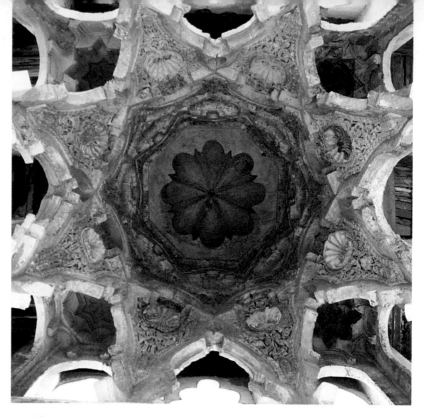

140 Islamic baroque. Marrakesh, Qubbat al-Barudiyyin, between 1106 and 1142, interior of dome. The heritage of Cordoban vaulting (cf. *ill*. 130) is enriched by burgeoning ornament and a new lightness and aspiration derived from the open-plan design.

gateway quite clearly derives from the desert residences of the eighth century. Numerous other Spanish Muslim castles echoed this form; but they did so principally with military intent, whereas in North Africa (as at Ashir or Raqqada) the association with palatial architecture persisted. More generally, the architectural vocabulary of Andalusia – horseshoe arches, roll mouldings, rib vaults, interlacing arcades – infiltrated the Christian architecture of the north and even crossed the Pyrenees, leaving its mark on the Romanesque churches of south-western France in particular, as at Le Puy, where even the cathedral door bears debased Kuficizing inscriptions.

The political vacuum left by the demise of the Cordoban caliphate was soon filled, and from an unexpected quarter. Deep in the newly Islamized territory of western Africa, in what is now Senegal, a puritanical movement was gathering momentum. Its members were

141 The Islamic counter-offensive. Rabat, Mosque of Hassan, tower; 1199. Unfinished, but probably planned to reach 85 m (279 ft) including its lantern. This gigantic size was a symbolic response to the advancing Christian *reconquista* of Spain. The exterior is of stone; the interior, with its succession of six vaulted chambers, is of brick.

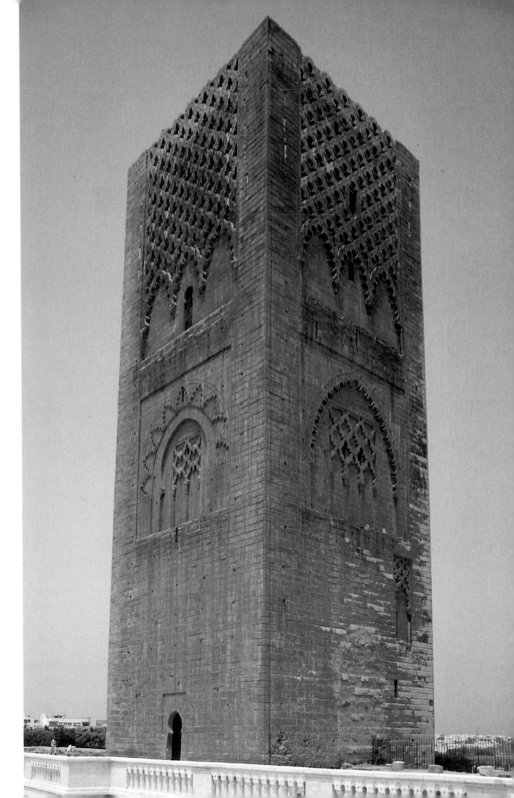

dedicated to the ideals of *jihad* (holy war), which they waged from fortified camps (*ribats*) along the frontier. Hence their dynasty bore the name Almoravid (*al-murabitun* – the men of the *ribat*). Their brand of ferocious piety appealed to the Berbers of North Africa, whose overwhelming support enabled them to storm into Spain and, for a space, recover most of the long-lost Muslim territory in the peninsula. Yet it is precisely their puritanical fervour which helps to explain why they produced so little in the visual arts. Their religious foundations in Spain have vanished completely, and the seriousness of that loss can be gauged by the sparse surviving evidence of their work elsewhere in the Maghrib, comprising principally the Great Mosques of Algiers (1097 onwards) and Fez (mainly 1135) and a 140 kiosk (presumably a fountain) once apparently part of the Great Mosque of Marrakesh.

The last two monuments in particular testify to the remarkable vigour and imagination with which Almoravid architects transformed the time-honoured motifs of interlaced arch and rib vault which they had inherited from Andalusia. Whereas in Spain itself the heritage of Cordoba was dissipated in increasingly finicky and small-scale ornament in which spatial values played a diminishing role (as instanced by the Aljaferia palace at Zaragoza), the buildings in Fez and Marrakesh, instinct with a formidable energy, are triumphantly three-dimensional. This dynamic manipulation of space combined themes earlier kept apart – ornamental arch forms and decorative vaults – to produce a distinctively Maghribi version of the *muqarnas*. The hallmark of these *muqarnas* systems – in contrast to contemporary Iraqi and Syrian versions of such themes – is that the exterior yields no hint of the internal configuration. At Fez, moreover – as in the almost contemporary Cappella Palatina at Palermo and the Qal'a of the Banu Hammad in Algeria – the *muqarnas* vault is built up over a rectangular space and is therefore not interpreted as a dome. Instead, it works visually like a suspended ceiling. It is significantly more evolved in design and complexity than contemporary examples in the eastern Islamic world. In the Mosque of the Dead attached to the Friday Mosque of Fez, as in the Marrakesh fountain, variously lobed and crinkled arch forms executed with truly sculptural verve are used to build up powerful contrasting rhythms. Thus architectural forms, not applied decoration, animate the building.

The coming of the Almohads brought a new impetus to religious 141 architecture, as shown by the huge congregational mosques which they built in Seville, Rabat and Marrakesh. Their keynote is a

184

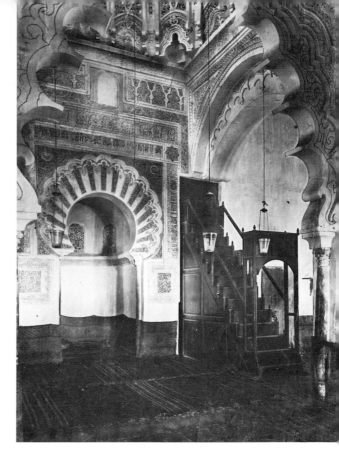

142 The long shadow of Spain. Tlemcen, Great Mosque, *mihrab*, *minbar* and dome, 1135–6. Dwarf arcades; cusped, interlaced and horseshoe arches; ribbed dome; and two-tone masonry all underline the defining role of the Cordoba mosque in Maghribi religious architecture; the patron, ʿAli b. Yusuf b. Tashfin, brought craftsmen from Andalusia to work in Tlemcen. However, cheap painted stucco now replaces expensive glass mosaics.

puritanical simplicity of design, unexpectedly relieved on the *qibla* axis by voluptuously lobed arch profiles. These mosques tend to enlarge the covered sanctuary at the expense of the courtyard, which shrinks dramatically. They all make much of the measured repetition of a single unit such as a bay or an arcade to create directed vistas and a sense of illimitable space; while their plain exteriors, articulated by little more than niches, exude a comparable austerity. All the more remarkable, then, is the contrast provided by the towering square minarets of these three mosques, all decorated with overwhelming richness, all dated to the last decades of the twelfth century, and all of them illusionistically rendered more gigantic still by the contrast with the low expanse of the mosque itself. In all three cases, each face of the tower is elaborately fenestrated (their interiors comprise a series of superposed vaulted chambers linked by a ramp) and bears a different set of latticed designs in raised stonework.

185

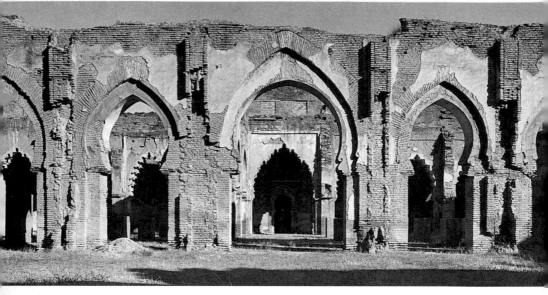

143 Dynastic mosque. In Tinmal, the Almohad capital, the self-appointed 'caliph' 'Abd al-Mu'min built a bijou version of the Cordoba mosque in 1153. It measures just 48 × 43 m (157.5 × 141.1 ft).

143　　But the masterpiece among these Almohad mosques, and indeed of later Maghribi architecture, is the mosque of Tinmal, the Almohad capital near Marrakesh. Here, too, the juxtaposition of plain and ornate is breathtaking; the eye moves from huge expanses of plain wall to intricately carved capitals – indeed, the Almohad Kutubiya mosque in Marrakesh has perhaps the most complex capital in all of Islamic architecture. Among other noteworthy features at Tinmal is the location of the minaret behind the *mihrab*, strongly salient from the back wall of the mosque (a major innovation, soon to be copied at the mosques of Algiers and Sale), with two sets of three projecting lateral portals and the three domed bays marking the corners and the centre of the *qibla* wall. This is part of the characteristically Maghribi T-shape, which is created by the junction of the central nave (wider than all the others) with the transverse aisle abutting the *qibla* wall. The vaults of this aisle run parallel to the *qibla* wall, not perpendicular to it like those elsewhere in the sanctuary. The area constituting the T is singled out from the rest of the mosque by a sudden quickening of the decorative tempo, evident in applied ornament, arch profiles and vaulting.

186

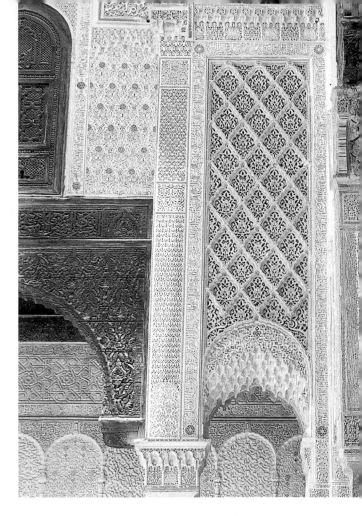

144 'Orient pearls at random strung'. Fez, Madrasat al-'Attarin, 1323. The wall (including the tiled dado below) is conceived as a kind of picture gallery, a series of individual panels of changing scales, media, designs, textures, tones, colours and depth; little care has been taken to integrate them into a single composition.

The demise of the Almohads left the way open for the creation of smaller principalities, of which three dominated the later Middle Ages in the Maghrib – the Marinids of Morocco (1217–1465), the Zayyanids of western Algeria (1236–1555) with their capital at Tlemcen, and the Hafsids of eastern Algeria and Tunisia (1229–1574). All three dynasties concentrated their patronage on architecture, and most other arts – such as pottery, textiles and metalwork – barely rose above the artisanal level in this period. The *madrasas* of the Marinids 144 deserve particular attention; these buildings reflect the orthodox Islam, propagated by a conservative religious élite, that flourished in cities like Fez, Taza and Marrakesh, rather than the popular Islam of the countryside which expressed itself through the veneration of saints, religious brotherhoods and descendants of the Prophet, and through countless modest shrines and mausolea of indeterminate date. Most of the *madrasa*s, by contrast, are firmly dated and are extravagantly embellished with glazed tilework, carved wood and intricate stucco ornament. The standard design featured an enclosed courtyard with a pool and two-storey façades. The lower floor served for lecture rooms and a prayer hall; while in the upper storey, quite removed from all this visual splendour, lay bare, comfortless and overcrowded cells for the theological students themselves.

145

From the sixteenth century onwards, most of the Maghrib fell under Ottoman rule and lost much of its local character. Nevertheless the grand public Ottoman mosques like the Fishermen's Mosque in Algiers were complemented by domestic architecture of an altogether lighter atmosphere, with fountains; painted and fretted woodwork screens, doors and fretted wood (*mashrabiya*) windows; and garish tilework.

The later medieval history of Muslim Spain, and of its art, is rather different. The Christian victory at the battle of Las Navas de Tolosa

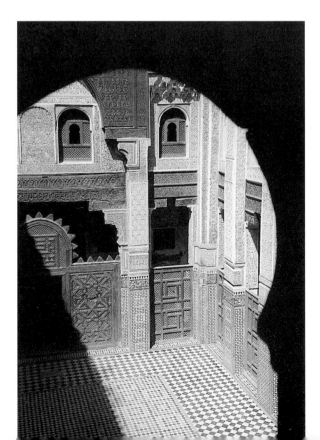

145 College life. Fez, Madrasat al-ʿAttarin: founded, staffed and endowed in 1323 by the Marinid sultan Abu Saʿid, who was present when the foundations were laid. The origins of many *madrasa*s in the teacher's own house are reflected here in the intimate domestic flavour and small scale. The contrast between the imposing and glamorous public face and the austerity of the students' quarters, safely out of sight, is striking.

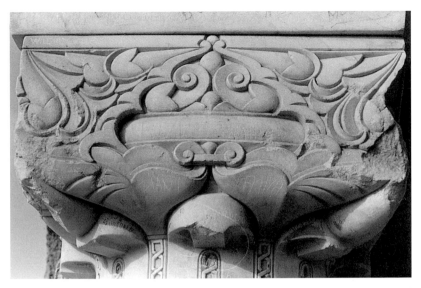

146 The afterlife of Samarran ornament. Marble capital from the unfinished Marinid palace at al-Mansuriya, Algeria; early 14th century. Such capitals of expensive stone echo the bevelled style (cf. *ill.* 27) and Almohad modes in their lavish carving and whimsical curvilinearity. This recalls the Maghribi fascination with exotic arch forms.

in 1212, with the consequent loss of Cordoba and Seville, was a catastrophe for the future of Islam in Spain. Yet Muslims continued to practise their arts and crafts under Christian patronage, as shown by the Alcazar at Seville (rebuilt by Pedro the Cruel in 1364), in many ways a reduced version of the Alhambra, and by the lustre pottery of Manises. Against all the odds, moreover, one Muslim principality managed to survive the general collapse by dint of the humiliating accommodations it reached with its Christian neighbours: the Nasrids of Granada (1232–1492). They maintained Islam and its civilization, together with the Arabic language, in Spain for over two and a half centuries, and with such panache and success that, according to an Arabic saying, 'Paradise is that part of the heavens which is above Granada'.

This emirate, despite its small size and constantly threatened position, took in refugees from elsewhere in Muslim Spain and its court welcomed historians and scientists, philologists and geographers, and above all poets. Some of the Islamic city's streets, baths, inns, villas, *madrasa*s, markets – even converted mosques and minarets – still survive. The wealth of the realm rested partly on its agriculture and

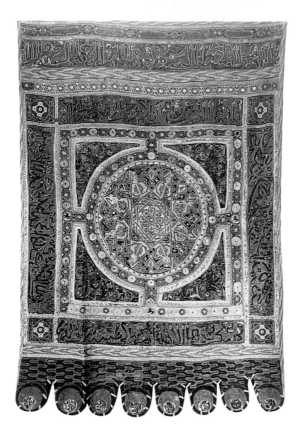

147 (*left*) Symbol of *jihad*. 'In God I find refuge from Satan' proclaims this Almohad banner, 1212–50. The inscriptions contain Qur'an 61:10–12, with its promises of Paradise to the faithful in holy war. The iconography features a central talismanic star and other celestial motifs, much like contemporary Qur'anic frontispieces.

148 (*opposite*) A Muslim monopoly under Christian control. Valencian lustre dish with abbreviated Arabic inscriptions (repeated 'good health'), early 14th century. Royal, ducal and other inventories, itemized orders and contemporary paintings indicate how coveted this ware was throughout Europe. The Muslim craftsmen worked predominantly in Christian territory; thus in 1458 a certain Juan Murci was executing orders for 200,000 tiles to be supplied to rulers in Naples and Valencia. The shields recall the armorial function of much Valencian ware.

partly on such products as textiles and lustre pottery. The range of Granadine art, which includes several objects and techniques not found elsewhere in medieval Islamic art, is quite remarkable. It includes writing desks, doors and caskets of marquetry work in wood and ivory, carved ivory and silver pyxides, jewelry, bridles, parade helmets, scabbards and swords decorated with cloisonné enamel, metal openwork mosque lamps and a spectacular array of textiles: 147   hangings, pillow-covers, capes, rugs, banners, mantles and curtains. These provide abundant proof that the textile industry of Muslim Spain maintained its vitality and its capacity to innovate right to the end, seemingly unaffected by the loss of almost all its earlier centres of production. The motifs tend to emphasize not the heraldic beasts that were the stock-in-trade of luxury textile designs across the Mediterranean world in previous centuries but instead defiantly proclaim their Islamic origins: interlocking motifs suggesting infinite

190

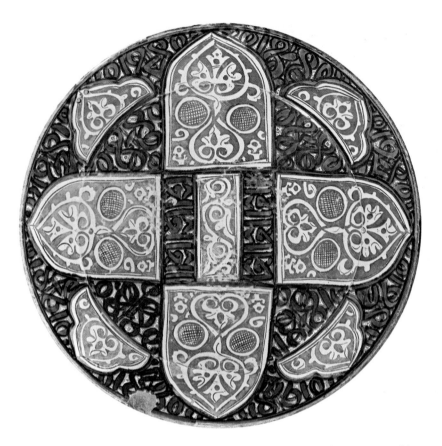

patterns, crenellations, and Arabic inscriptions with mottoes like 'Power belongs to God' and 'Glory to our Lord the Sultan', as well as more light-hearted messages, like 'I am made for pleasure, for pleasure am I'. The wide distribution of these luxury textiles can be deduced from the frequency of their appearance in medieval Spanish and Portuguese paintings of Christian content. To the very end, then, Islamic textiles maintained their ancient associations with wealth and authority.

Spanish lustreware had similar associations. It was made, often for 148 Christian patrons, with western coats of arms and Christian inscriptions such as 'Ave Maria', at various centres including Manises, Paterna and Malaga (hence 'majolica'), and was widely exported, especially in the form of great dishes and apothecaries' jars (*albarellos*). Pride of place in this technique, however, must go to a speciality apparently unique to Granada – the so-called Alhambra vases, huge amphora-like containers more than 1.20 m (4 ft) high, decorated in lustre or lustre and blue, and furnished with decorative handles. Some bear apotropaic motifs such as the *khams* or sacred hand, suggesting that their contents (wine? oil? perfumed water?) required protection. For the potter, their size alone posed a daunting technical challenge; the firing of lustrewares was a tricky operation at the best of times, and a kiln capacious enough to hold pieces this big would not generate constant heat. Hence the traces of uneven firing which they bear. Well do some of them bear the single word 'power' (*al-mulk* – also the title of a Qur'anic *sura* or chapter) repeated like a mantra in a closed circuit around their bodies. Other vases are inscribed with wishes for good health, good fortune, prosperity, pleasure, or with the motto 'Power belongs to God'. Or they may apostrophize themselves in flattering terms, a popular convention in later Moorish art. There is a certain irony and pathos in the fact that these, by far the largest and most spectacular examples of all Islamic luxury wares, were produced in a tiny principality situated on the outer fringes of the Muslim world and doomed to rapid extinction.

149

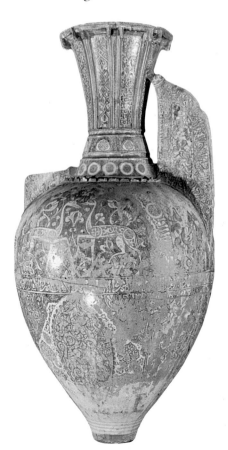

149 'The artist's hand has embroidered me like a robe of silk'. Wing-handled lustre storage vase, Malaga, *c.* 1400. Here pottery approaches architecture. The gold and blue palette – typical of Spanish lustre – was termed 'gilded' and 'silvered' in contemporary texts. The Arabic inscriptions, of different scale, type and colour, repeat the same message: *al-yumn wa'l-iqbal*, 'good fortune and prosperity'. The stylized Tree of Life below the affronted animals evokes Paradise. H. 135 cm (53.1 in).

Much the same can be said of the Alhambra itself, the only large-scale medieval Islamic palace to survive, admittedly much repaired over the centuries. It is not so much a palace as a fortified royal city set athwart a mountainous outcrop dominating Granada, with the River Darro below and remote vistas of the Sierra Nevada beyond. The complex originally contained six palaces, of which five remain, plus numerous subsidiary buildings and gardens. Like much of Nasrid art it is delicate, even over-refined, and fastidiously choice execution. The literary sources speak of Moorish landscape architects; this is their handiwork. The Alhambra brings the forces of nature into play at every turn: water in movement – trickling, running, cascading, spurting – or still, in tranquil expanses; carefully barbered trees and bushes; sunken flower beds; sudden glimpses of mountains or gardens framed in a casement, or, more ambitiously, miradors and belvederes cunningly placed to exploit sight lines over an entire landscape; and, above all, light. The Alhambra studiously manipulates contrasts of light and dark, with bent entrances, shafts of sunlight angled into shadowy interiors, dim passageways suddenly opening into a courtyard open to the blazing sun, and light reflected from placid ponds or walls clad in glistening tiles.

Frequent destruction and new buildings (which have come and gone as architectural fashions change) have wrecked the original carefully planned processional sequence which channelled petitioners to the royal quarters. The principal elements are largely datable between *c.* 1333 and *c.* 1391. Two of these stand out. First in date is the Comares palace. Its entrance façade evokes a vast petrified Nasrid hanging, its staggeringly complex yet still two-dimensional ornament articulated by doors to left and right and multiple windows. Blank walls on either side focused attention on the centre, where the sultan sat on his throne, itself raised on three steps, to deliver public judgment. To the east lay the Hall of the Ambassadors, a private audience chamber whose lacy insubstantial architecture is paradoxically encased in a huge bastion, its unadorned walls an unmistakable metaphor of brute strength. The ceiling within represents in schematic form the seven heavens of the Islamic cosmos, above which is the throne of God Himself, whose protection thus extended to the ruler, God's earthly deputy, enthroned below. Close by this hall were the private quarters of the sultan, plus four apartments for the four wives permitted by Islamic law; each apartment was two-storey, with suites for summer and winter. But the largest and most scenic feature of the Comares palace is the Court of the Myrtles, focusing on a sheet of

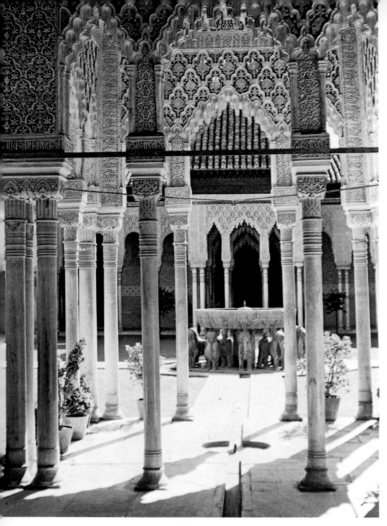

150 Self-advertisement. 'Incomparable is this basin! Allah, the Exalted One, desired/That it should surpass everything in wonderful beauty'. Court of the Lions, Alhambra, *c.* 1375. The lions are taken from an 11th-century palace; they spouted water, a restful sound in this secluded spot. In the rising and falling rhythms of these delicate pencil-like ringed columns, architecture melts into music.

water bordered by aromatic shrubs. It lends an axial emphasis to the complex while its water serves both as a cooling device and to reflect the surrounding structures.

150 The most famous element of the Alhambra is the Court of the Lions, set at right angles to the Court of the Myrtles. It is essentially a classical villa for the private recreation of the monarch, with a shaded portico and a garden courtyard. The latter is divided into four quadrants, perhaps to suggest the seasons, perhaps to suggest in miniature the world itself; at the centre stands the Fountain of the Lions,

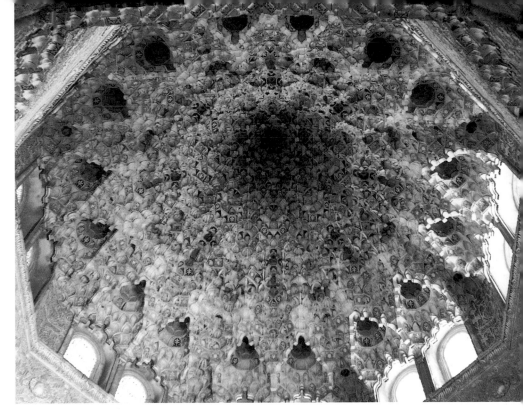

151 'It surpasses the stars in the heavens' wrote Ibn Zamrak of this *muqarnas* vault, the Dome of the Two Sisters in the Alhambra; *c.* 1380. The 23 stanzas of his poem inscribed here evoke a rotating heavenly dome which mirrors the changing constellations and the eternal cycle of day and night. They also touch on other interrelated themes – fertility, gardens, money, victory, service, textiles, jewels and divine protection – thereby revealing contemporary attitudes to the building.

a theme with resonances of the Solomonic Temple. Four halls, again axially grouped, served for private entertainment such as music – hence their acoustic ceilings – and official functions. The master-piece here is the Dome of the Two Sisters, a *muqarnas* composition 151 involving over five thousand cells; the structure bears an inscription by the local poet Ibn Zamrak linking it to the constellations. This conceit is taken up by the multitude of reflections caused by the play of light on this honeycombed surface, which evokes the revolving heavens mentioned in the inscription. The emigration of artisans from Muslim Spain ensured that echoes of the Alhambra and its decoration persisted in North Africa for centuries, though none of its many descendants rivalled it as a machine for gracious living.

CHAPTER EIGHT

The Ilkhanids and Timurids

The robbery and murder of a caravan of merchants from Mongolia in 1217 by Muslim customs officials in Central Asia unleashed a deadly retribution. From 1219 the Iranian world was devastated by repeated invasions of Mongol hordes, originally commanded by Genghis Khan and later by members of his family. These campaigns culminated in the sack of Baghdad and the extinction of the ʿAbbasid caliphate in 1258. The whirlwind nature of the Mongol conquests compounded the sheer terror caused by their apparent invincibility, by their awesome cruelty and by their essentially alien nature – they were, after all, a people who were not Muslims, spoke no Islamic language and for whom the norms of Islamic culture and society were foreign. All this left an indelible mark on their victims. Moreover, this was not mere conquest. The Mongols waged total war and inflicted on much of Iran an eco-catastrophe from which it never recovered. Canals were destroyed, orchards felled, wells blocked up, fields sown with salt; the very cats and dogs were killed. After the sack of the great city of Merv, the Mongols forced a muezzin to give the call to prayer and then slaughtered the survivors as they crept out of their hiding places. Altogether, the loss of life amounted to genocide. Only artisans were spared, to be sent back to Mongolia – where no trace of their activity remains. Vast areas, especially in north-east Iran and Central Asia, were depopulated, and refugees streamed westwards. In the field of the visual arts, this brought to Egypt and the Levant ideas and techniques from the area between Iraq and Afghanistan.

Gradually a new political order arose from these ruins. At first it had little in common with the past. Iran was relegated to a mere province in a pan-Asiatic empire which at its height comprised much of the Eurasian land mass from Korea to east Germany – an empire whose continuous extent is unparalleled in world history. Karakorum in Mongolia, and later Peking, where the Great Khan resided, was the new centre of power, and the Golden Horde (covering much of Russia) and the Ilkhanid realm (comprising Anatolia, Iraq, Iran and

Central Asia) were its sub-states. The Pax Mongolica imposed on this vast tract of land, and maintained by fearsome penalties inflicted on wrongdoers, dramatically facilitated communication between East and West. For the first time in history, it was safe to travel overland from Europe to China. Merchants like Marco Polo took full advantage of the opportunity, and Christian missionaries trekked to the Great Khan's court bearing messages from the Pope, leaving vivid accounts of their journeys.

The Christian powers, who at first equated the Mongol ruler with the legendary Prester John, a Christian monarch believed to rule in the heart of Asia, saw the new order as a heaven-sent opportunity to give the death-blow to Islam, and initiated diplomatic moves to this end. For their part, the Mongol khans, especially in Iran, maintained an active correspondence with European rulers, principally with an alliance against the Ayyubids and Mamluks, who ruled Egypt and Syria, in mind. They saw these European monarchs as suppliants and the language of their letters is arrogant and high-handed. Western hopes of converting the Mongols were in any event ill-founded. In religious matters they showed a tolerance remarkable in the medieval period; they themselves practised by turns their ancestral shamanism, Buddhism, Christianity and eventually Islam, of both the Sunni and the Shi'ite persuasion. This tolerance created a golden age for Christians and Jews, who repeatedly rose to high administrative office. There can be no doubt that this openness to other cultures and beliefs was a key element in the formation of Ilkhanid art. But the Mongols also imposed their own civil code, the *yasa* first promulgated by Genghis Khan, which had little in common with the *shari'a* code that had traditionally governed Muslim life.

The centre of Ilkhanid power was in north-western Iran, whose fertile uplands were a potent attraction to the still-nomadic Mongol élite. Here Abaqa Khan (1265–82) built a palace on the ruins of a spot already sacred to the Sasanians, Takht-i Sulaiman ('The Throne of Solomon'), centred on a perpetual lake in the crater of an extinct volcano. These ancient resonances were deliberately exploited – and enriched by theological undertones – by some of the leading Persian intellectuals of the time when the site was refurbished. Lengthy and carefully chosen quotations from the Persian national epic, the *Shahnama* ('Book of Kings'), are incorporated into an iconography of markedly Chinese character, in which animal and landscape themes of Far Eastern origin – trees, clouds, grass and fabulous beasts like phoenixes and dragons – predominate. Yet Takht-i Sulaiman, for all its size and complexity, its free-standing kiosks and its technical innovations in *muqarnas* vaulting, is still exceptional in its time; it took some eighty years before the arts of Iran had recovered from the destruction wrought by the Mongol invasions.

That they did recover was in large part due to the greatest of the Ilkhanid rulers, Ghazan Khan (ruled 1295–1304). He established his capital at Tabriz, which briefly became perhaps the major international metropolis of the time, a magnet for ambassadors, merchants and artists from most of the known world, where Persians and Mongols mingled with Arabs, Turks, Chinese, Armenians, Byzantines and western Europeans. The Italian republics, notably Venice, Genoa and Pisa, maintained an especially high commercial profile. It was Ghazan, an energetic and far-sighted ruler, who took the momentous decision to embrace Islam and thereby to anchor his own people in Iranian life and culture. This conversion, in which the Mongol ruling class participated, only confirmed the growing power of the Iranian bureaucracy and triggered an explosive expansion of output in the visual arts, in which a revival of national sentiment and of Islamic piety are unmistakable. The balance of power had shifted. Ghazan founded a suburb in Tabriz named after himself where, in the shadow of his own gigantic tomb tower, institutions of learning proliferated. He commissioned his vizier, Rashid al-Din, a physician of Jewish extraction, to write (though perhaps 'editing' would better describe the actual process) a history of the Mongols in the context of a much larger history of the world. Parts of this great enterprise

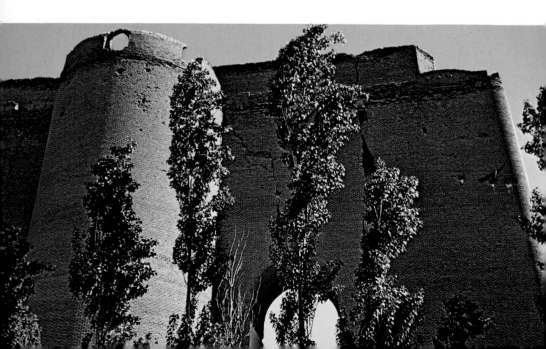

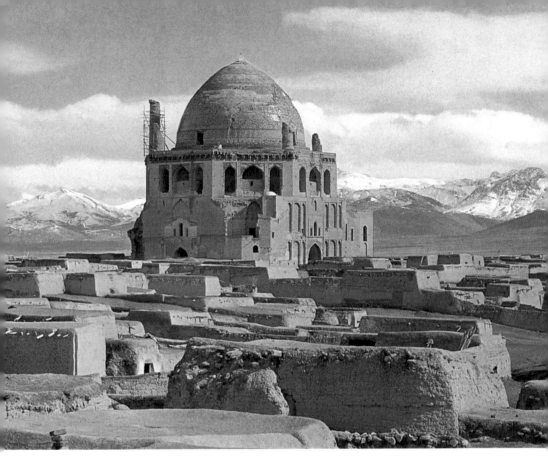

152 (*opposite*) Sheer mass. Mosque of the vizier
'Ali Shah, Tabriz, *c.* 1315; the *qibla* wall. Its
monumentality, echoed in other imperial
Ilkhanid buildings, stimulated rival Mamluk
buildings in Cairo. The vanished entrance
portal was built to eclipse the Sasanian palace
arch at Ctesiphon near Baghdad – evidence
that this symbol of pre-Islamic majesty
remained a touchstone eight centuries later.

153 (*above*) Iran's Taj Mahal. Mausoleum of
Oljeitu, Sultaniya, 1304–15. This complex
building, echoing both the Dome of the Rock
(also in its vast empty precinct) and nomadic
Turco-Mongol tents, fits into a long line of
royal mausolea in the eastern Islamic world.

154 (*right*) A numinous space. Interior of
mausoleum of Oljeitu. This overwhelmingly
volumetric interior soars to 53 m (175 ft). Its
inscriptions are of politico-religious intent,
evoking the Abrahamic Ka'ba and the conquest
of Mecca and – more indirectly – Medina and
Jerusalem, the three holiest cities of Islam.

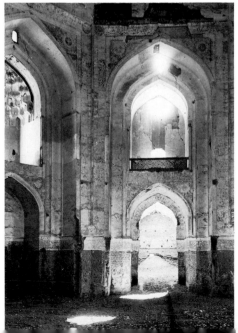

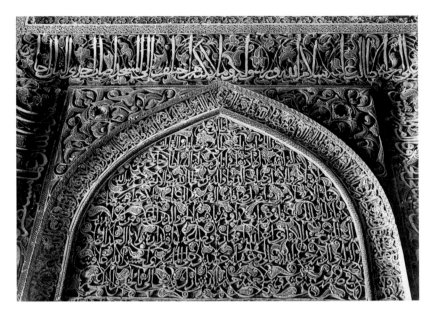

155 Stucco as sculpture. *Mihrab* in the Friday Mosque, Isfahan, 1310. Its inscriptions stand proud of floral motifs which recall an undulating bed of water-lilies. They are signed by Haidar, a pupil of the celebrated Yaqut al-Musta'simi, and mention the twelve Shi'ite *imam*s, thus reflecting Oljeitu's conversion to Shi'ism.

have survived, perhaps because Rashid al-Din ordered multiple illus-trated copies of his work to be distributed at regular intervals to the major cities of the Ilkhanid realm. Simultaneously, Ghazan reformed the *yasa* to bring it closer to the *shari'a* and embarked on an ambi-tious building programme, which was designed to provide every village in the country with its own mosque, financed by the revenues of the bath (*hammam*).

His brother and successor, Oljeitu, was an equally lavish patron of architecture, even founding a new city, named Sultaniya ('The Royal'), to act as capital. Its cynosure was the mausoleum of Oljeitu himself, still one of the finest buildings in Asia. Structurally it was at the forefront of building technology, with its vast pointed dome rising, it seems, directly from the octagonal chamber below but with the intermediary of a spectacular vaulted gallery. Recent research has highlighted its similarity to Brunelleschi's Duomo in Florence. It can be seen as one of a long line of Islamic reinterpretations of the essen-tial schema of the Dome of the Rock and as another indication of

153
154

the desire of the later Ilkhanids to identify themselves with their adopted culture. Craftsmen from many areas of the Ilkhanid domains were conscripted to contribute to this vast project, which involved a huge precinct with numerous subsidiary buildings, and they disseminated the latest fashions and techniques on their return home.

A veritable building boom, at its height between 1300 and 1340, especially in such central Iranian cities as Qumm, Isfahan, Yazd and Abarquh, but continuing for decades thereafter, was triggered by these vast imperial projects at Tabriz and Sultaniya. Existing mosques were expanded and enriched, as shown by the prayer hall, *mihrab* and *madrasa* added to the Friday Mosque of Isfahan. As for new mosques, the Mongols favoured established types, such as the 4-*iwan* plan, as at Varamin and Hafshuya; the covered sanctuary, as at the Masjid-i 'Ali, Quhrud and the recently destroyed Friday Mosque at Barzuk; and the isolated dome chamber, as at Kaj, Dashti and Aziran. The mosque of 'Ali Shah at Tabriz is atypical, for it consists only of a courtyard and a *qibla iwan*. Like the tombs of Ghazan and Oljeitu, it illustrates the huge scale of some Mongol foundations. The Mongol contribution lay principally in a refining and attenuation of Saljuq forms; one may compare the relation of Gothic to Romanesque. Twin-minaret portals best expressed this new trend. The elaborate articulation of Saljuq transition zones was toned down, while in decoration the emphasis gradually shifted from brick patterning to glazed tilework, which brought a dramatic infusion of colour to Iranian architecture. New accents such as saffron and green enriched the palette of the craftsmen, and tile mosaic with floral, geometric and epigraphic decoration became widespread. So too did wall painting, especially in mausolea; the designs were often stencilled and

155

156

152

156 A classical Iranian mosque. Friday Mosque, Varamin, 1322–6. Generously proportioned (according to the 2:3 ratio familiar since 'Abbasid times, and based on a grid of equilateral triangles), this traditional 4-*iwan* structure stresses the longitudinal axis by a deep portal and a mighty dome at opposite ends.

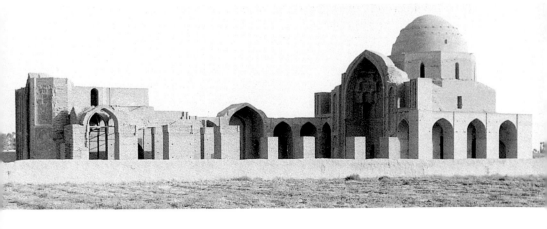

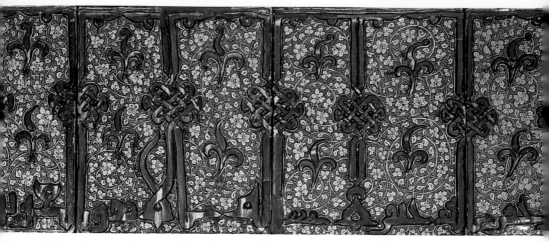

157 'There is no God but He, the Mighty, the Wise' (Qur'an 3:6) proclaims the text on these four huge flawlessly executed lustre tiles, Kashan. *c.* 1300. Each tile 57 × 47 cm (22.4 × 18.5 in).

owed much to Qur'anic illumination, as a group of mud-brick buildings in Yazd and Abarquh show.

The Mongol period saw a major shift of emphasis in the building of mausolea, with most tomb towers being built to serve religious (specifically Shi'ite) purposes rather than secular ones, and often decorated internally with lustre tiles. The concomitant popularity of religious shrines, often of Sufi character, as the focus for local as well as imperial patronage can be seen in such sites as Natanz, Bastam, Linjan and Ardabil, with their pronounced welfare function. These shrines, continually added to over the centuries, both depended on and fostered local piety, and they also had an important role in the local economy through the land they owned.

157 Mongol ceramics are dominated by lustre tiles, which were produced in great quantities – especially in Kashan, where, as inscriptions show, the tradition was sometimes handed down from father to son for generations. Several entire *mihrab*s composed of these rectangular tiles have survived. The production of such tiles seems actually to have increased during the Mongol period, though even in this area a hiatus of about twenty-five years (*c.* 1230–55) is apparent and was presumably caused by the chaotic aftermath of the Mongol invasions. Lustre tiles of star or cross shapes, often with interlocking monochrome glazed tiles to act as a foil, created huge shimmering dados in religious buildings and palaces. Very often the individual tiles would each bear a Persian inscription rendered in a hurried

202

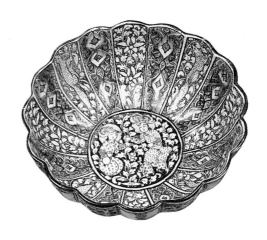

158 (*right*) The fashion for the Far East. Pottery bowl with lobed sides, Sultanabad type, early 14th century. The roundel depicts two Mongols of high rank. The panels feature a running fox, arabesques and foliage of Chinese inspiration.

159 (*below*) Textiles: portable wealth, portable propaganda. Silk and gold-thread slit tapestry roundel, early 14th century, perhaps a royal table cover. Images such as the tortoise and crane by a fishpond and the lotus scroll, and the overall aesthetic link it to tapestry weaving (*kesi*) from Chinese Turkestan and thus to Uighur culture. But most of the iconography is Islamic, as are the benedictory inscriptions.

scrawl all along its outer edge. Floral or animal motifs are the staple decoration of these tiles. Some Qur'anic inscriptions on these tiles, in defiance of orthodox Islamic practice, have a background in which birds feature among arabesque scrolls. In the larger rectangular tiles in which living creatures dominate the design, an effective combination of relief and lustre painting was devised.

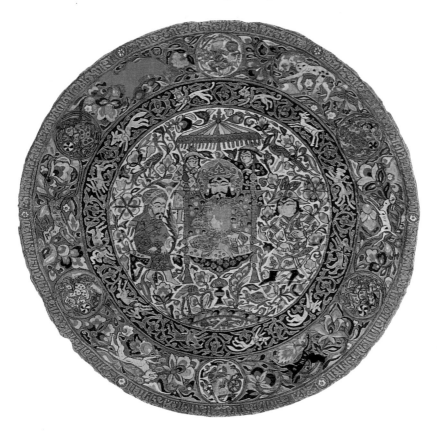

While many other wares of Saljuq type continued to be made under the Ilkhanids, two major new types of pottery appear. *Lajvardina* is a simplified successor of the *mina'i* technique. The courtly scenes of the earlier ware are replaced by geometric and epigraphic themes and by Far Eastern mythical creatures. Gold overpainting set against a deep, royal blue glaze makes *lajvardina* ware one of the most spectacular ever produced in Persia. The other new Ilkhanid ware is dowdy by comparison. Traditionally associated with the Sultanabad region, it is heavily potted and makes frequent use of a grey slip with thick outlines, while another type displays black painting under a turquoise glaze. The drawing is of indifferent quality, but the ware as a whole has a special interest as a classic example of the way Chinese motifs invaded the Persian ceramic tradition. Earlier, Chinese techniques and shapes alone had inspired the Persian potter; but from now on his iconographic repertoire drew widely on Chinese sources. Dragons, phoenixes, mandarin ducks, cloud bands, peonies and lotuses are all standard Ilkhanid themes, and they are treated with a new naturalism also inspired by China. Such Chinese elements are equally marked in the relatively few surviving Ilkhanid textiles.

In metalwork as in ceramic production, the Mongol invasion fatally disrupted a flourishing industry. The ravaged province of Khurasan, in particular, never again supported a major metalworking industry. After a gap in production of almost a century, which can be paralleled closely in architecture and painting, the industry revived – but in new centres. One was in Central Asia; another was in Azerbaijan, the principal centre of Mongol culture; but it was southern Iran that really came to the fore. This area had been spared Mongol devastation, but was, of course, open to Mongol stylistic features. Hence there appear in the metalwork of Fars such features as the peony, the lotus, flying ducks, *ju-i* heads (a tri-lobed motif) and Chinese phoenixes. The figures, slim and narrow-waisted, have something of the elegance that characterizes the figures of late fourteenth-century Persian painting, a link that extends also to their costume. A general readiness to adopt alien fashions would explain the presence of geometrical patterning of Mosul type and of the bold elongated *thulth* inscriptions that were the hallmark of contemporary Mamluk metalwork. But this same school seems to have popularized the use of Persian poetry on metalwork, and its epigraphic formulae celebrating Solomon and Alexander are rooted deep in the Persian tradition.

In the field of the arts, apart from architecture, pride of place in

158

159

160

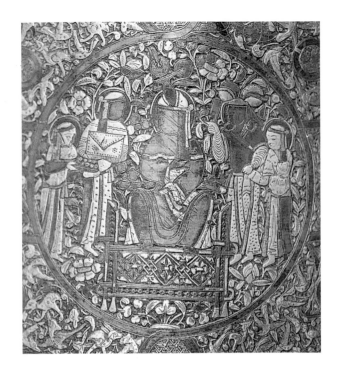

160 Women in authority. Detail of a candlestick made for the Inju ruler of Fars, Abu Ishaq (reigned 1341–56). This, one of four decorative roundels with enthronement scenes derived from contemporary manuscript illustrations, presumably depicts his queen, who wears a version of the *baqtaq*, the headdress worn by married Mongol women; her presence on two of the four roundels corresponds to the conspicuous honour paid to royal women in Mongol iconography.

the Ilkhanid period goes to the art of the book. Ilkhanid scribes and illuminators, especially those of Mosul and Baghdad, rivalled the best Mamluk work and may indeed have laid the foundations for it. Characteristic of this school is the use of very large sheets (up to 72 × 50 cm, 28 × 20 in) of Baghdad paper and correspondingly large-scale scripts, especially *muhaqqaq*. The vaults in the gallery of Oljeitu's tomb owe much to the designs in the frontispieces and carpet pages of these Qur'ans, of which a good two dozen have survived.

Among the various traditions of Islamic manuscript painting – Arab, Persian, Turkish and Indian – Persian painting, which effectively begins with the Ilkhanids and attained its classic style under the Timurids, must take precedence on several scores. For diversity it is without parallel in Islam; for sheer output it rivals even India; and while the Arab world can boast slightly earlier work, it cannot match the continuity of the Persian tradition. The origins of that tradition are probably destined to remain obscure, though textual evidence establishes the continuity of this art from the Sasanian period. Iranian book painting for the first five centuries of Islam is thus an almost total blank and must be reconstructed with

205

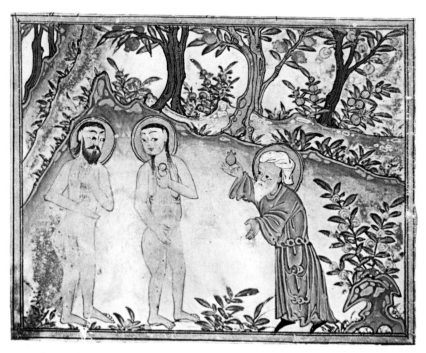

161 The Garden – and the Fire. The *Chronology of Ancient Nations* by the 11th-century polymath al-Biruni discusses all the calendrical systems known to him, often with an Islamic slant. But the Zoroastrian story of the evil spirit Ahriman tempting Misha and Mishyana, the first man and woman, reflects Genesis iconography. Perhaps Tabriz, 1307.

161 the help of painted pottery, and a few wall paintings from Samanid Nishapur and Ghaznavid Lashkar-i Bazar, as well as the probably Saljuq manuscript of *Varqa va Gulshah* ('Varqa and Gulshah'; see p. 100). The first really useful clues are provided by the late Saljuq painting practised in Iraq (see pp. 125–32). This probably reflects contemporary Persian work, to judge by the painted Persian pottery of the time, just as the paintings of al-Biruni's *al-Athar al-Baqiya* ('Chronology of Ancient Nations'), dated 1307, echo the style of the Baghdad school. From the eleventh to the fourteenth century, both Iran and Iraq were frequently part of the same political unit, so these close links are to be expected; and indeed, both Tabriz and Mosul have been suggested as the provenance for this manuscript. Its emphasis on calendrical systems, which caters to the same interests as Hulegu Khan's great observatory in Maragha (1258), testifies to the Mongol interest in science, also manifest in illustrated bestiaries and

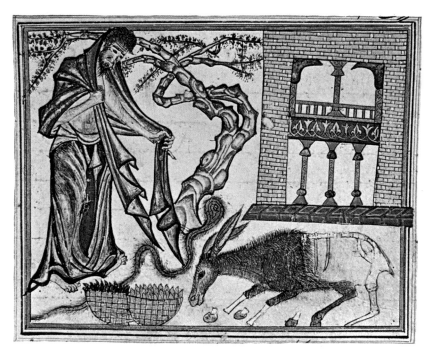

162 Religious pragmatism. The images of Rashid al-Din's *World History* are multi-confessional; f.13b illustrates Qur'an 2:261 (cf. The Valley of the Dry Bones, Ezekiel 37:1-14), which tells how God causes a man to die and be resurrected, along with his donkey and food, a century later. Note the Chinese conventions for tree and stream. Tabriz, 1314.

encyclopaedias such as the *Mu'nis al-Ahrar fi Daqa'iq al-Ash'ar* ('The Free Men's Companion to the Subtleties of Poems') by al-Jajarmi.

The Biruni manuscript is a fortunate survival, for it documents the invasion of the established pictorial idiom of eastern Islam by totally alien influences, especially from the Far East. But the resultant degree of flux in fourteenth-century painting is, nevertheless, surprising. Several distinct styles flourished, some of them owing little to each other and quite remote in spirit and in style from the pre-Mongol traditions. The Biruni manuscript, with its emphasis on non-Islamic heresies and faiths, especially Christianity, its astrological content, and its choice of key Shiʿite themes, is a case in point. The *Manafiʿ-i hayavan* ('On the Usefulness of Animals', produced in the 1290s in Maragha), essentially a bestiary, and the manuscripts illustrating Rashid al-Din's *Jamiʿ al-Tawarikh* ('World History') share the stress on Biblical themes. In content, 'On the Usefulness of Animals'

162
163

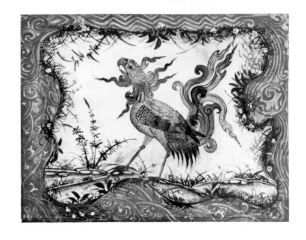

163 Chinese art Islamized. *On the Usefulness of Animals*, Maragha, 1290s. 'The Simurgh, found in inaccessible islands . . . is fearless beyond all other animals. He can carry off exceedingly large animals like the elephant and the rhinoceros. . . .' Muslims, like Europeans, had their 'Marvels of the East' literature, part fantasy, part reality. This gaudy bird echoes the Chinese phoenix.

– of which several other contemporary versions are known – belongs firmly within the orbit of those practical treatises long popular in Mesopotamia and issuing from an ancient Byzantine and classical tradition. But this bestiary inhabits a different world from that of its Arab equivalents. The clue lies in the artists' partiality for drama. They invest essentially undramatic subjects with a portentous power wholly at variance with the stiff, woodenly articulated animals of Arab bestiaries. Some of the painters obey the formulae of Mesopotamian painting for details of plants, landscape, drapery and facial features. Other miniatures are infused with a new Chinese spirit expressed in the treatment of landscape details and especially in the overlapping planes that lend depth to a composition. But, as in

164 'They came, they sapped, they burnt, they slew, they plundered, they departed.' The Mongols at work, as described in the *World History* of Rashid al-Din, (f.124b).

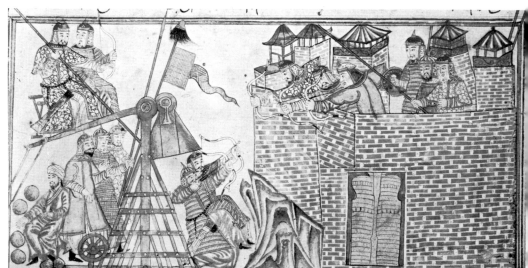

later times, Persian painters were never fully attuned to the artistic conventions that underlie Chinese painting. They preferred to borrow, and frequently to use out of context, eye-catching individual motifs such as exotic creatures (the phoenix [often representing the *simurgh*, the bird of Persian legend], giraffes, elephants), plants (peonies, lotuses), blossoming trees, and the conventions for rendering water, fire and clouds.

The manuscripts of the 'World History' of Rashid al-Din are on an altogether different scale. Their provenance in the cosmopolitan city of Tabriz guaranteed the paintings a remarkably mixed ancestry in which Chinese, Byzantine and Uighur (Eastern Turkish) elements mingle with Persian and Arab strains. The large oblong format usually employed for these paintings allowed the artists ample scope for scenes expressing the savage lust of battle as well as for solemn tableaux of enthroned monarchs. Their ferocious battle scenes, full of 164 authentic Mongol military detail, mirror the invasions that had traumatized the Persian psyche a century earlier and whose memory was clearly still green. Conversely, their scenes from the Old and New Testaments, the Buddha cycle and – for the first time in Islamic art – the life of Muhammad reflect the Mongol curiosity about religion. One manuscript, in London, is prefaced by dozens of stereotyped royal portraits that are pastiches of Chinese models even to details of dress and pose. The same obedience to formula governs the many court scenes in a contemporary codex of the *Diwan* ('Collected Poems') of Mu'izzi. But whether the scenes depicted are inventive or merely routine, the hybrid style associated with the atelier of Rashid al-Din is instantly recognizable. So muted are the tones and so dominant the role of line that many paintings resemble tinted drawings.

Some impressive court scenes were produced in this style, and it lingered for several decades. By 1330, the fashion for illustrated *Shahnama*s bulked large in southern Iran, under the Inju dynasty. Here national sentiment was fostered, perhaps because the area was not under direct Mongol rule. The dating and provenance of the so-called 'small' *Shahnama*s pose a different set of problems. Firm data have 165 proved hard to establish and good cases have been made for attributing these manuscripts to Baghdad and Tabriz; even Anatolia is a possibility. At all events it is a *Shahnama* that is the undisputed masterpiece of the last years of Mongol rule. This is the incomplete Great Mongol *Shahnama*, whose scale may reflect the growing commitment of the Mongols to the land that they were governing. It is presumably a royal manuscript made for the last Ilkhanid ruler, Abu Sa'id (1316–36).

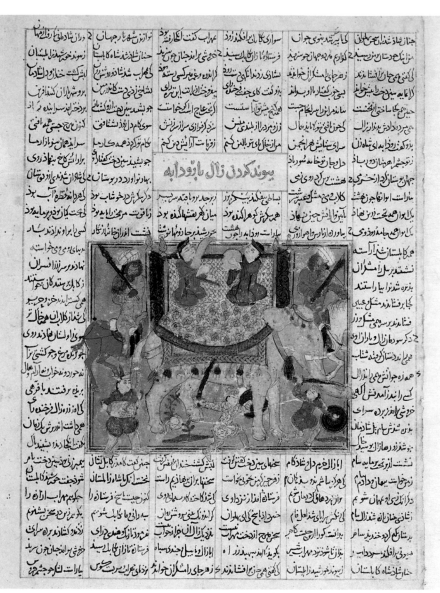

165 (*above*) Pre-nuptial festivities. Musicians riding an elephant celebrate, according to the caption, 'the physical union of Zal with Rudabah'. 'Small' *Shahnama*, provenance uncertain, *c*. 1300. Firdausi's text sets the event in Kabulistan (modern Afghanistan), where there was indeed an 11th-century elephant park.

166 (*opposite above*) The resurgence of Iranian myths. In the Great Mongol *Shahnama* (Tabriz, *c*. 1330) the tale of Bahram Gur, legendary lover and hunter, is reinterpreted as a moral evolution from irresponsible playboy to just ruler. When, at his lover's request, his arrow pins together a gazelle's head, ear and hind leg, she reproaches him for his demonic spirit and he tramples her to death.

167 (*opposite below*) The Mongol way of death. The bier of Iskandar, from the Great Mongol *Shahnama*. The unrestrained expression of grief flouts Muslim norms but mirrors Mongol practice and European art. The lavish appointments match literary accounts of the mausoleum of the Ilkhan Ghazan.

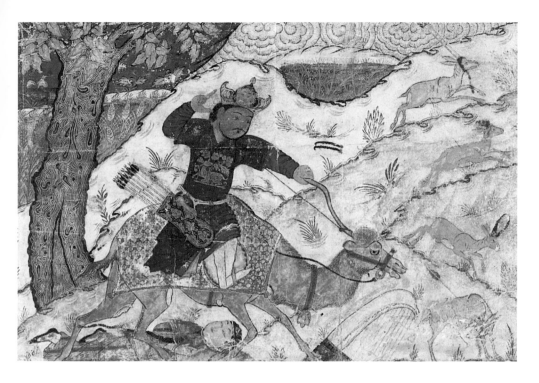

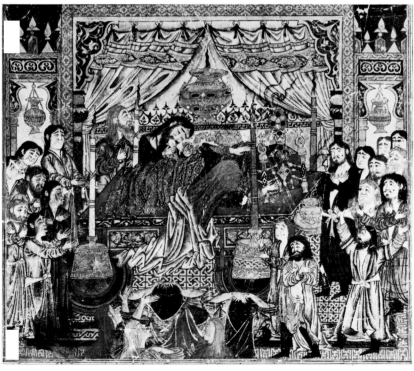

Fifty-eight of its original two hundred or so illustrations are known. In certain paintings ambition and execution do not fully coincide; this is a style in flux. It is notable especially for the dense design and spatial complexity of many of its paintings, their subtle gamut of colours, and a marked predilection for drama and violent action. Full of elements from China and western Europe alike, alive with contemporary allusions, and of an emotional power never recaptured in later versions of this text, it expresses at every turn millennial Iranian ideas of royal

166   legitimacy, and is therefore an apt metaphor for the resurgence of Iranian national sentiment in later Ilkhanid times. So by the end of this period, as in the case of Greece and Rome many centuries before, captive Iran had made captive its conqueror. The Great Mongol

167   *Shahnama* is thus an appropriate envoi to the whole period, ushering in the dissolution of the Mongol state and the re-establishment of native Iranian centres of power in much of the country.

    After the collapse of Mongol central authority in 1336, Iran disintegrated into several independent political entities, each with its own geographical centre of gravity. Of these the most important were the Jala'irids who ruled western Iraq and Iran and the Muzaffarids who controlled central and southern Iran. Both devoted their major patronage to architecture and to painting. Jala'irid architecture is best

168   represented by the *madrasa* and *khan* of Amir Mirjan in Baghdad, both built in the later 1350s in the style of intricate carved terracotta ornament and bold transverse vaulting first developed in late ʿAbbasid Baghdad. Typical of their spatial subtlety is the triple-domed prayer hall in the *madrasa* and the fully operational set of rooms in the upper storey of the *khan*, accessible via a cantilevered gallery, a design echoed in a *Maqamat* illustration.

    In book painting the Jala'irids took over the mantle of Mongol imperial patronage, experimenting both with new messages for familiar texts and with new relationships between text and image. The later fourteenth century saw the incubation of the Timurid 'classical' style which was to dominate Persian painting for over two centuries. The Muzaffarids built energetically in Isfahan where several mausolea, *madrasa*s and minarets datable to *c.* 1340–70 survive; in Yazd, which developed its own style of painted ornament closely allied to Qurʾanic illumination (as in the Shamsiya *madrasa* and a series of mausolea); and in Kirman, as in the portals of the Friday Mosque and the Masjid-i Pa Minar, which display a transitional style between Mongol and Timurid modes both in structure and in such decorative details as cable mouldings and tile mosaic.

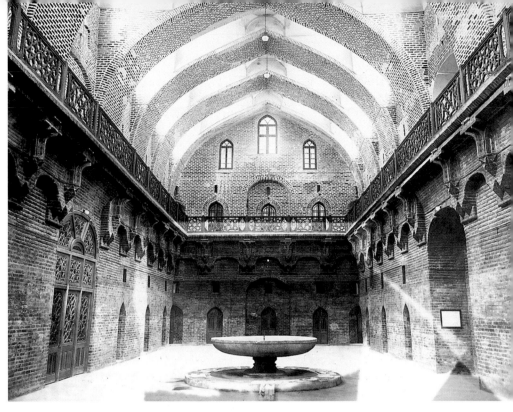

168 Mercantile cathedral. Interior of Khan Mirjan, Baghdad, 1359, a hotel-cum-warehouse: accommodation upstairs, storage space below. The revenues it generated paid for the upkeep of the neighbouring *madrasa* erected by the same patron. The endowment inscription is signed by a Qur'anic calligrapher.

The last two decades of the fourteenth century saw the rise to power of a conqueror scarcely less fearsome than his ancestor Genghis Khan. Timur the Lame, whose larger-than-life memory (as 'Tamburlaine') galvanized the imagination of Renaissance Europe, was an illiterate tribal chieftain who gradually built up a confederation of Turco-Mongol tribes from Central Asia and beyond, launching them on a series of victorious campaigns that lasted until his death in 1405. These frenetic conquests proved transitory; their memory was their heritage. The Iranian world, India, Anatolia, Syria – all fell to him, with horrendous destruction and loss of life even though he posed as a pious Muslim. Craftsmen were spared from these massacres and transported to his capital Samarqand, which they beautified with spectacular buildings, including now vanished palaces with wall paintings depicting Timur's victories. They also worked in

213

other Central Asian cities like Kish and Yasi. This empire fell apart on his death as the standard Turkish practice of dividing the patrimony among the various sons asserted itself.

None of his successors had his military genius, but they applied themselves with equal fervour to the arts of peace, and rapidly acquired a taste for Persian culture, as shown by the pocket anthologies of classic Persian poetic texts which they ordered for their personal use. Samarqand under Ulugh Beg became renowned as a scientific centre; the gigantic quadrant of his observatory still survives and the astronomical tables he drew up were in use at the University of Oxford as late as 1665. Shahrukh and his son Baisunqur, ruling at Herat, devoted themselves to literature and painting respectively; the 1420s saw an ambitious attempt to complete the 'World History' of Rashid al-Din by bringing it into contemporary times, and histories of Timur were written and illustrated. Painting also flourished under Iskandar Sultan in Isfahan and Shiraz, and later under his cousin Sultan Ibrahim in the latter city. Each of these princes established his own court and kept an eye on what his relatives were doing in the cultural as well as the political sphere. Thus emulation was a constant spur to achievement. Yet the cultural values espoused by these Timurid princes were not exclusively Persian; Chaghatay or Eastern Turkish was spoken at court, poetry was composed in that tongue and the famous *Mi'rajnama* ('Book of the Ascension') of 1436 depicting the Prophet's journeys to Heaven and Hell has its primary text in Chaghatay with abbreviated cribs in Persian and Arabic.

The fifteenth century saw the Timurids consistently losing ground to their enemies, notably the Aqqoyunlu or 'White Sheep' Turcomans who dominated central and western Iran and eastern Anatolia from the 1430s, while in the last years of the dynasty the Uzbek Khans encroached on their Central Asian territories. Eventually the Timurid 'empire' had shrunk to Herat and its surroundings, and the much reduced revenues available to royal and aristocratic patrons sufficiently explain why there are few paintings in the great manuscripts and why the decoration of the major buildings is concentrated at a few points only. Yet at the last moment this self-consciously exquisite civilization produced yet another adventurer, Babur, whose dreams of empire were destined to be realized in India, where he founded the Mughal (i.e. Mongol) dynasty in 1526.

As with the Ilkhanids, so with the Timurids architecture and the arts of the book take pride of place over other art forms. With the

169 Here lies 'the Scourge of God'. Gur-i Amir, the tomb of Timur, Samarqand, from 1404. The high drum, stilted and fluted melon dome and glazed bricks spelling out sacred messages (such as 'God is Eternal') and the names of Allah and Muhammad all serve to transform the familiar schema of the domed square. By degrees this became a dynastic mausoleum.

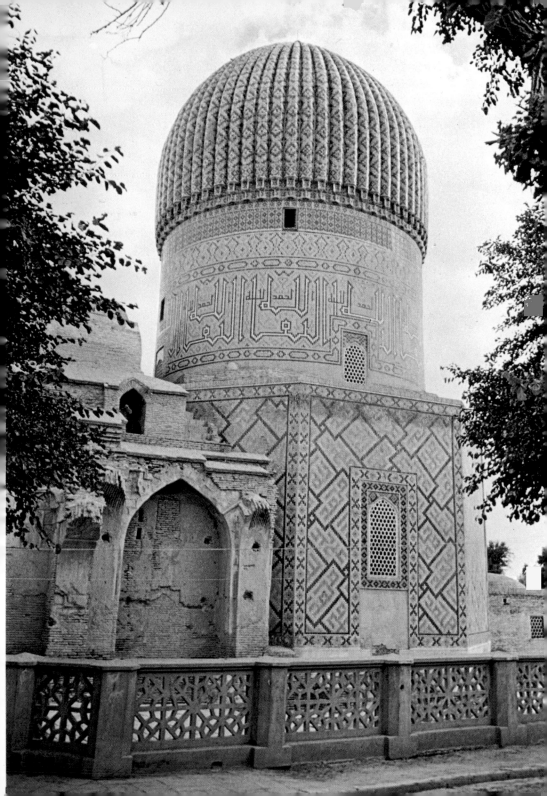

irruption of Timur and his hordes into Iran at the end of the fourteenth century, the desolation of the Mongol conquest repeated
itself. Craftsmen were once again transported, but this time to
Transoxiana, where the signatures of men from Isfahan and Tabriz
have survived in architecture and metalwork.

Imperial Timurid architecture reflects political realities in that its
centre of gravity is squarely within the north-eastern Iranian world.
Thus the areas of Khurasan and Transoxiana replace north-western
and central Iran as the source of major innovations in design as in
structural and decorative techniques. Yet the continuity of Ilkhanid
and Muzaffarid modes is manifest, helped no doubt by the voluntary
or enforced migration of craftsmen from central and southern Iran to
the centres of Timurid power, and by the fact that Timur's campaigns were less destructive in these areas than elsewhere.

The Timurid period marks the apogee of colour in Iranian architecture, both in sheer technical expertise and in the astonishing
variety of designs and textures. Colour transforms exteriors and
interiors alike, yet it is not allowed to run amok. Most Timurid
buildings project a solid sense of the structural skeleton itself, which
the use of colour enhances but does not overwhelm. This delicate
balance was apt to be lost in subsequent centuries. The equilibrium
between structure and decoration meant that brick, the basic building material, was available to serve as a foil, both in colour and in
texture, to the applied ornament. The designs themselves, for
example medallions and arabesques, can often be matched in other
media and many may well have originated in the royal ateliers, to be
circulated later for use in bookbindings, carpets, textiles, manuscript
illumination, pottery and woodwork as well as architectural ornament. Hence, perhaps, the tendency for general decorative schemes
– applied on an architectural façade, say, or a vault – to be subdivided
into individual and seemingly unrelated panels so that the overall
144   effect is that of a picture gallery with paintings of varying size hung
at different levels. Arabic and Persian poetry, felicitously described as
'orient pearls at random strung', suggests itself as an intriguing
parallel. Sometimes the decorative scheme is strongly sculptural, as in
the use of glazed medallions standing proud from a glazed surface, or
the multiple levels of Timurid vaults. More common, however, is a
contrast of texture, for example glazed terracotta juxtaposed with
smooth glazed tiles, or carved stucco set against painted plaster, or
contrasts of marble and glazed tilework, wood and ivory. Yet the use
of snow-white *muqarnas* domes or bottle-green dados reveals

Timurid craftsmen experimenting with the potential of a single colour to dominate an interior.

Colossal size is the defining feature of some of the most characteristic imperial Timurid buildings – the Rigistan and Gur-i Amir in Samarqand and Timur's own palace at Shahr-i Sabz, whose *iwan* apparently soared to 40 m (131 ft). Indeed, the portal now takes on major significance as the cynosure of a façade, often dwarfing the actual building behind it, as at Anau. At the shrine of Gazur Gah near Herat, it may symbolically suggest entry to the hereafter. Flanking minarets placed behind the tomb at the far end of the building make some of these *iwan*s illusionistically still more lofty. Many such portals function as huge screens or hoardings inscribed with religious or political messages, but others are proudly salient and of spatially adventurous design. Perimeter walls, too, take on a new importance which is reflected in the overall brick and glazed ornament which they bear. These are buildings meant to be experienced in the round, not designed with a single viewpoint in mind. The popularity of ribbed domes, high drums and multiple minarets (as in the Bibi Khanum mosque in Samarqand and the *madrasa*s of Herat) again reveals Timurid architects to have been fully alert to the scenic dimension of their buildings.

Fifteenth- and sixteenth-century drawings found in Istanbul and Tashkent contain, among much other material, detailed notations for the layout of ground plans and the construction of *muqarnas* vaults. Their use of gridded paper and modular units provides independent documentary evidence for what could be deduced from the monuments themselves – that a mastery of geometrical concepts and of proportional relationships was needed to control these vast spaces and to order them into harmonious, symmetrical designs. It is size above all that empowers such factors as axiality, rhythm, repetition, anticipation and echo to yield their full effect. Thus in the 4-*iwan* courtyard *madrasa* of Ulugh Beg in Samarqand (1417), the component parts are all interdependent and logically related to each other, while at the Shah-i Zinda – a necropolis largely intended, it seems, for Timurid princesses – the individual mausolea are not sited haphazardly but operate in concert, forming a processional way towards the tomb of the eponymous saint. A long monumental staircase creates a suitable air of expectancy and ensures that from the outset pilgrims are channelled towards the tomb along the desired route. It is a textbook case of the capacity of Timurid architects to think big and to exploit space to the full. The whole site seems to have been

170

169

171, 172

deliberately designed as an open-air gallery displaying the latest decorative techniques. Perhaps there was a certain competitive edge too. It is no surprise that major Timurid artists such as Qawwam al-Din Shirazi were figures of consequence at court.

A fascination with the expressive potential of vaulting can be sensed in the more experimental Timurid buildings. Gone now is the Saljuq and Ilkhanid preoccupation with the tripartite elevation of a dome chamber – base, transition zone, dome – and in its place there reigns a much more fluid transition from one plane to the next. Typically a network of small vaults, often of rhomboidal form, cloaks the upper reaches of a building (with simpler, sturdier vaults behind them doing the actual work); these give way eventually to the dome itself, which rises serenely above the apparent confusion below. The polychrome vaults of Khargird and Herat, instinct with dynamic tension, create a vortex of frantic pyrotechnic energy which constantly teeters on the brink of chaos. Yet this explosive power is of course entirely controlled, as can be understood at once from a plan of such a vault. The heavenly associations of domical vaults, complete with fixed and shooting stars and a central solar motif, are unmistakable.

Relatively little high-quality metalwork has survived, though miniatures of the period (whose obsessive detail makes them an excellent guide to contemporary luxury objects) show that ewers with long curved spouts were developed at this time. A few spectacular but isolated survivals give a clue to this largely vanished industry. They include a candlestick base formed by knotted dragon heads, tall

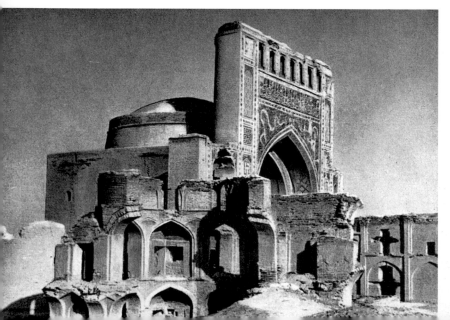

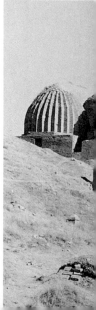

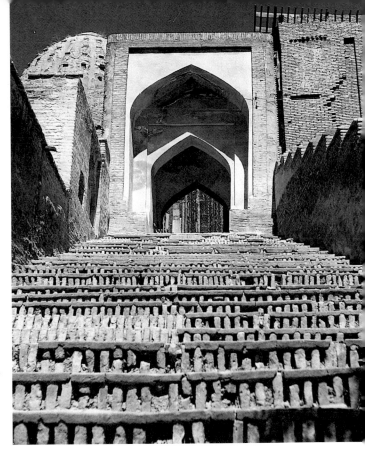

170 (*opposite*) The holy man as a source of authority. The shrine complex of Shaikh Jamal al-Din, Anau, 1455–6. The buildings apparently comprised a mosque, *madrasa* and convent (*khanqah*), all domed, plus accommodation for visitors, dervishes and pilgrims around the courtyard; a lofty portal featured spandrels bearing images of dragons, presumably as talismans.

171 (*right*) Gateway to death – and life. Entrance to the Shah-i Zinda complex, Samarqand, mainly *c.* 1350–1450; dedicated to the cult of the saint Qutham b. al-'Abbas, a cousin of the Prophet. He allegedly met Khizr (guardian of the Water of Life) and continued to live in splendour under his own tomb.

172 (*below*) City of the dead. General view of the complex of Shah-i Zinda, Samarqand. The desire to develop an expressive skyline explains the emphasis on hill-top sites and exaggeratedly high drums.

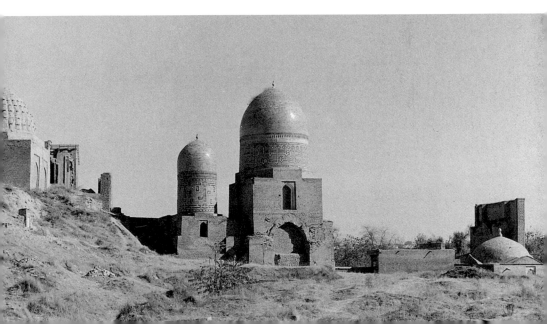

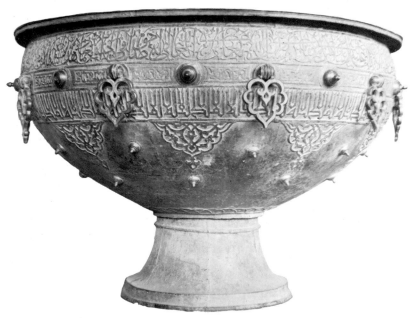

tubular candlesticks with a succession of bold annular mouldings, and a pair of massive bronze cauldrons, now in St Petersburg and Herat respectively, both made in the 1390s. The closest analogies for these impressive vessels, which are virtually undecorated apart from their inscriptions, are in the metalwork of Daghestan in the Caucasus. In most Timurid metalwork, the Saljuq and Mongol motif of a figural scene within a cartouche seems to have been definitively superseded by closely knit floral designs. A new style heavily dependent on manuscript illumination is found on Khurasani inlaid metalwork in the later fifteenth century, while the same province generated simultaneously a style of engraved metalwork that leads without a break into the Safavid period. Persian poetry is a staple feature of the decoration of much Timurid metalwork; it often has Sufi over-tones. The inlaid brass jugs that were a speciality of Herat shortly before 1500 illustrate these features.

Recent research has demonstrated that the tally of surviving Timurid ceramics is not nearly as meagre as it was once thought to be. The vogue for chinoiserie continued unabated. Indeed, side by side with such traditional techniques as lustre, the quality of which was appreciably lower than in earlier centuries, the Persian potter

173 Amassing credit for the hereafter. Bronze basin intended to serve water to pilgrims visiting the shrine of the Sufi *shaikh* Ahmad Yasavi. Inscriptions on the basin state that Timur ordered it in 1399 for this shrine; they also quote the particularly relevant Sura 9:19 and the Prophetic *hadith* 'He who builds a place for drinking for holy purposes, God will build for him a pool in Heaven'. Diam. 2.45 m (8 ft).

now produced blue-and-white wares inspired by imported porcelain of Ming type. The ultimate origin of these wares is disputed, but reciprocal influences between China and Persia are certain. Timurid copies of this Chinese porcelain body are also known. Quite different in style is a category of pottery made in northern Iran from at least the 1460s until the seventeenth century. These ceramics were all found in the Caucasian village of Kubachi, a famed metalworking centre; presumably they had been exchanged for local metalwork. The earlier pieces of this school are painted in black under a bluish-green glaze and eschew figural designs in favour of floral cartouches or scrollwork and epigraphic motifs.

The origins of Timurid painting are mysterious. The exact nature of the debt it owes to the early Jala'irids, whose activity in this field was mentioned above (see p. 212), is still a matter of lively dispute, and the potted history of earlier Persian painting with which the librarian Dust Muhammad prefaced the *muraqqa'* (album) of the Safavid prince Bahram Mirza in 1544 is tantalizingly incomplete and obscure in its treatment of the fourteenth century. The backbone of his account is not chronology but a sequence of masters and pupils, and it is no easy matter to match their reported output with the fragments that now survive in Istanbul and Berlin. But there is no doubt that a whole series of key decisions had been made by the time that the *Mathnavi*s (poems in rhyming couplets) of Khwaju Kirmani was painted for Sultan Ahmad Jala'ir at Baghdad in 1396 by a certain Junaid, the first Persian painter of the new age whose signature survives on his work. Hence the sheer assurance and the dazzling virtuosity of this masterpiece. The size of the book has decreased; paintings are much fewer in number; text is sometimes whittled down to a brief two-line panel placed at will in the picture space; and the full-page illustration has now come to stay. A high rectangular format with a correspondingly high horizon permits an uncluttered arrangement of numerous spatially distinct figures. True, the emotional range has been toned down and the sense of drama evaporated in a dreamlike fantasy world. But the technical skill of the artist is now staggering. It embraces the preparation of the surface, the application of paint, the purity of colour, the balancing of hues, the effects of crescendo and diminuendo in the composition and in the distribution of colour, and the pinpoint accuracy of the smallest detail. Moreover, while the paintings are often physically no smaller than the greatest Ilkhanid paintings, they contain very much more. This is truly miniature painting. Everything is calculated; these are images that demand a great deal of the viewer, and they do not yield up their secrets lightly.

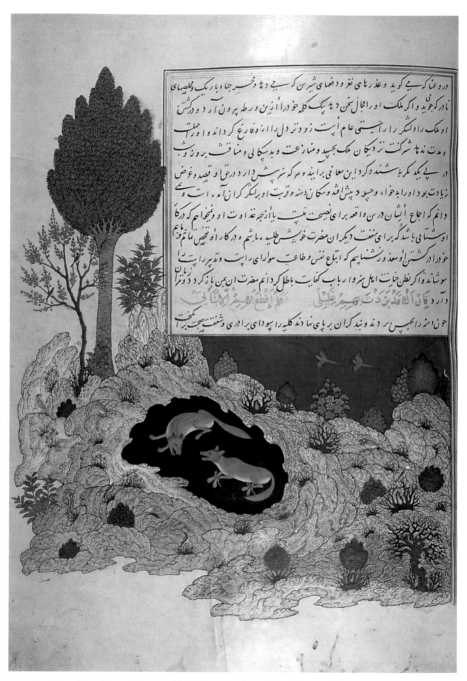

درونما کے سے گوید و عذریای نغز و دنیای شیرن کے سبے دہا و خسرجها بار یک و جلمهای
نادرکه گوید واگر ملک و انجال سخن دہا یک که خود را ازین ورطه برون آرد و درکشن
او ملک راو لشکر راآهستہ ای عام اپت زودتر دل را از و فارغ که داند او مجلت
و مدت ندانا شرکت نزدیکان ملک بجمید و منازعت و بدسکالی و منافت بروزوش
در پے یک یک مکه باشندواگرد این معنی برآبید و سر که نهرپش دارد درحیا و قصدو عض
زیادت بود و او رابدخواه و حبود پیش افتده و مکان زدنه و قبت او برکبک گران آمده است و سے
دانم که اجماع ایشان در سن واقعه برای نصیحت یا از جهه غذاوت و نمخواهم که درکا
او شتای باشد که برای منفت دیکران مضرت خویش طلبه هاشم و در کار او نقص تمام کزم
خود را در کشتن او و معذ ورنشام سم بر ابتاع نفس و طاعت مولادی راپت و تقدیر راپت ا
سوشاندو که نظر جایت اپل منزو رباب کفایت باطل کرد دانم مضرت این همن باز کرددو زدار
آرد و قال الله بدردت بهم علی کلم اقطع بهم الاپای
خون دمنه راجفس مرده وند کران بر پای نها دند کلیا را سپودای برا ری و شغفت حبت کفت

174 A mirror for princes. Dimna visited in prison by Kalila, from *Kalila wa Dimna*, a collection of animal fables with moral and political applications. Herat, 1429 (f.56a). The calculated technical perfection so characteristic of Baisunqur's atelier led to a certain stiffness in the treatment of figures and landscape, though new accommodations are forged between written and painted surface.

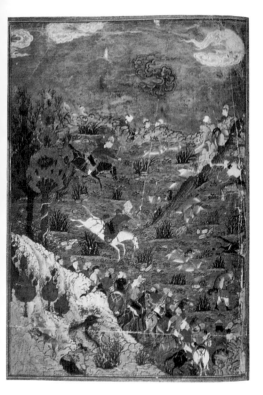
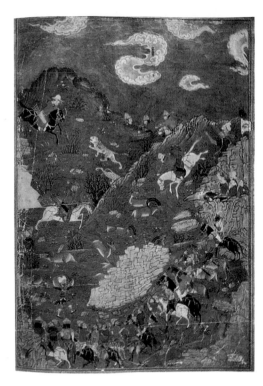

175 Hunting: the quintessential royal pastime. This double frontispiece of *c.* 1470 may depict the then ruler of western Iran, Uzun Hasan. It shows a grand *battue*, or mass hunt, in which the game is driven for many days until trapped in the constricted killing fields. Plunging vistas and the semi-circle of spectators draw the eye to the frenzied slaughter at the heart of the painting. Leering grotesques people the rocks.

Persian painting had now found itself and henceforth generations of artists strove to achieve perfection in this style. Important centres from *c.* 1390 to *c.* 1420 included Baghdad and Shiraz, the latter especially under the rule of Iskandar Sultan, but this style unquestionably reached its peak in the work of the academy founded at Herat by the celebrated bibliophile Prince Baisunqur b. Shahrukh (1397–1433), who in the intervals of the dissipation that plunged him into an early grave found time to oversee the production of fastidiously choice illustrated copies of the great classics of Persian literature. Some forty artists were active in his atelier, including not only painters but also scribes, illuminators, gilders, tent-makers, designers, bookbinders, leatherworkers and sculptors; some were proficient at several crafts. Moreover, their status had risen to the extent that some were boon companions of the prince himself. The great masterpieces of this

223

174   Herat school that survive include two copies of the *Kalila wa Dimna*, an *Anthology*, a *Gulistan* ('Rose Garden') of Sa'di (1426) and at least one *Shahnama* (1429), for which Baisunqur – who had commissioned a new edition of Firdausi's masterpiece – himself wrote a preface. This had a tenth of the illustrations of the Great Mongol *Shahnama* (see pp. 211–12), and that difference alone betrays the new aesthetic. Imperial Timurid painting was produced for connoisseurs, so the painters took care to load every rift with ore.

Several other quite distinct styles developed in the fifteenth century. One was a simplified recreation of the manner (including the format) of the Rashid al-Din manuscripts, which was used for primarily historical texts produced at Herat for Timur's son Shahrukh (ruled 1405–47). Another was a vigorous, bold, minimalist style whose keynote is action, featuring huge inflexible figures woodenly disposed within a ruthlessly simplified landscape; this was developed under the patronage of Ibrahim Sultan, a brother of Baisunqur, at Shiraz. The same city was later a major centre for a third style commonly dubbed Turcoman after the ruling dynasty of

175   western and southern Iran. Commercial production predominated; its hallmarks were a revelling in picturesque if fanciful landscape detail in an astonishing range of greens, and squat, jowly figures with rosy cheeks. These features were heightened and enriched in court Turcoman painting after about 1480, especially under Sultan Ya'qub in Tabriz, in several fragmentary Nizami and *Shahnama* manuscripts. These attain a psychedelic exuberance of colour allied to complex, multi-planar compositions often with a sense of illimitable distance not hitherto encountered in Persian painting. The scale and ambition of these pictures explains clearly enough why the projects of which they were part remained unfinished (see *frontispiece*).

The patronage of the last Timurid prince, Sultan Husain b. Mansur b. Baiqara (reigned 1468–1506), was on a scale to rival that of his contemporary Lorenzo de' Medici in Florence. Herat flourished as never before and many believe that here Persian painting reached its apogee. In these decades the names and achievements of painters – such as Qasim b.'Ali, Aqa Mirak and, above all, Bihzad – begin to attract the notice of chroniclers. Yet these are perhaps not the competing geniuses of Renaissance Italy but might rather be seen as colleagues (and courtiers) in a royal atelier, pooling their talents, developing an increasingly accomplished and seamless house style and maybe even working together on a picture. Often, therefore, Western scholars bent on attributing this or that painting to a given

224

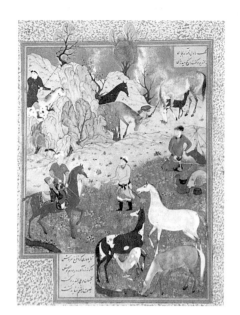

176 The ruler rebuked. In this scene from Sa'di's *Bustan*, copied in Herat in 1488 for Sultan Husain Baiqara, the prince, who has lost his way while hunting, comes across his own horsemaster and, not recognizing him, strings his bow to shoot. His unthinking aggression disrupts the peaceful, ordered scene. The horsemaster knows his own charges by sight and fearlessly tells the prince to follow his example.

artist seem to be chasing a will-o'-the-wisp. Moreover, the nature of Timurid connoisseurship is difficult to pin down, for the critical vocabulary it uses has no unambiguous set of western equivalents. What defines this late Herat school? Once again, the pictures are few in number in any one manuscript, and thus each one matters. The singular intensity of colour and vibrant chromatic contrasts owes much to the Baisunquri academy, but the delight in spatial complexities, variegated poses and individual types is new. None of this amounts to realism; these painters, like their predecessors, customarily favoured the general at the expense of the particular, and their paintings testify as much to intellectual abstraction as to patient observation. Figures are sharply differentiated, but the sense of a living, unique personality is generally absent. Quite apart from these factors, however, is a new spirit reflected both in what is chosen for illustration and in what is omitted, as well as in the manner of storytelling. It seems that a democratic spirit was in the air, a quietly subversive set of values that exalted the common man and his daily tasks and made him a mirror for the selfishness of his 'betters'. Hence an unprecedented emphasis on daily life – on a building site, in a bath, at pasture, in a cemetery – with people buying and selling, cooking, digging, cutting wood and ploughing. Often these humble scenes are a metaphor for the spiritual realities of the Sufi path. Thus form and content combine in a profoundly satisfying synthesis.

176

CHAPTER NINE

The Safavids

The dynasty that made Iran Shi'ite venerated as its ancestor and took its name from a saintly but not Shi'ite *shaikh*, Safi al-Din (d. 1334), the head of a sectarian Sufi order based at Ardabil in north-western Iran. The masters of this order exercised gradually increasing religious and political authority, until by the late fifteenth century they were a force to be reckoned with in eastern Anatolia and north-western Iran, with several charismatic leaders. For almost two centuries after the fall of the Ilkhanids in 1336, apart from the meteoric career of Timur (see pp. 213–14), Iran had lacked cohesiveness or relatively fixed boundaries. This period was also one of religious ferment which witnessed a flowering of folk Islam, Sufism and extreme Shi'ism. The Safavids combined these three elements, turning the order at Ardabil into a revolutionary and at times messianic Shi'ite movement originally dominated by Turkish tribesmen (the *qizilbash* or 'red-heads') from eastern Anatolia and Azerbaijan, and creating a successful political system which from 1501 was quickly imposed by fiat and terror on the country as a whole. A Turcoman military aristocracy held power under the authority of the shah himself, though their internal clan feuds, their rebellions and their antipathy to the Persian bureaucracy continually shook the body politic. Yet the shah needed both the 'Men of the Sword' and the 'Men of the Pen'; and the second Safavid shah, Tahmasp (1524–76) eventually created a third force at court, a corps of *ghulams* (slaves) comprising Georgian, Armenian and Circassian converts to Islam, to stabilize the situation.

The Safavids taught that their legitimacy depended on their descent from the family of the Prophet Muhammad, on their authority as masters of the order at Ardabil and on the divinely ordained office of shah as the shadow of God on earth. These ideas were propagated by a hastily assembled body of theologians, many of them from the Levant, Iraq and Bahrain, who with Iranian converts

177 The Masjid-i Shah (now Masjid-i Imam), Isfahan, largely 1612–30. This spectacular blue–tiled mosque epitomizes one era, one style and one man – Shah 'Abbas, the greatest Safavid ruler. Though its portal terminates the long axis of the great *maidan* or piazza, the rest of the mosque is set at an angle from it so as to be correctly oriented towards the *qibla*. Thus sacred and secular geometry diverge.

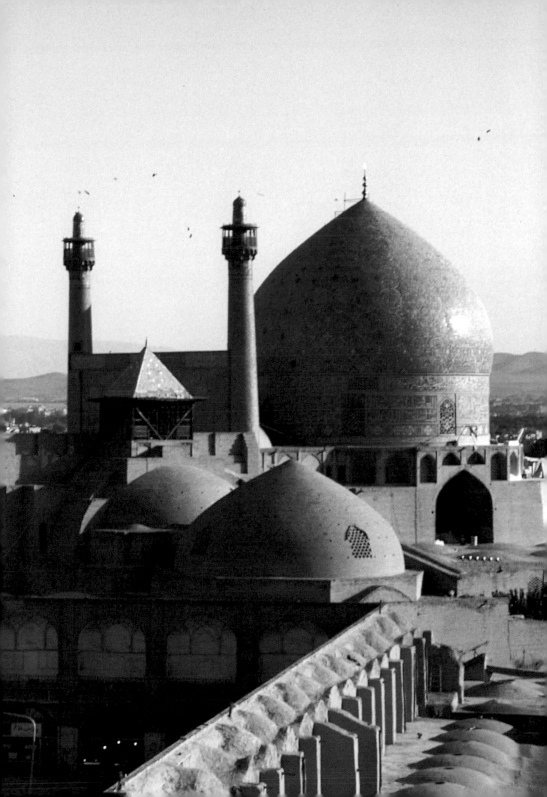

from Sunnism created a new religious establishment. It was for such teachers of religious law (*mujtahids*) to exercise their personal judgment (*ijtihad*) until the ultimate return of the Mahdi, the Hidden (and twelfth) Imam. In later Safavid times their power at court grew significantly. The regime was thus thoroughly theocratic. By making Shi'ism the official religion the Safavids forged an ideology that not only strengthened the state but also helped to create a new sense of national identity, and so enabled Iran to escape being absorbed into the empires of the neighbouring superpowers – although its borders were frequently contested and the shah had to fight a war on two fronts. It was the Safavids who made Iran (with the old Shi'ite centres of Iraq) the spiritual bastion of the Shi'a against the onslaughts of orthodox Sunni Islam, and the repository of Persian cultural traditions and self-awareness. They largely Persianized a country whose Turkish, Arab and Kurdish elements had hitherto been stronger, and to some extent they ruptured the cultural as well as religious ties that had earlier bound Iran to the Islamic commonwealth. At long last Shi'ism had found a 'national' home.

Yet for the indigenous Iranian population Twelver Shi'ism was at first alien, and powerful opposition manifested itself, especially in the east of the country. In much the same way the rule of the Ottomans in Anatolia, the Near East and North Africa, and perhaps even of the Uzbeks in Central Asia and the Mughals in the Indian subcontinent, can be interpreted as an imposition of religious conformity which coincided with a hardening of political, national and even religious boundaries. This, then, was the age of the Islamic superpowers; and, significantly, all of them shared the same Turco-Persian rather than Arab culture. Thus Islam, like Europe, emancipated itself from its medieval heritage by creating larger political groupings. The rulers of these superpowers were keenly competitive, alert to match claims (e.g. to the caliphate) with counter-claims. Their horizons were wide. Isma'il, the first Safavid shah, bore the title of Persian Emperor (*Padishah-i Iran*) with its implicit notion of an Iranian state stretching from Afghanistan as far as the Euphrates, and from the Oxus to the Persian Gulf.

The long reign of Isma'il's son Tahmasp helped to establish Iran's role vis-à-vis its neighbours, to tone down religious extremism and to control the power of the clergy. But it fell to Tahmasp's grandson, Shah 'Abbas I (ruled 1587–1629), to set the country on the road to greatness by creating an efficient standing army (in which the role of the *qizilbash* was much reduced and that of the *ghulams* strengthened) and a centralized administration, and thereby to lay the foundations of the modern Iranian state in its political, religious and geographical aspects. And that state he regarded in some sense as his personal property, which he governed (and milked) through the hierarchical administrative apparatus of his court, headed by the Grand Vizier and the Intendant (*nazir*), the latter functioning in effect as treasurer. It is under the Safavids that one can trace more clearly than ever before the stirrings of a national sentiment that would eventually become, centuries later, a fully-fledged nationalism, and for which the territorial integrity established by the Safavids was a necessary precondition.

The Safavids continued the attempts of the Ilkhanids to foster closer diplomatic ties with the European powers, as evidenced by the frequent exchange of embassies with the various courts of Europe in order to cement alliances against the Ottomans. Similarly, they were alert to the political and economic implications of the opening of the sea route to the Far East in 1496, which diverted Ottoman pressure away from Iran to the Red Sea and the Indian Ocean; the Dutch, the English and the Portuguese were permitted to establish trading posts on the Persian Gulf, where Indian merchants also settled. For the Iranians, this meant revenue from customs dues, while for the European powers such posts were essential if they were to control the increasingly lucrative East India trade. The inevitable clash of interests, however, resulted in frequent hostilities, especially with the Portuguese. Attempts were also made to avoid Ottoman customs dues by relocating the silk and spice routes to the north across Russia. Much Safavid silk reached Europe, especially the Habsburg domains and Scandinavia, in this way (see p. 250). Indeed, some textiles and carpets were made specifically for the West, and bear (not always accurately) the arms of royal and noble houses. Conversely, Europe exported muskets, mail shirts, clocks, Italian paintings, Chinese porcelain, Japanese screens and even plants, fruits and vegetables unknown in Iran, and Shah ʿAbbas had several Europeans in his permanent service. The dramatic increase in commercial and diplomatic relations with the European powers was fostered by a tolerant and multi-racial society in Iran. Colonies of Armenians, Georgians and Hindus were settled in villages or key towns, while western orders such as the Augustinians, Carmelites and Capuchins founded religious houses in Isfahan and other major centres as part of a world-wide missionary campaign which also embraced China, Japan and the Americas at this time.

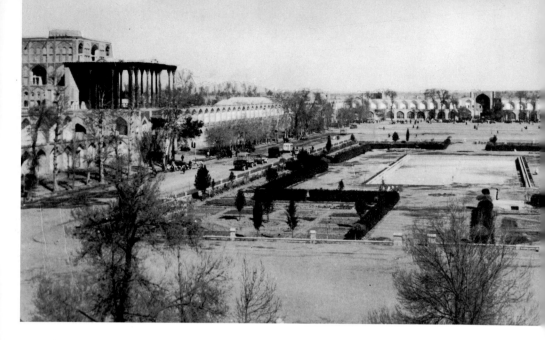

178 'Isfahan is half the world' runs the Persian proverb. This enormous open rectangle – the *maidan* – was the nerve centre of a capital to which visitors flocked from East and West.

179 An Islamic invention. Portal arch, Masjid-i Imam, Isfahan. The *muqarnas* or honeycomb vault has many functions in Islamic architecture: it articulates a curved space, dissolves surfaces, bridges contrasting spaces, and creates a frame for related but discrete motifs (see *ill.* 50). Directly over the door is the Shah's name.

The principal achievements of the Safavids were architectural. Pride of place goes to the expansion of Isfahan masterminded by Shah 'Abbas I from 1598 onwards; it is one of the most ambitious and novel schemes of town planning in Islamic history. This resulted in the famous *maidan*, which, with its measurements of 512 × 159 m (1680 × 523 ft), is perhaps the largest piazza in the world; the Chahar Bagh esplanade and royal quarter linking the *maidan* with the river (the Zayandarud); and the huge covered bazaar. It may be no coincidence that a mere two decades earlier the Mughal emperor Akbar had built a sumptuous new capital from scratch at Fathpur Sikri. The Masjid-i Imam, the Masjid-i Shaikh Lutfallah and the interdependent complex of *madrasa*, *khan* and bazaar built by Shah Sultan Husain are the finest public buildings of the time.

Yet it would be a mistake to regard any of them as fundamentally original buildings. The Lutfallah mosque (1602–19) and the Masjid-i

178

230

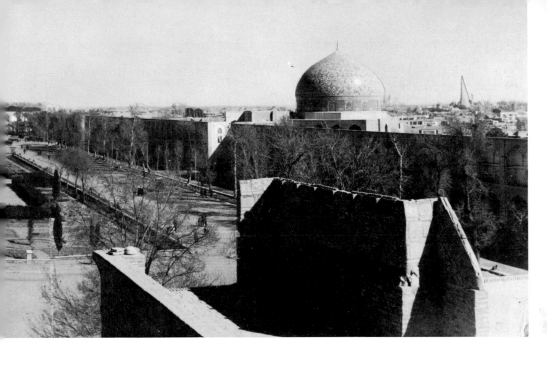

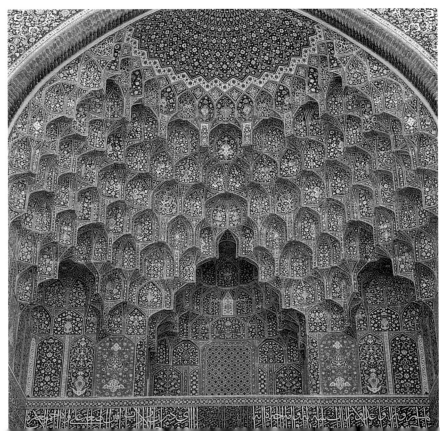

Shah (1612–30), each repeat a familiar schema – the domed square chamber and the 4-*iwan* plan respectively. Their exceptional size and splendid decoration make it easy to overlook their essential conservatism. In the Masjid-i Shah (now renamed the Masjid-i Imam) this huge scale allows the incorporation of dome chambers behind the subsidiary *iwan*s, a rectangular pool which serves as the focal point of the courtyard, ample facilities for ablution, a winter prayer hall and *madrasa*s flanking the main prayer chamber. Yet visually all is subordinated to the sheer bulk of the portal and *qibla iwan* and the principal dome chamber. As for the Lutfallah mosque, the structural complexities of earlier domed squares have been toned down dramatically, leaving a vast and minimally articulated inner space which is organized mainly by its ornament – for example, the bright blue cable mouldings which define the pendentives or the two-dimensional honeycomb ornament of the inner surface of the dome. Exterior and interior alike accord a major role to plain unglazed brick, which serves as a background to sparingly applied glazed tilework in floral and geometric patterns; the interplay between these two accents seems illusionistically to confer a glazed sheen on the plain brick. The façades of both mosques open on to the great *maidan*, which was the centre of the new city, and both have bent entrances, so that the mosques themselves are correctly orientated but do not compromise the regularity of the façades defining the square. Those façades are kept low so that the major buildings which punctuate them stand proud of their surroundings. Here, as in so much Safavid architecture, one may detect an innate sense of theatre and a delight in the grand scale.

The high officials of the Safavid court, often in response to direct pressure from the shah, built widely in Isfahan, including several mosques (e.g. the Masjid-i Hakim), but as a group these do not display any marked originality. The complex of Shah Sultan Husain on the Chahar Bagh (1706–15) is a resounding coda for Safavid Isfahan: deeply traditional in its core plan – this is one of the largest Iranian *madrasa*s – spacious throughout, its key areas (and those alone) richly decorated with glazed tilework, and the whole creating an agreeable sense of *rus in urbe* with its pools, trees and gardens. Moreover, the complex worked in economic as well as aesthetic terms, for it comprised a huge caravansarai and bazaar adjoining the *madrasa,* and the revenues of the secular establishments funded the religious foundation. Indeed, such complexes flourished throughout Iran in Safavid times, whether these were shrines (Ardabil, Qumm,

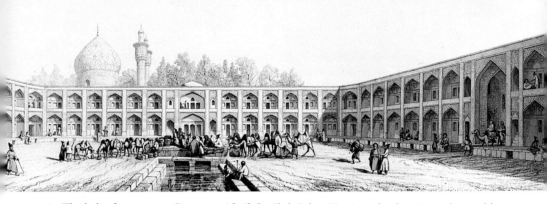

180 The hub of commerce. Caravansarai built by Shah Sultan Husain with adjoining *madrasa* and bazaar; Isfahan, 1706–15. Spacious and austerely practical, it could accommodate hundreds of animals and their loads, while the two-storied arcades held living chambers.

Mashhad and Mahan – many of them comprehensively remodelled in this period) or institutions that were both religious and secular (for example the foundation of Ganj ʿAli Khan at Kirman).

Isfahan is notable for its secular architecture too, especially the royal palaces like the ʿAli Qapu, Chihil Sutun and Hasht Bihisht. Embowered in gardens and embellished with verandahs, wall paintings and fanciful *muqarnas* vaults, they expressed to perfection the luxurious lifestyle of the court. The ʿAli Qapu ('Sublime Porte') is an arched portico crowned by a flat-roofed balcony with wooden columns, from which the shah and his entourage could watch spectacles in the *maidan* below. Like several other Safavid palaces, it was designed to be seen frontally or at an angle, not from behind. The formal gardens and watercourses into which it leads were once scattered with courts, two-storey open-plan kiosks, and pavilions, of which one, the Chihil Sutun ('Forty Columns'), has a flat-roofed portico with wooden columns, following pre-Islamic Persian practice. This precedes the shah's throne room. The sculpture in the surrounding garden may also be intended to evoke ancient imperial memories. The Chahar Bagh ('Four Gardens'), an avenue lined with trees, streams and the palaces of the nobility (evocatively named after roses, mulberries, nightingales and Paradise itself) gave access to the capital from the south – a curtain-raiser nearly a mile long. Massive bridges, such as the Pul-i Allahvardi Khan with its thirty-three arches, or the Pul-i Khwaju featuring not only sluice gates but also pavilions for the

181

royal party which served as vantage points from which to watch regattas and other water sports, linked Isfahan with some of its suburbs.

In secular architecture the network of *khan*s or caravansarais erected across the country by Shah 'Abbas I deserves special note. Most of them follow a 4-*iwan* plan, with the space in the corners serving for stables while the entrance and domed vestibule define the major axis. Features common to many caravansarais include a single massive portal, with an entrance high enough to admit a loaded camel; kitchens in the corners; and adjoining enclosures for tethering animals. Caravansarais in the open country were often built at intervals of a day's journey – about 25 km (16 miles) – along the major trade routes. Those in the towns (often very numerous; Isfahan, for example, had nearly two thousand in the seventeenth century) served not only to house and feed travellers, but also as warehouses and centres for a particular trade or group of merchants.

However, Safavid art has tended in modern scholarship to be dominated by the undeniable glamour of the Isfahan of Shah 'Abbas, to the detriment of the Iranian art produced in the previous century under less charismatic rulers. The penalty for this over-exposure has been a seriously distorted perspective of early Safavid art, in which it

180

181 A Sasanian tradition revived. The Allahvardi Khan bridge, Isfahan, stretches 300 m (984 ft). Designed to carry traffic and regulate flooding with its massive buttresses; it also has pleasure pavilions.

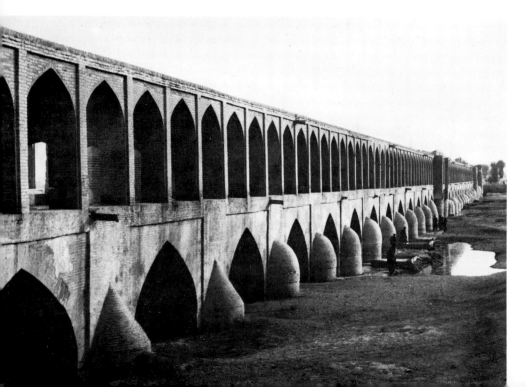

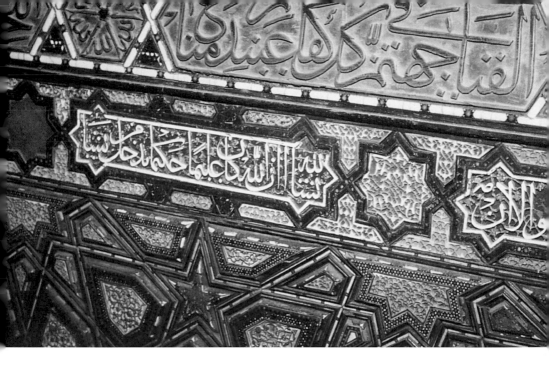

182 Sandalwood and ivory sarcophagus of the dreaded Shah Isma'il I, founder of the Shi'ite Safavid state – 'on seeing him, outsiders would prefer to turn to stone' – at the shrine of Shaikh Safi, Ardabil, *c.* 1524.

is underestimated and seen merely as a curtain-raiser for what was to come. The surpassing quality of book painting and of carpets in the early sixteenth century suggests that such an attitude is a cardinal mistake, and that it would be worth investigating other media in an attempt to redress such an injustice. The lack of substantial art-historical research on the reign of Shah Isma'il has been a major barrier in this respect. So too has the poor survival rate of the buildings produced under his patronage, and the fact that Ardabil, the first major centre of Safavid power and art, has been unaccountably overlooked by art historians – except for its architecture. The shrine has, of course, been comprehensively pillaged over the last two centuries and the process continues to this day. What survives comprises not only architecture but metalwork (including several standards or 'alams), carving in wood and stone, and tilework. The constellation of talent seen displayed in the decorative arts of Ardabil makes a re-assessment of early Safavid work imperative. It is worth noting that, despite Shah Isma'il's disastrous defeat by the Ottomans at Chaldiran in 1514 and the consequent loss of eastern Anatolia, he did manage

235

to bring under his control all of Iran including much of Afghanistan and some of the neighbouring territories north of the Oxus and the Araxes rivers. This gave him a far more extensive financial base than had been enjoyed either by the Timurids or by the Turcoman dynasties, and it therefore allowed him correspondingly greater latitude in his patronage of the arts.

The Ardabil material in architecture and the minor arts is also of vital importance in highlighting the continuity between late Timurid and early Safavid work; if that continuity is not recognized, the transition to the mature Safavid style under Shah 'Abbas I is lost, and instead one is faced with an abrupt and perplexing juxtaposition of two essentially unrelated styles. Finally, Ardabil is important in that, for the most part, it is a kind of time capsule in which the arts of early Safavid Iran are displayed side by side and medium by medium, to create an ensemble in which, for once, the decorative arts can be seen in context, enhancing each other and almost bandying themes across the space of the shrine.

182   The sarcophagus of Shah Isma'il I has the traditional rectangular form, but is of quite special splendour. Timurid imperial woodwork, as demonstrated by the doors in the Gur-i Amir and the shrine of Khwaja Ahmad Yasavi, had effectively marked the technical limits of fine, filigree carving in wood. At Ardabil the carvers struck out in another direction, drawing inspiration from work on a much smaller scale, such as boxes inlaid with ebony and ivory. The geometric strapwork which forms the skeletal structure of the decoration is familiar enough; but its interstices are ornamented with grace notes applied almost parsimoniously at key points, in black-and-white marquetry. Tiny spots of green (probably stained bone or ivory) add an extra touch of luxury. The borders are marked by further clusters of marquetry in a sprightly dancing rhythm.

183   Many doors in the shrine are entirely silver-plated, and some are gilded too. A common design is a curvilinear lattice work whose slight rises and dips in plane create an undulating quilted effect. Multiple mouldings constitute the only added ornament, so that these doors project a powerful sense of harmony and serenity – an excellent foil for the more assertive accents of tilework, carpets and carved wood.

Ardabil also sets the scene for subsequent developments in the visual arts, which continued to cluster around the capital city as the court removed first to Qazvin and finally to Isfahan, ever further distant from the sensitive frontier with the Ottomans. In this respect

236

the Safavids continued and consolidated a process which can already be detected under the Timurids, whereby most art of top-flight quality in the principal media was produced in the immediate orbit of the court. In practice this spelled the disappearance of provincial ateliers of the first rank, though it did not exclude occasional lavish patronage on the part of a provincial governor, for example at Mashhad or Kirman.

The Safavid capture of Herat in 1507 meant that the Timurid library and its craftsmen, including Bihzad, fell into Safavid hands and were eventually transported to the new capital of Tabriz, under the patronage of Shah Isma'il I. His successor, Shah Tahmasp, himself a painter, even expanded the royal atelier. Early Safavid painting combined the traditions of Timurid Herat and Turcoman Tabriz to reach a peak of technical excellence and of emotional expressiveness which for many is the finest hour of Persian painting. The master-piece of the age is the *Shahnama-yi Shahi* ('The King's Book of Kings', formerly known as the Houghton *Shahnama*) which, with its 258 paintings, was the most lavishly illustrated *Shahnama* recorded in all of Persian history and which monopolized the resources of the

184
186

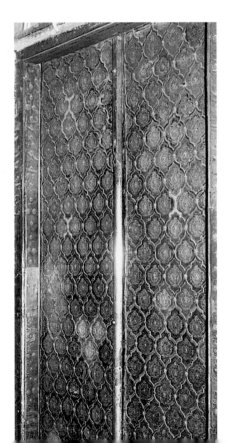

183 'O Opener of Doors!' is an inscription commonly associated with gateways and doors in the 15th and 16th centuries. The reference is to God; and the notion of a saintly person as a gate was commonplace – 'Ali, for example, was called the Gate to the City of Knowledge. Such associations enrich these and other silver-faced and gilded doors at the Ardabil shrine, 1611–12. Each door leaf has a carpet-inspired ogival lattice design of 114 blossoms, one for each *sura* of the Qur'an.

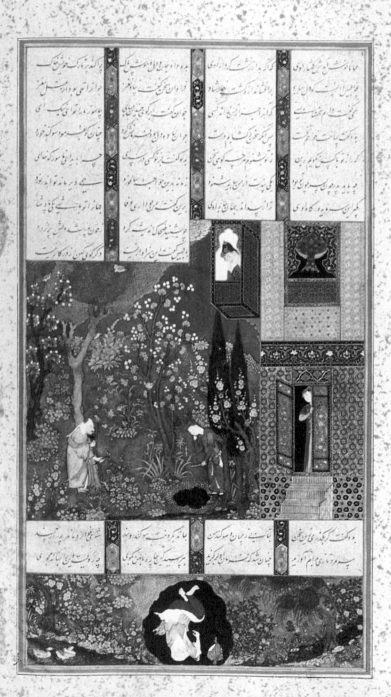

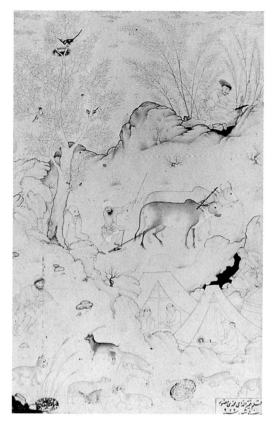

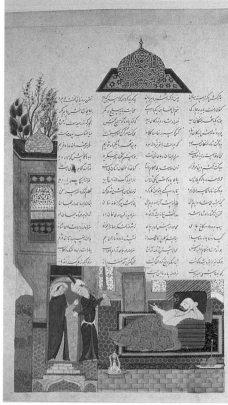

185 Pastoral idyll. Everyday rustic occupations rendered by Muhammadi, 1578, in a minimalist aesthetic employing the unusual technique of tinted drawing and the play of light and dark accents.

186 War yields to love. Royal Turcoman *Shahnama*, Tabriz, *c.* 1505. The single romantic episode in the 600-year life of the *Shahnama*'s greatest hero, Rustam.

royal atelier for a generation. Its pictures lay special stress on the war between Iran and Turan (Central Asia) and may thus reflect contemporary political concerns. It has justly been termed 'a portable art gallery' because all the most illustrious painters of the time contributed to it. Its lissom, eternally youthful figures are apparently an original creation. Perfection proved hard to sustain, and before long artists were overreaching themselves, for in some works of this school (e.g. the *Khamsa* or 'Quintet' of Nizami in the British Library, dated 1539 and 1543) so much detail is crammed into the composition that its fastidious precision fails to make its full effect. Similarly, the colour range may be so kaleidoscopic that the very richness confuses the eye.

184 (*opposite*) A dream world. *Shahnama* of Shah Tahmasp, Tabriz, *c.* 1525: the death of King Mirdas. This scene, distanced as if viewed from the wrong end of a telescope, typifies the contemporary blend of preternatural clarity with an other-worldly palette and subtly exaggerated spatial relationships. Here a virtuous king is treacherously lured to his death, thus triggering disaster in the body politic.

It could be argued that the manuscript page had too limited a scope to accommodate the increasing complexity of these compositions.

In his middle years, Shah Tahmasp became a religious extremist, which resulted – among many other, more significant, changes – in his losing interest in painting and disbanding the royal atelier. The court style associated with Qazvin, which became the capital in 1548, is marked, despite certain exceptions (like the *Haft Aurang*, the 'Seven Thrones', of Jami in Washington), by a palpable decline in quality. Compared with the best Tabriz work, landscape becomes simpler, with large areas given up to a single colour (as in the *Shahnama* of Isma'il II, 1576). Figures tend to increase in size and they exhibit a curious stiffness. Yet in courtly tableaux, youths and maidens are rendered with a consistently suave line. No trace remains of the vigorously differentiated types of the school of Bihzad, and the earlier obsession with detail gradually disappears. In the later sixteenth century, the enforced change of patronage, which meant that the day of the luxury book was effectively over, led the best artists (such as Muhammadi, who specialized in figure studies and tinted drawings of carefully understated scenes of peasant life) to produce single leaves that were eagerly collected by connoisseurs and bound into albums. Figure studies – of pages, prisoners and princes, among others – were a popular subject for such leaves, which became the forte of the Qazvin school. Their subjects came to include genre scenes of the utmost delicacy, with pastel shades enhancing the composition. The sequence of drawings, paintings, ornament and specimens of calligraphy is carefully calculated so that facing pages contrast with, complement or mutually enrich each other, and it is possible to recognize the development of themes. It is therefore misleading to regard such an album (*muraqqaʿ*) as a scrapbook. There is nothing random about it. This sea-change brought artists out of the court and into the public market, a process which accelerated the break with traditional anonymity and the rise of the artist – for example Sadiqi Beg or Siyavush – as a personality.

It is hard to account for the radical change in taste and style in seventeenth-century painting. Technically it is easy enough to point to the fashion both for single-leaf paintings and for tinted drawings in the later sixteenth century; but while presaging the divorce of painting from book illustration, neither of these developments fully implied the shape of things to come. Some time around the end of the sixteenth century – and the timing accords too well with the change of capital to Isfahan in 1597 to be coincidental – a massive and apparently unofficial deregulation of the traditional codes of practice governing book painting took place. It is not clear whether this was market led   precipitated perhaps by a terminal turn for the worse in official patronage for illustrated books – or whether the pressure for change came from the painters themselves, or at least from a few strong-willed radicals among them. But the results are perfectly plain to see. They govern execution, subject-matter, output, patronage and expense. As with all such revolutions in taste, the pace of change was uneven, with some able painters stubbornly hanging on to traditional ways. But the logic of the new style was inexorable. It brooked no rivals. Book painting as it had been understood for the previous thousand years was now finished, for the most part relegated to the bazaar.

For centuries, paintings had served to illustrate and explain the great classics of Persian poetry. Now, that increasingly elaborate, refined symbiosis had been shattered, and Persian painting lost its tap root. And once the tradition had been broken it could not simply be reinstated. Hence some of the best Iranian paintings of the later Safavid period and thereafter that are still produced in the context of the luxury book remain stubbornly divorced from a continuous text; they serve as frontispieces or are inserted into earlier volumes like the British Library Nizami of 1543. Some painters turned to   187 other media, experimenting with book-covers or (under European influence) with full-length oil-paintings. Lacquerware, too, developed significantly in the Safavid period, being used principally for secular book covers, and drawing on the lyric and epic themes created by book painters. But lacquer doors and boxes are also known and these have a wider repertoire, including for example audience scenes. Clearly, later Safavid painting will not fit neatly into pigeon-holes.

The principal change in painting on single leaves concerns subject matter. That sense of an intellectual construction, a hard-won and hard-edged abstraction of reality, that stamps earlier Persian painting and prevents it from disintegrating into a self-indulgent dream world, has gone. The subject-matter on which it had traditionally been exercised is no more. Perhaps a new style had of necessity to be fashioned to match the new subject matter. Hitherto the Persian painter had come to terms with the world around him by miniaturizing it, by viewing it as it were from the wrong end of a telescope, and then recomposing selected elements of what he saw in his mind's eye. Now he holds a distorting mirror to reality. Sometimes he may

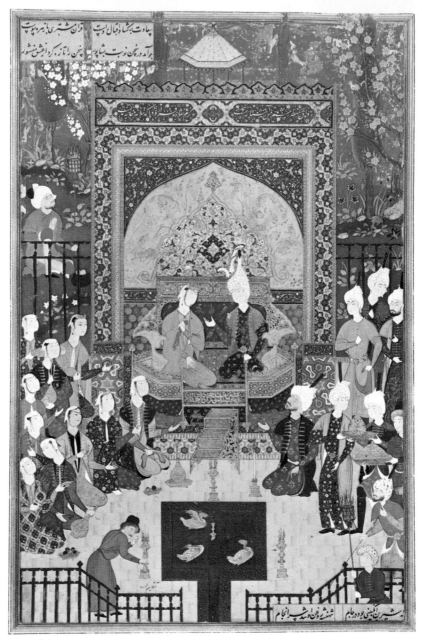

187 The past as myth. Nizami, *Khamsa*, Tabriz, 1539–43. In this icon of imperial majesty drawing on pre-Islamic Persian legend, Khusrau and his consort Shirin spend the evening listening to stories told by her maids. The scene evokes Scheherezade and the 1,001 nights.

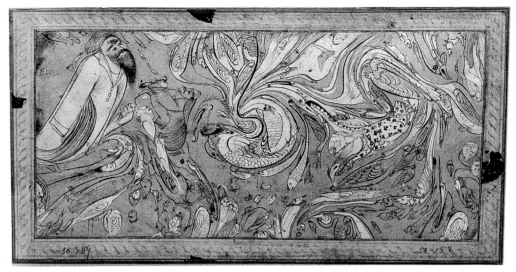

188 A taste of Ecstasy? Using techniques recalling marbled paper, this hallucinatory image of a mystical journey evokes the swirling rhythms of a cosmic dance. It celebrates the unity of being (*wahdat al-wujud*), a concept elaborated by Ibn al-ʿArabi and variously described as monism or pantheism. Thus created forms dissolve into each other. The composition suggests infinity, for the frame cannot confine it.

capture the exaltation and ecstasy of a mystical vision. More often, far from keeping his own distance, and forcing us to keep ours, he thrusts his discoveries right under our noses. More than a hint of the fairground freak can be sensed in some of the images served up by seventeenth-century painters. Studies of single figures dominate, and they are decidedly unheroic. Seedy dervishes, Sufi *shaikh*s, bagpipers, grooms, beggars, ageing painters, ne'er-do-wells, merchants – a whole gamut of portraits of the middle and lower reaches of society (for the grandees of the court are not depicted) meets the eye. Their likenesses are seized with formidable accuracy and speed, a notable achievement for an art form that, minor exceptions apart, had for centuries disdained portraiture. Yet despite the searching realism of some of these portraits, perhaps a juster term would often be carica-tures – for, while serious portrait studies of profound psychological insight, of intimacy and tenderness, are not lacking, the main body of this material has an altogether robuster tone, and is frequently downright coarse. Satire and knockabout humour are the driving forces behind most of the images. Hence the unsparing focus on drunken, pot-bellied holy men, or on dervishes built like storks, smoking pipes of opium and wearing fur hats tilted at rakish angles. Hence too the unflatteringly exaggerated length of nose or chin.

188

190

243

No-one could gainsay the bite and individuality of these mainly low-life character studies. Yet they are only half the story. Some of the self-same artists lent their talents to an altogether different genre of painting, at once vulgar and louche: the high-gloss pin-up. Pert androgynous pages with inviting smiles and thighs of awesome girth subside gracefully onto clumps of grass, proffering cups of wine. Or they pose smirking for their portraits, dressed in the height of European fashion, from the saucy feather in their hats to the jewelled buckles on their kid boots, and holding some newfangled import from the West, such as a turnip. Their poses are often of a coy and studied awkwardness. Their faces – full moons with rosebud mouths, as contemporary taste would have seen them – exhibit perhaps the final degradation of the Buddha image in Persian painting. All concrete sense of the individual human form is dissipated in these spineless, indeed altogether boneless, forms, mere confections of elegant line. More rarely the theme is definitively a girl, or a pair of lovers, sometimes depicted in explicitly erotic poses, with wraps of filmy lawn incompetently veiling their nakedness. Thus cloying sweetness alternates with startling grossness. This again marks a new departure in Persian painting.

The execution of these leaves is as novel as their themes, and is intimately related to the scale of their output. The same coldly efficient, mannered, economically linear style is employed throughout. Once again, and here in the most unexpected context, the Islamic capacity to geometricize forms finds expression. The very large quantity of these pin-ups to survive has done much to skew modern understanding of Safavid art, and it should caution against evaluating them very highly. It proves, of course, that they were extremely popular – but no more. Indeed, close inspection suggests that they were produced almost mechanically. Colouring is flat and simplified, laid on in broad washes. Expressions are of a uniform simpering blandness. The background setting for the figures is as exiguous as it well could be, a clear indication that it was regarded as being of no importance. And the virtuoso mastery of line cannot disguise that the lines themselves are remarkably few. Here, then, was a way to make a lot of money with minimum effort. The attraction is on the surface: what you see is what you buy. The conservative nature of public taste in this genre explains why it is difficult to tell the work of the various masters apart; but that same similarity reveals also how much each of them subordinated his own individuality to the dictates of fashion. Many such leaves were inscribed with the

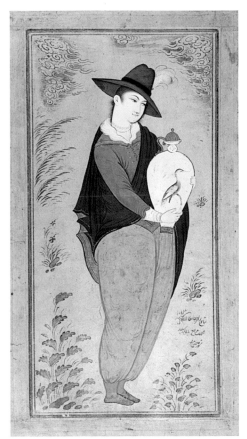

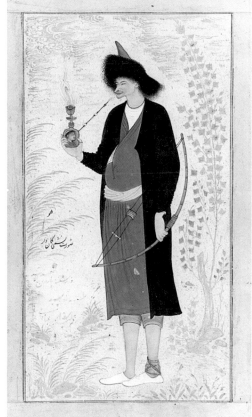

189 (*left*) The androgynous centrefold. Note, for example, the disproportionately tiny feet.

190 (*right*) Sly humour. Inscribed 'He [is God]. Portrait of Nashmi the Archer. Completed on Tuesday, 4 Rabi' II 1031 [10 January 1630]. Work of the humble Rida'-yi 'Abbasi'. This dishevelled character, with his cadaverous face and one stocking at half-mast, has clearly fallen on evil times.

name of the artist, the place and date of execution and the identity of the sitter; and the works of certain masters – Sadiqi Beg, Rida'-yi 'Abbasi, Mu'in Musawwir, Muhammad Qasim, Habiballah – were eagerly sought after. Contemporary gossip pounced on their personalities and eccentricities. Sometimes they worked at home.

What of the patrons who bought these leaves, and the prices they paid for them? An anecdote about Sadiqi Beg reveals him using two of his drawings in part payment for a poem written and recited in his honour, and asserting that each work could be sold to merchants for

3 *tumans* (worth £7 in English seventeenth-century money – a very considerable sum). It appears from this story that there was a market for his work as far afield as India – and indeed many Persian specialists in the various arts of the book found a good living both at the Ottoman and the Mughal courts.

Carpet fragments of thirteenth-century date from Saljuq Anatolia, and even earlier survivals from Islamic Egypt, show that this art was well developed in some parts of the medieval Muslim world, and literary sources amply corroborate this, mentioning dozens of carpet types and production centres of which no tangible evidence survives. Persian paintings of the fourteenth and fifteenth centuries, with their close focus on detail, flesh out this picture and reveal the remarkable range of contemporary carpet types. But the Safavid period is the earliest from which a critical mass of physical evidence has survived – enough to allow the history of this art form in Iran from 1500 to 1700 to be written. The reason, perhaps, is that the Safavids turned a cottage industry into a national one. Shah ʿAbbas I founded carpet factories at Isfahan and Kashan. The weavers, who sometimes sign their work (e.g. Maqsud Kashani or Ghiyath al-Din Jami), display consummate technical mastery across a wide spectrum of materials – silk, wool, gold and silver thread – and techniques, from flat weaves (*zilus* and *kilims*) to pile carpets knotted coarsely or so closely as to total eight hundred knots per square inch. Red, white, yellow and blue are by far the most popular colours, irrespective of the design. Gigantic carpets were produced; in 1539–40, the Ardabil shrine was graced, at the behest of Shah Tahmasp, with a pair of carpets, the larger and better preserved one comprising some thirty-three million knots and measuring *c.* 11 × 5.40 m (36 × 18 ft).

191

As in the Timurid period, no significant barriers operated between most media in the matter of design, and thus many of the motifs and themes encountered in carpets can be paralleled in contemporary tilework, wall painting, lacquer, metalwork, manuscript illumination and illustration, and so on. So close are the analogies with contemporary Safavid book painting, in particular, that some of the most complex carpets can be regarded as paintings executed in a different medium. This has its disadvantages, as can be seen with modern rugs bearing portraits of statesmen – for the language and range of expression natural to a carpet is being ignored, indeed suppressed. What, then, made the design of carpets distinctive? Perhaps

191 A woven Paradise. The larger Ardabil carpet (1539–40), of superlative technical quality, is saturated with the imagery of heavenly light. At its dead centre is a pond with floating lotus blossoms – perhaps the Qurʾanic Pool of Kauthar. The carpet bears verses by the poet Hafiz and a signature: 'Except for thy haven there is no refuge for me in this world;/Other than here, there is no place for my head./Work of a servant of the court, Maqsud of Kashan, 946'.

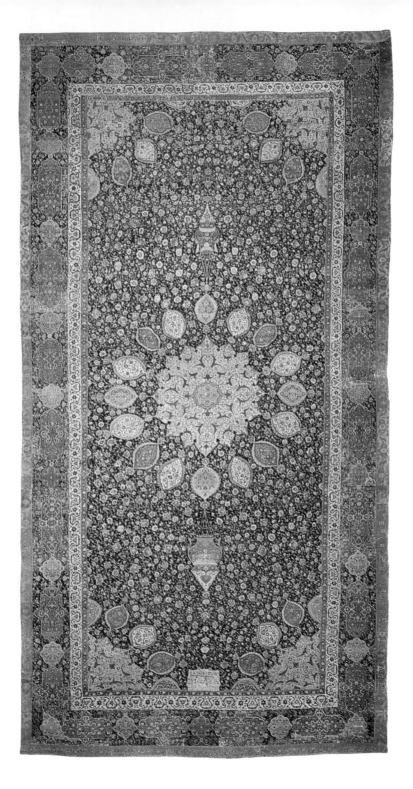

more than in any other art form, carpet design manipulates multiple levels of pattern, sometimes five at a time, using colour as the principal means of distinguishing the different schemes. The designs are often predicated on constantly shifting viewpoints, which add further complexities and lend the ensemble extra dynamism. As with many panels of tilework, moreover, the design is deliberately not complete but is only a portion of an unimaginably large but thoroughly disciplined composition. Hence the viewer receives intimations of infinity, even eternity, all the more affecting because they are not explicit.

Various major categories of design may be distinguished, though they continually overlap – for example, borders comprising cartouches with animal scenes enrich otherwise abstract designs. Garden carpets perpetuate a type known as far back as the Sasanian period, when the rug known as 'The Springtime of Khusrau' was a national treasure. This was divided into four plots, each representing one of the seasons and depicting appropriate flora, all executed in gold and silver thread and precious jewels. Safavid garden carpets seem to reflect simultaneously a side view and a bird's-eye view, though drastically schematized, of water-channels stocked with fish, flower-beds, terracing, pavilions, ponds and fountains. The poems inscribed on them compare them to roses and tulips. Sometimes peacocks and lesser birds, lions, leopards, hares and deer can be glimpsed in the foliage; their colours (as in Safavid tilework) may bear no relation to nature. The other-worldly associations of the garden theme are always subliminally present. A second category consists of hunting scenes conceived as a sequence of loosely linked vignettes, with the border sometimes depicting an alfresco royal reception, lutanists and even angels (major examples survive in museums in Boston and Milan, the latter dated 1522–23). The so-called animal rugs, in which creatures of various species frolic or attack each other, can be classified alongside the hunting rugs. A third type can be described rather inadequately as a medallion carpet because its centrepiece is usually a huge circular or oval medallion with numerous smaller medallions orbiting around it. The Ardabil carpets are the most distinguished examples of this variety, and display the extra refinement of a mosque lamp hanging from the inner circle of smaller satellite medallions – all silhouetted against a ground of deep indigo which makes the carpet like a window on to the Milky Way. Placed on the floor directly beneath the dome, it evoked that dome and thus the heavens. Further themes in these two carpets contain references to

248

Paradise as described in Islamic tradition; other carpets depict angels or houris. Quite another type is the vase carpet, in which vases of various sizes form the leitmotif of the composition. A last major category is represented by the floral rugs, in which multiple flowering sprays of various sizes, linked by thin tendrils, spill across the field.

These carpets, though essentially court art, were actually made in numerous manufactories throughout the Safavid realm, though opinions differ over allocating types of rugs to specific places. Tabriz, Qazvin, Kashan, Isfahan, Herat and Kirman were all major centres, though it was common for a single centre to produce several different types of rug. The finer carpets represented a considerable investment in time and money, and it is therefore not surprising that they bear quite full inscriptions; the London Ardabil carpet is signed by one Maqsud Kashani, who styles himself 'servant of the court', and bears the date 1539–40. A carpet in the Najaf shrine was donated, says the inscription, 'by the dog of this shrine, 'Abbas' (Shah 'Abbas I). The strongly pictorial character of so many Safavid carpets plainly owes much to Safavid book painting, a borrowing which extends even to the concept of pictorial space, as in the adoption of the high horizon and stepped planes and the plethora of small-scale detail; but it has a much more marked anti-naturalistic quality (for example in the choice of colour), which suggests that even figural images were seen in some sense as abstract motifs, and the roster of Chinese motifs far exceeds the norms of contemporary painting. Cloud collars, undulating cloud bands, cranes, phoenixes, dragons, lotuses, peonies and numerous fabulous creatures (as in the Sanguszko carpet in New York) – all are grist to the mill, though their context owes very little to China. Nor is it certain whether they retain their Chinese significance or whether they have acquired new symbolic meanings (the dragon/phoenix combat, for example, emblematic of happiness in China, may now refer to dualist beliefs). This obsession is still imperfectly explained in current scholarship; not even Safavid pottery is so saturated in Chinese motifs. On the other hand, many of the finest carpets were made as presents for foreign potentates or for commercial export to the West. The horizons of the Safavid carpet industry were therefore very wide. But while it did not ignore the immemorial past of carpet production in the Near East – the abstract, usually geometric designs of tribal weavers – its supreme masterpieces bear a very different kind of iconography. As a result, they had no root in the medium itself; for all their splendour and majestic scale, they were an intrusion.

Architecture, painting and carpets may fairly claim to represent the principal achievements of the Safavids in the visual arts, but this was a productive period in many other media too. Textiles were produced in various materials – printed cotton, silk, shorn velvet, reversible brocades in gold and silver thread, and embroidery – not only in Isfahan but also in Yazd and Kashan. Similarly, textile factories were established by royal command all over the realm, from Shirvan to Isfahan, Yazd, Kashan, Mashhad and Kirman, each with orders to 'weave in its own manner'. Here too much of the production was for export, and notable painters like Rida'-yi 'Abbasi were co-opted to provide designs. Velvets, brocades and block-printed cottons were made in huge quantities. 'They last forever', as Chardin said. Hence they survive in great quantity, and they too were exported – an entire room in Rosenborg Castle in Denmark was hung with them. Their designs bear once again the unmistakable imprint of book painting, with themes like dallying lovers, winsome pages, picnics, horsemen leading prisoners of Turkish stock, huntsmen on foot or mounted, animal combats, floral patterns and the familiar episodes of Nizami and Firdausi. The absence of serious themes of religious or political iconography is noticeable. Reds and yellows are especially favoured colours. While some of these textiles were intended as hangings and tent decoration, most were garments naturally intended for the wealthy, and advertised the luxury of the Iranian court. They attracted admiring notice when worn by Iranian ambassadors abroad, and were often sent as gifts to European potentates.

The last decades of the sixteenth century saw a vigorous revival of the pottery industry in Iran, which despite occasional fine – even dated – pieces had been in the doldrums. Safavid potters developed new types of Chinese-inspired blue-and-white wares, due perhaps to the influence of the three hundred Chinese potters and their families settled in Iran by Shah 'Abbas I, and indeed some of the vases made in Kirman and depicting swirling dragons are a passable pastiche of Chinese work, a comment that applies equally to their semi-porcelain body. Much of this 'chinoiserie' pottery was produced in response to European demand. More typically Iranian designs, however, also appear on such pieces. Subtler references to Chinese originals include the so-called Gombroon ware, which depends for its effect on distinction of form and on its white translucent body, to which celadon slip may be added. Lustre enjoyed a revival under Shah 'Abbas and was produced in great quantity, but it has a rather

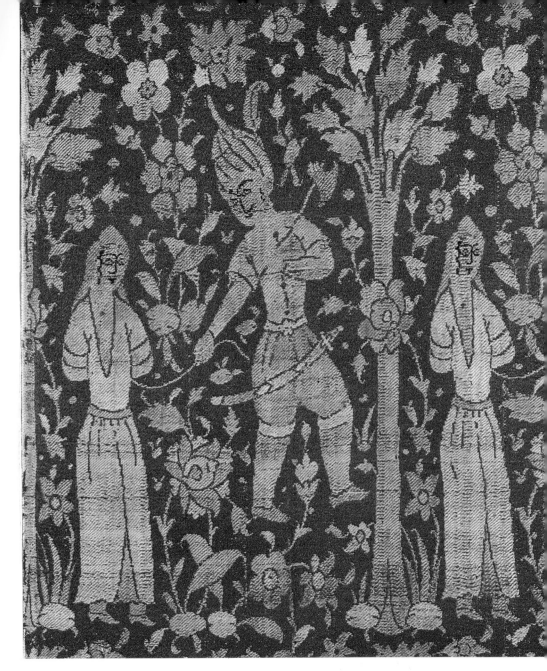

192 A royal monopoly. Silk textile with warriors leading prisoners (detail), late 16th century. The French traveller Tavernier notes that in Safavid Iran there were more people engaged in silk-weaving than in any other trade; in Kashan 'one single city quarter boasts of one thousand houses of silk workers,' according to his fellow-countryman Chardin. Kashan received more silk per year than London did broadcloth.

brassy sheen which, combined with an emphasis on underglaze blue, results in pieces inferior to earlier lustre in aesthetic quality. The decoration is restricted to vegetal motifs. Polychrome ware was produced in great quantities in Kirman. Figural designs on such Safavid pottery as eschews chinoiserie echo the mannered style of the painter Rida'-yi 'Abbasi, whose idiom in fact dominates all later Safavid figural art; they also recall, more generally, Safavid carpets and textiles. Later Kubachi ware has a much wider and brighter 193 colour range and often has a central medallion enclosing an engaging portrait bust executed with rapid strokes in typical late Safavid style.

The Safavid pictorial manner lingered long after the fall of the dynasty and, in an enfeebled state, remained the staple of Qajar potters. This staleness, combined with the widespread popularity of cheap European ceramics from the eighteenth century onwards, brought about the final demise of fine wares in Iran, though Mashhad and Kirman, the major centres of Safavid production (neither city being noted for its pottery in earlier times) continued to 194 produce blue-and-white ware with black outlines into the nineteenth century. Only in architectural tilework did the Safavid tradition continue with undiminished vigour after the fall of the dynasty, with new colour schemes favouring yellow and pink, an unprecedented emphasis on relief and themes of European origin.

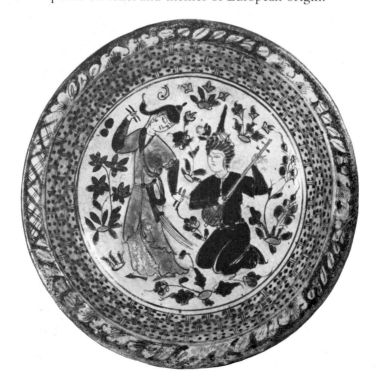

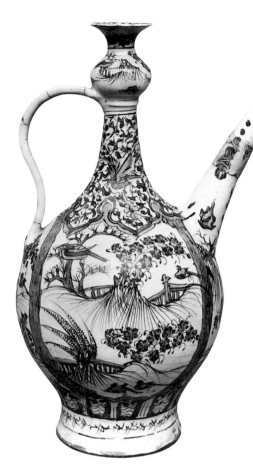

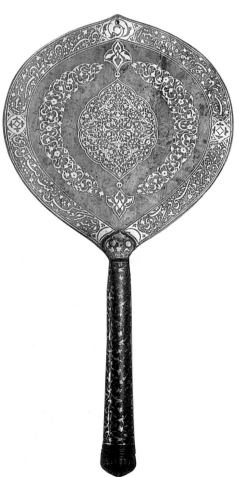

194 (*left*) The shadow of China. Ewer, early 18th century. The Persian potter has imitated Chinese blue-and-white export wares, as in the simplified and weakened renditions of Chinese landscape conventions, and has achieved a semi-porcelain body. But the all-over decoration on the neck betrays Islamic taste.

195 (*right*) The mirror as mystical metaphor? Steel mirror inlaid with gold, early 17th century. For Sufis, the mirror connotes man's inner jewel, the heart. Through spiritual exercises the mirror of the heart is polished and the rust of sin is removed. Thus the heart can worthily receive the experiential knowledge (*ma'rifa*) of God. The inscription may parody these Sufi associations: 'Tell the mirror-maker: "Don't bother polishing it."/ The mirror will become unclouded when you look in it'.

193 (*opposite*) Courtly imagery popularized. 'Kubachi' earthenware dish with polychrome design of a castanet dancer and a *rabab* player. North-west Iran, 17th century. The drawing is Iranian but the colouring owes something to Turkish underglaze painted wares.

In metalwork, the engraved technique developed in Khurasan in the fifteenth century retained its popularity well into Safavid times, and indeed that province, now supplemented by Azerbaijan, continued to be a major centre for this medium. It is curious that Safavid metalwork has been so long neglected even though it produced significant innovations in form, design and technique. They include a type of tall octagonal torch-holder on a circular plinth, a new type of ewer of Chinese inspiration, and the almost total disappearance of Arabic inscriptions in favour of those containing Persian poetry, often by Hafiz and Sa'di. The content of these verses is frequently religious and is apt to have a strong Sufi tinge. Dense arabesques and floral designs were more to contemporary taste than figural motifs, even though such motifs dominated the other visual arts of the period. Perhaps they would have coexisted somewhat uneasily with the huge fields of epigraphy which are the major visual accent on these pieces, and which find their ideal foil in the low-key vegetal background which expands effortlessly to fill the remaining available space. Inscriptions are now allotted a greater surface than ever before, in bold zigzags and cartouches as well as the more familiar encircling bands. A few pieces commissioned by Armenian patrons juxtapose lines from Persian mystical poets with Armenian inscriptions. Armenian architecture and pottery produced in Iran proper uses Iranian modes in just the same unselfconscious manner even though their iconographic message is unmistakably Christian: a silent testimony to the religious tolerance practised by the Safavid state.

195 Safavid brasses were apparently often tinned to simulate silver, though the most luxurious metalwork, of which only a few pieces are known, was inlaid with gold and incrusted with jewels. Other lost types of Safavid metalwork can be reconstructed with the help of ceramic copies. But some of the best Islamic armour extant – stirrups, shields, battle-axes – fashioned in iron and especially steel, was produced by Safavid smiths. Important pieces include a group of scimitars (shamshirs) from Khurasan, as well as steel banners inlaid with Twelver Shi'ite invocations. 'Damascening' (watering and gold overlay or gold inlay) and openwork were the most common decorative techniques used for such objects, which often bear lengthy inscriptions. Safavid metalwork, like so many of the other visual arts, remained the standard for subsequent artists, and Zand and Qajar work perpetuates its shapes and decorative conventions, though the execution tends to lose itself in a meaningless intricacy.

CHAPTER TEN

The Ottomans

The Ottoman empire began modestly, as a principality at the western vanguard of the Turkish campaign to Islamize Anatolia and bring down the Byzantine empire. A mêlée of small and often mutually antagonistic emirates (*beyliks*) had arisen to fill the political vacuum in Anatolia after the final fall of the Saljuqs of Rum in 1308 and the decline of Mongol authority soon afterwards. The Ottomans gradually consolidated their position in western Anatolia and expanded their territories at the expense both of Byzantium and their Muslim neighbours, changing their capital in the process from Iznik – right on the Byzantine frontier – to Bursa, further south. A series of ambitious and able rulers in the later fourteenth and early fifteenth centuries enabled them to survive a catastrophic defeat by Timur in 1402 and to expand into Europe, first via Greece and then the Balkans. The noose around Constantinople tightened inexorably and in retrospect it is remarkable how long the city was able to survive. It fell to the charismatic young sultan Mehmed II, after a prolonged and gallant defence, in 1453. The name Qustantiniya continued on the coinage, but Istanbul now claimed much of the thousand-year heritage of the Byzantine empire – a message driven home by the silhouettes of the mosques which quickly dominated the city's skyline.

The psychological boost provided by this victory can be said to have launched the Ottomans on the road to a world empire; in the course of the next century they had established themselves not just as the principal Islamic state but as a superpower – the only medieval polity both to achieve this distinction and carry it into the modern age. Neither their Safavid nor their Mughal contemporaries could match them for power or territory – or perhaps even wealth. For two centuries and more after the fall of Constantinople this was an empire on the move, transforming much of the Mediterranean into a Turkish lake, its persistent encroachment into Europe finally turned back as late as 1683 at the Siege of Vienna. So powerful was its grip on the lands it had acquired that even the long decline of the eighteenth and early nineteenth centuries saw only minor losses of territory. Even later, when Turkey began to be described as 'the sick man of Europe', Ottoman possessions in Asia remained firmly within the empire.

What was the secret of this success? Several answers can be proposed. First, this was a thoroughly militarized state; yet, far more than its Islamic predecessors, it was open to technological advance, a true gunpowder empire. Second, it presented itself as the consummate Islamic state, fully integrating government and Islamic law (the *shari'a*). The Ottomans took over from the Mamluks the mantle of the leadership of Sunni Islam and the Ottoman sultan subsumed into his own titles those of the caliph, thus ending the shadow 'Abbasid caliphate that had survived in Cairo until 1517. Yet the Islam propagated by the Ottoman state was not only that of the *'ulama*, the men of theological learning, which was apt to become arid and legalistic; for the sultans also sponsored certain Sufi orders and were on intimate terms with their leaders. Thus they had a tap-root to popular piety, and the flourishing of the dervish lodge (*tekke*) in their dominions is clear proof of this. Thirdly, this was not only a militarized but also a quintessentially bureaucratic state, with well-established hierarchies in all the affairs of government. The Ottoman *millet* system formalized and protected the position of non-Muslim minorities in the body politic; the *devshirme* policy systematically uprooted young Christian boys from their native lands and brought them to the capital for service in the palace or in crack regiments. The Ottoman archives, which survive in abundance, document the workings of this bureaucracy, for example the way that the Iznik potteries were run and financed, or how building campaigns were managed. Fourthly, the Ottomans were staggeringly wealthy. Their empire stretched from Hungary to the Yemen, from Algeria to Iraq. With such taxation revenues to draw on, it is little wonder that the Ottomans did not – though to their ultimate cost – evince serious interest in the Americas, India, the Far East or the burgeoning of international seaborne trade. Finally, they wielded the weapon of propaganda most effectively. They were thoroughly international, as witnessed, say, by the contents of the Topkapi Saray (see p. 280) or by their welcome of Western experts in art, the sciences and military techniques. Yet they also represented the culmination of five centuries of Turkish rule in the Islamic world, and that heritage manifested itself culturally, socially and politically in numerous ways. But they also stood for the whole of the Islamic world, for example as guardians of the Holy Places of Mecca, Medina and Jerusalem. They were the very image of the infidel so far as Europeans were concerned, and their pomp and ceremony was recorded with a sense of awe by European ambassadors and travellers.

Ottoman art is in a category of its own within the wider world of Islamic art. It certainly has its own distinctive character in the major media such as architecture, ceramics, book painting and textiles, and its products bear witness to the massive financial resources of the most powerful empire of its time. Yet the remarkable uniformity of much of the Ottoman visual arts gives one pause. On the technical side, much that was produced attained the highest standard of excellence. But this superlative execution is liable to be offset at times by a cold, rational formalism that drains the life out of the work. The perfection itself has a somewhat forbidding, hard-edged quality. Cases in point are the austerity of so much architectural decoration or the combination of high-gloss surface and a rather restricted decorative repertoire in Iznik wares. It seems permissible to suggest, on the basis both of the relatively static nature of much Ottoman art and of its high technical quality, that government control had a consistent and decisive impact on the art of the period. On the credit side, this kept very large numbers of artists occupied and ensured that their work met the most exacting standards. But there was a price to pay, most evidently in architecture, where the existence of centrally produced blueprints is well documented, but plainly in other fields too – in a word, standardization. Top-flight artists paradoxically had less freedom of manoeuvre than less able ones; they were palace employees rather than subject either to their own preferences or to the demands of the open market.

Ottoman architecture is unique in the Islamic world for its unswerving fidelity to a single central idea – that of the domed square unit. This basic theme announces itself on a tiny scale at the very beginning of the Ottoman period, in the mosque of Ertughrul at Soghut, datable to the early fourteenth century. Over the next five centuries it was developed with a singular intensity of purpose. It is, so to speak, the spinal cord running through the body of Ottoman architecture; it controls every major development of that style and its influence can be felt even in peripheral areas. The intrinsic simplicity of the domed square unit as a structural form made it ideally suited to function on any scale, large or small, without sacrificing clarity or monumentality. It readily accommodated, too, numerous appurtenances – domed buttresses, semi-domes, porticoes, domed cloisters, courtyards and minarets. Possession of this solid structural core

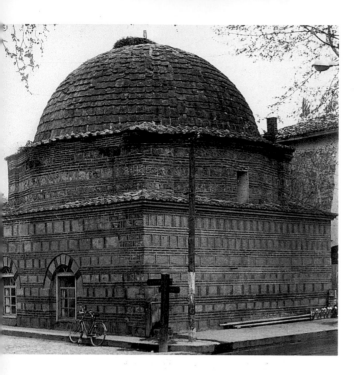

196 The seed of greatness. Haci Ozbek mosque, Iznik, 1333. This is the earliest Ottoman mosque dated by inscription. Ottoman Islamic power began in the far west of Anatolia and this mosque is an early symbol of that sovereignty, appropriating former Byzantine territory. The cloisonné masonry (stone framed by brick) is a technique of Byzantine origin.

enabled Ottoman architecture to retain its quintessential character intact, independent of superficial local detailing in materials or decoration, throughout the many provinces of the empire. From Algeria to Iraq, from Syria to the Yemen, a distinctively Turkish Ottoman architecture effortlessly imposes its presence.

This feat is all the more impressive when one recalls that the domed square unit had already had a long history in Islamic architecture even before the coming of the Ottomans. But in, for example, the Iranian tradition between, say, 800 and 1700, for all that the domed square recurs repeatedly for many centuries and in most major building types, it never acquired the exclusive status which it enjoyed in Ottoman times. The same could be said of Syria, Egypt, the Maghrib or India. Instead, the domed square is merely one of several equal and mutually dependent architectural forms: the portal, the *iwan*, the hypostyle hall, the two-tier façade and so on. Ottoman architecture, however, somehow suppresses these other forms, though without discarding them completely, and in so doing elevates the domed square to premier rank. It fashions a new balance of component parts, arranged according to a much more explicit hierarchy than before. And the domed square tends to invade areas from which it was formerly excluded, and swamp them. Thus high courtyard façades give way to shallow arcades covered by a succession of domes, becoming effectively a sequence of domed square units; the same is true of hypostyle halls.

This consistency does have its drawbacks. It can lead to a certain inflexibility, a tendency to apply a rote solution, devised at the drawing board, irrespective of the peculiarities of the site. The degree of centralization necessitated by so vast an empire encouraged a strong bureaucratic input into architectural design, a process formalized by the creation of a special department of state charged with preparing blueprints for repeated use. This system effectively tied the hands of provincial architects and imposed a perhaps undesirable uniformity on their work. They could choose – it was only practical that they should do so – whether to use naked brick or to coat it with plaster, whether to have their masonry plainly dressed or striped. They had a comparable freedom with applied decoration. But in the crucial matter of managing space – which of course lies at the heart of all architecture – they clearly had to work within parameters imposed from outside. Thus the vigorous local traditions which had characterized the Islamic lands bordering the Mediterranean, and beyond, for almost a millennium, suffered a serious decline. Pre-Ottoman traditions in most of these areas had positively benefited from the absence of central governmental control, in that individual provinces, and often even individual towns, had managed to develop their own distinctive styles of architecture. No doubt this phenomenon had much to do with political independence. But whatever caused it, the fact of this diversity is undeniable; strong local roots nurtured it; and its vitality had ensured continuous change and evolution across a broad front encompassing form, structure and ornament. Regrettably, the Ottoman conquest put a damper on this process. More than that, it brought Ottoman architectural forms to places where they simply did not belong. A building like the Fishermen's Mosque in Algiers stands out like a sore thumb, a metropolitan Turkish import into a solidly Maghribi landscape. The political implications are just as inescapable as those attached to the architecture of the British Raj in India. This was cultural imperialism at work.

Ottoman architecture could fairly be termed mosque-driven. The unchallenged prestige of the mosque made it the natural focus of royal patronage. Thus it became the most public showcase for innovation, ensuring that new ideas were disseminated quickly and that they had the *imprimatur* of the most venerated building type of all. Moreover, virtually all the significant stages in the evolution of

196
197

mosque design were accomplished in the capital – first Iznik, then Bursa, finally Istanbul – which naturally conferred on them a metropolitan glamour. And the extremely large size of so many of the imperial Ottoman mosques, with their courtyards, made them perhaps unexpectedly useful models for quite different building types such as caravansarais, *madrasas* and elements of *külliyes*, foundations centring on a mosque but comprising multiple buildings. Indeed, the core forms of Ottoman architecture, domes and courtyards, are basically interchangeable; a domed square with a vaulted two-bay porch can as easily be a mausoleum as a mosque. But it is the dome that dominates. Hence the various illusionistic devices adopted to magnify the size of the dome – such as the low roofline of the adjoining cloister, porch or sanctuary, or the siting of the climactic dome at the highest point of a sloping site.

197 Calligraphy writ large. Interior of Ulu Cami, Bursa, 1396–9. Huge calligraphic panels used as wall decoration are an Ottoman speciality, as is mirror writing. Here the central panel reads 'The Guide' (*al-hadî*), one of the 99 names of God. Note the multi-domed interior.

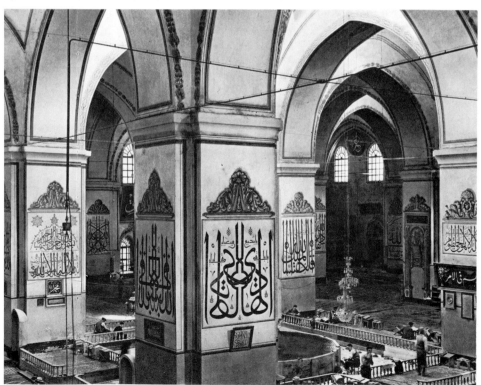

The concentration of major mosques in Istanbul can be explained in political terms as part of a sustained attempt to transform the visual aspect of the ancient Christian city of Constantinople and to give it a new Islamic identity as Istanbul. In the roughly contemporary Safavid and Mughal empires, too, the capitals – Isfahan, Agra, Delhi – were given massive face-lifts by means of ambitious building programmes, and the resultant architecture had an unmistakably scenic purpose. But the well-nigh obsessional focus on huge mosques which characterizes Istanbul for the century or so after the conquest of the city – it is even recorded that a detailed model of the Suleymaniye was on a show in a public procession held in 1582 – is noticeably absent in these lands. Of course major mosques were erected, but palaces, bazaars, mausolea and piazzas account for much of the new building in India and Iran. And the demographic pressures caused by an influx of Muslims into a previously Christian city can only partially explain this frenzied building campaign. Competition between successive sultans must also be taken into account. And given that the first great mosque erected by Mehmed the Conqueror in Istanbul was itself a very substantial building, the sultans who succeeded him had little option but to follow him down the same path. For that simple human reason the imperial mosques of Istanbul are unreasonably large and plentiful. Presumably the expansion of the city beyond its Byzantine walls meant that there was less premium on space and that architects were able to spread themselves. Moreover, since there was plainly no overriding liturgical need for so many large mosques, their architects designed them to serve additional functions. Hence the *külliye* or composite foundation saw an unprecedented expansion in this period.

Several other factors also encouraged the rapid evolution of a dynamic innovatory style in sixteenth-century Istanbul. For example, architects paid close attention to the work of their rivals, identifying the weak spots in their designs and improving on them in their own work. The increasingly compact and concentrated silhouette of mature Ottoman mosques owes much to the intelligent observation of failure. That visually satisfying sense of interdependence between component parts, that carefully staggered sequence of supporting elements, which lend these mosques their air of confident, four-square stability, is a prime example of this pragmatic approach. And of course each new variation on the familiar theme could be conveniently examined at close quarters, because virtually all the major mosques were in Istanbul. Another contributory factor was

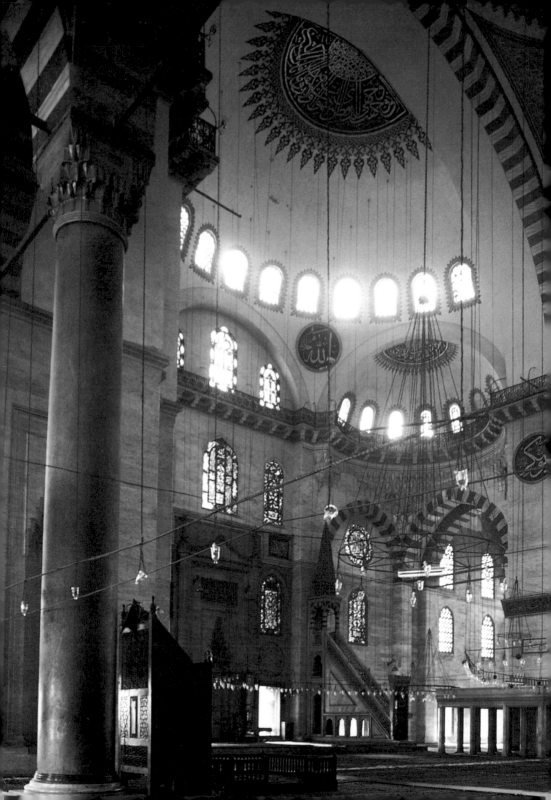

the creation of a government department, a kind of Ministry of Works, to oversee the continuous building campaigns launched by the sultans. This created a pool of administrative expertise which greatly facilitated the rapid completion of these complex projects. One should remember, too, that the Ottomans constituted the largest and most dreaded power in Europe and western Asia, controlling as they did an area of almost a million square miles. It was only fitting that their architecture should reflect this fact. Foreign embassies flocked to Istanbul and reported back admiringly on the scale and magnificence of the new buildings there. Thus the propaganda dimension of these mosques was an integral part of their contemporary context; and the colossal financial resources of the Ottoman empire allowed the sultans to exercise patronage on a scale perhaps unmatched since the high days of the 'Abbasid caliphate.

The increasing size of these mosques brought daunting technical problems in its train. Hence the introduction of ever more refined systems of buttressing, experiments with semi-domes, more lavish fenestration with a consequent reinforcement of the adjoining masonry, and so on. Since the self-same process had taken place in early Christian and Byzantine architecture it is not surprising that Ottoman architects happened independently on many of the same discoveries – though for obvious religious reasons their buildings did not incorporate the cruciform element so important to Christian architects. Yet the catalyst was undoubtedly the conquest of Constantinople, which brought Ottoman architects face to face with the greatest of Byzantine monuments, Haghia Sophia, and the various churches related to or developed from it. This encounter, moreover, took place at a cusp of history when the Ottoman state enjoyed boundless self-confidence and was expanding its boundaries, when revenues were ample and when the new masters of Byzantium were laying claim to its ancient heritage. The time was, in short, perfect for propaganda gestures, and architecture was the obvious medium. It was entirely natural for Turkish architects to study Haghia Sophia intensively, learn from it and resolve to outdo it. Thus all major Ottoman mosques in Istanbul were built in full awareness of the challenge posed by Haghia Sophia, and they were in some sense in its shadow.

Yet for all the indisputable similarities between Haghia Sophia and the great Ottoman mosques from the Fatih Cami (1470) onwards –

198 The apogee of Ottoman power. Interior of Suleymaniye mosque, 1556; the dome, whose diameter (26.6 m, 87.3 ft) is half its height, rests on eight piers. The epigraphic roundels with the names of Allah, Muhammad and the four Rightly Guided caliphs were designed by Ahmad Karahisari, the premier calligrapher of the time. The mosque glorifies Suleyman the Magnificent as the upholder of Sunni Islam, repository of the sultanate and the caliphate.

tiered elevation, grouped windows, cascading volumes, prominent semi-domes and domed turret-like buttresses – the differences are manifest; and it must also be recalled that such features also occur in earlier Ottoman buildings, though in a less developed form. Where Haghia Sophia exploited mystery and ambiguity, the Ottoman style put a premium on clarity and logic. While the exterior of the great Byzantine church is treated largely as a shell for the interior, Ottoman mosques maintain a scrupulous balance between the two.

199 Where Haghia Sophia visually plays down the mechanics whereby the great dome is supported, partly by dim lighting and partly by
198 decoration, such mosques as the Şehzade, the Suleymaniye and the Bayezid Cami are flooded with light and glory in their great free-standing piers which carry the central dome; the spatial divisions are muscular and clear-cut. The decoration of the vaults, in which designs familiar from manuscripts and carpets (but now vastly inflated) predominate, further emphasizes these divisions by virtue of being concentrated in selected spots. A totally different aesthetic governs the way that the billowing volumes of Haghia Sophia flow into each other with little perceptible transition. Where the Byzantine church suggests, its Ottoman successors display.

The central figure in sixteenth-century Ottoman architecture is Sinan (c. 1491–1588), probably a Greek convert to Islam; he rose to become Chief Architect (effectively Master of Works) and was responsible for something over one hundred buildings in his exceptionally long working life. He is the most famous of Islamic archi-
200 tects, both for his own work – crowned by the Selimiye mosque in Edirne, finished in 1575 when he was over eighty – and for the plans generated by his office, which were exported throughout the Ottoman empire and were duly executed by his subordinates or by local builders using local detailing. Here, if anywhere, is an Islamic equivalent to Sir Christopher Wren; and, like Wren, Sinan placed his stamp on an entire city. He it was who fleshed out the rather stark and unadorned external elevation of Ottoman mosques with a whole battery of articulating devices: single- or double-entrance porticoes, porches, gates, fountains, windows, turriform buttresses, grilles, variegated fenestration, and, above all, the interlocking volumes of the domes and semi-domes clustering around the great central cupola, with a new type of slender, pencil-shaped minaret of great height (up to 70 m or 230 ft) defining the key points of the

199 The challenge. Interior of Haghia Sophia, Constantinople, founded 537. Following a common Muslim practice, Mehmed II commemorated his capture of the city by turning its great church into a mosque. The 15th-century historian Tursun Beg specifically notes that this same sultan 'built a Great Mosque based on the design of Haghia Sophia, which not only encompassed all the arts of Haghia Sophia, but moreover incorporated modern features constituting a fresh new idiom unequalled in beauty'.

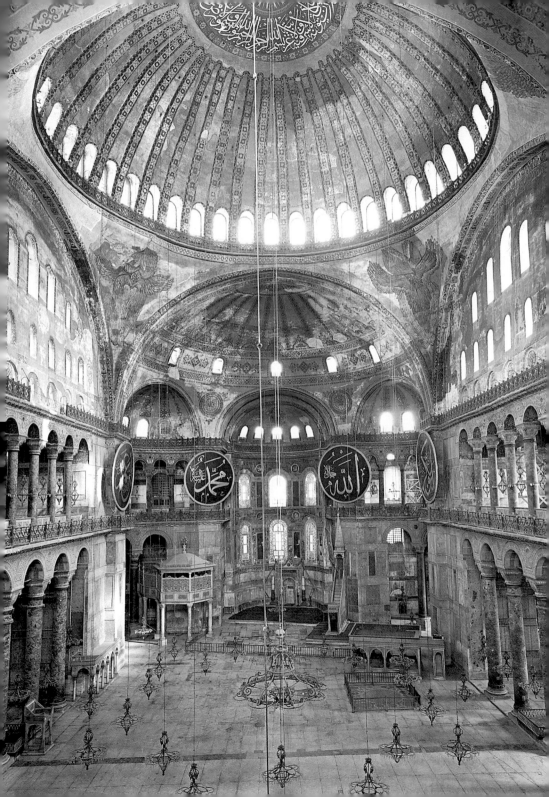

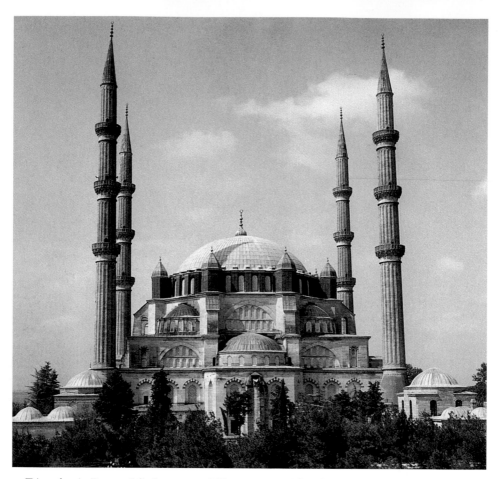

200 Triumph – in Europe. Selimiye mosque, Edirne, 1569–75. This, the masterpiece of Sinan, the greatest Ottoman architect, has the first Muslim dome whose diameter equals that of Haghia Sophia.

perimeter. His finest mosques are great grey mountains of masonry, but as complex and coordinated as a fugue. This is truly architects' architecture. The details of mouldings, two-tone voussoirs, embrasures, *muqarnas* hoods, door-frames and the like reveal a fastidious attention to detail, but they are placed parsimoniously and scarcely counteract the prevailing tone of austerity. The knife-edge sharpness of the stonework is its own ornament. The interiors are more colourful, with floral and geometric designs painted red, blue and 205 yellow, calligraphic roundels, stained glass and Iznik tiles, the latter

266

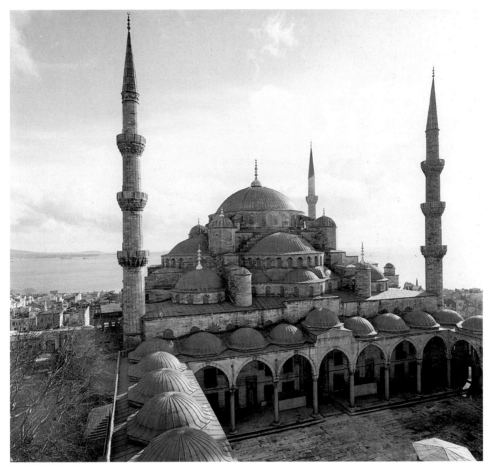

201 The end of the road. Complex of Sultan Ahmed I (the Blue Mosque), Istanbul, 1609–17. Sinan's students worked in his idiom but could not match his vision; this mosque is noted for its 21,000 Iznik tiles.

sometimes used, as at the Rustem Pasha mosque, to cover most of the interior. This balance between structure and decoration was gradually lost after the Sultan Ahmed complex of 1609–17; thereafter   201 Turkish architecture entered a baroque phase which emphasized loftiness, profuse sculptural detail and a restless curvilinearity.

The sterling craftsmanship, the confidence in marshalling huge spaces, the long experience in working with modular designs easily adaptable to different functions, the structural know-how accumulated in the course of building campaigns throughout the empire –

all this gives Ottoman architecture its distinctive stamp. It is manifest in the chains of caravansarais built along the major trade and pilgrim routes, in joint foundations and above all in the great *külliyes* for which the vast revenues of the Ottoman state were available. Some of these complexes are on a scale without parallel in Islamic architecture, like the Bayezid II complex at Edirne or the Suleymaniye, where the mosque is merely the centrepiece of a congeries of buildings which include an asylum, medical college, boys' school, kitchen, hostel, cistern, *hammam*, two mausolea and four *madrasas*.

202

The largest complex of all is mainly secular in character, namely the Topkapi Saray – more a royal city than a palace and thus a distinctive Turkish version of a building type also known in Nasrid Granada, Safavid Isfahan and the Mughal capitals of Delhi, Agra and Lahore. Hadrian's palace at Tivoli shows how ancient this tradition was in the Mediterranean world. The scores of buildings scattered over the many courts of the Topkapi Saray were erected over a period of some four centuries, and many were repaired again and

203

202 Welfare institution. Complex of Bayezid II, Edirne, begun 1484. It included a hospital with attached medical college and a separate section for the insane; the Islamic medical tradition led the world in the Middle Ages.

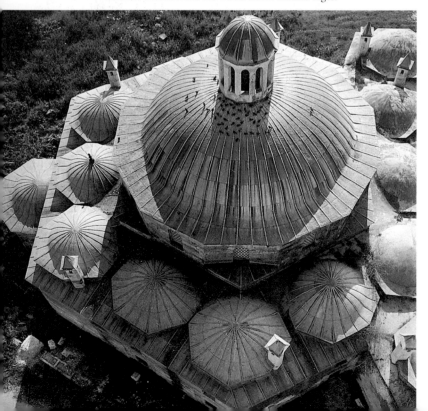

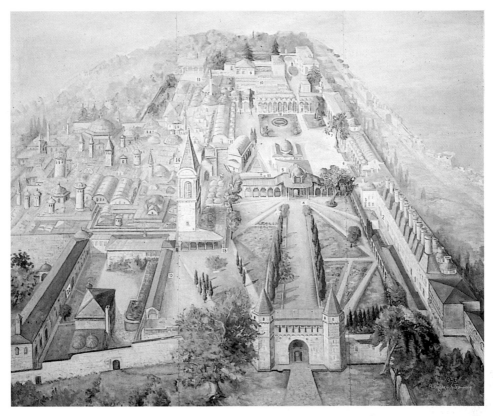

203 Nerve-centre of the empire. Bird's-eye view of the Topkapi Saray palace, Istanbul, 15th–19th centuries. Despite its huge size, much of it has an intimate, domestic atmosphere. It borrows from the Byzantine imperial palace the notion of a city within a city. The informal layout gives little hint of the extreme luxury of its interiors.

again. They housed an army of servants and retainers; the royal harem and the various corps of eunuchs; and of course soldiers and civil servants. The absence of grand structures of imposing scale, on the lines of contemporary European palaces, is noteworthy. Indeed, many of the buildings are diminutive and are not articulated into an overall design of any pronounced axiality or symmetry. The atmosphere is by turns formal and domestic, which is entirely appropriate since the Topkapi Saray ministered to both the public and the private aspects of the sultan's life.

It is ironic that the most famous and popular of all Ottoman art forms – Iznik pottery and tilework – was executed in a cheap and

269

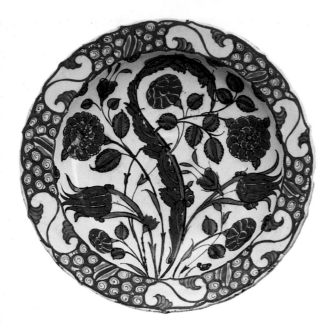

204 (*left*) Ceramic innovation. Iznik dish, later 16th century. The factories at Iznik rose to prominence just before 1500 when the Ottoman court began to oversee their management, and steadily increased the range, quality and quantity of their output over the next century. The palette was consistently modified, notably with the introduction of a brilliant tomato red after 1560. Roses, carnations, tulips and hyacinths predominate.

humble material. This is the best-known and most coveted of all Muslim ceramic wares. Iznik wares owe their name not only to their intrinsically high aesthetic and technical quality, but also to the fact that very great numbers of these wares, both tiles and individual pieces, survive, often in excellent condition. Moreover, if a comparison is made, say, with the Iranian world between 1000 and 1200 – a period which saw at least a score of different types of glazed wares being produced – the difference clearly lies in the way that Ottoman potters concentrated their efforts in a single direction. Here the dominating influence of a government-sponsored and government-financed industry can be recognized immediately. Iznik pottery was an official enterprise whose gigantic output required much bureaucratic supervision and financial control. Production quotas were enforced, salaries were pegged at levels judged appropriate to the particular skills of the workmen, designs created by the palace studio in Istanbul were sent to the potters' workshops for transfer on to pottery and tiles. The wares – a royal monopoly – were exported throughout Europe, and although the heyday of Iznik was the sixteenth century, the style, and its various provincial derivatives in Syria and elsewhere, lasted at least another century. As in the case of public architecture, this strong government interest tended to standardize production and to reduce variety while maximizing

205 Divine illumination. *Mihrab* of mosque of the vizier Sokollu Mehmed Pasha, built by Sinan in 1571. The white marble, the hanging lamp, candles, sunburst inscriptions and battery of windows above the *mihrab* all harp on the theme of light. Indeed, the Sufis developed around the Light Verse (Qur'an 24:35), traditionally associated with *mihrab*s, an intricate language for describing mystical experience.

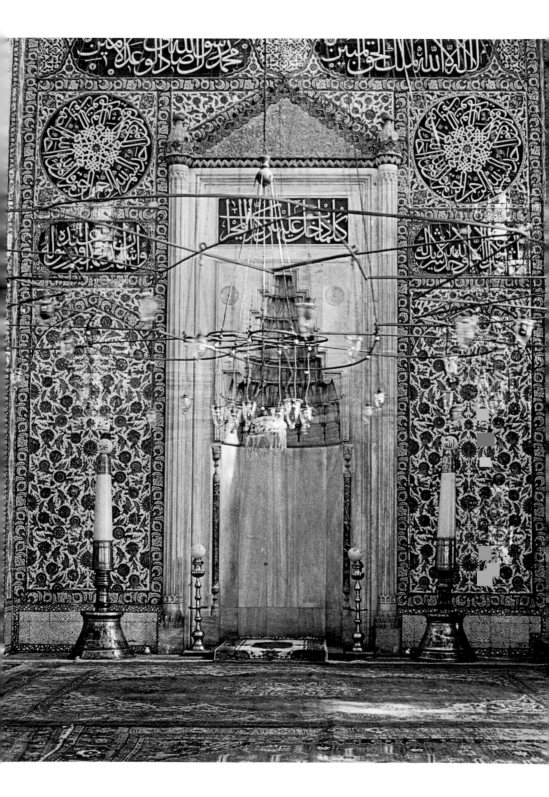

output. And while Iznik became the main centre for high-quality glazed pottery, other provincial production centres declined or were, indeed, completely eclipsed. But of course the concentration of ceramic production in a single centre was nothing new in Islamic art.

Recent research has pinpointed the evolution of the characteristic Iznik motifs and compositions and has developed a basic chronology. Although some pieces bear double- or triple-decker Qur'anic inscriptions, representations of ships, birds and snakes, as well as geometric or chinoiserie designs, the favoured subject-matter for Iznik wares, especially tiles, was floral motifs and the distinctive feathery *saz* scrolls. Carnations, hyacinths, tulips and other flowers recur in endless combinations. Set in apses in a *qibla* wall, they turn a *mihrab* into a paradise garden. The palette is limited and extremely distinctive: white, light and dark blue, purple and a vivid tomato or oxblood red. Most of these tones are used for foreground and background alike. The best Iznik ware owes its reputation to the purity and strength of these colours, and the decline of the industry can be detected in the gradual falling off of colour rather than design.

The arts of the book in Ottoman times drew their initial inspiration predominantly from those of Iran under the Timurids and their rivals, the Turcoman Aqqoyunlu, in the later fifteenth century. In some of the associated specialities – for example, in most Qur'anic illumination and in the illustration of verse romances – they did not progress significantly beyond this heritage. But for the most part they struck out on their own. In the field of book painting, for instance, entire cycles of religious images were devised, almost for the first time in Islamic art. This involved the creation of literally hundreds of new images. The *Anbiyaname* ('Book of the Prophets') of 1558 is an early attempt at this genre, but pride of place naturally goes to the six-volume illustrated life of the Prophet Muhammad, the *Siyar-i Nebi* (1594), whose images of the founder of Islam, with a white veil and a gigantic flame halo, sometimes attain a visionary intensity. Illustrated guides to Jerusalem and to the Holy Cities of Arabia, entitled *Futuh al-Haramain*, became popular during the sixteenth century. Despite their strongly abstract nature, expressed for example in the simultaneous adoption of multiple points of view and in their indifference to accurate spatial relationships, they have the bright colour and lively directness of a cartoon strip.

In secular painting, too, which accounts for most of the illustrated manuscripts of the period, there were important developments, inspired perhaps by a desire for realism – a quality pursued more

204

consistently than ever before in Islamic art. The thirteenth-century illustrations of the *Maqamat* of al-Hariri had held up a satirical mirror to daily life; the Timurid *Zafarnama* ('Book of Victories') and perhaps the lost Ilkhanid *Chingiznama* ('Book of Genghis Khan') had chronicled military exploits in a loosely epic style. But Ottoman painters, when they reverted to this subject matter, approached it in the spirit of a diarist or journalist, and inflated it to a major artistic genre. The process began modestly enough with the versified *Selimname* of *c.* 1525, but by *c.* 1558 it reached its apogee with the *Suleymanname* of ʿArifi. This history in verse has more in common with a newsreel as it patiently chronicles the ups and (occasionally) the downs of the sultan's campaigns. Its great set pieces of sieges and 206 battles often extend over two pages. Sometimes an illustrated manuscript was devoted to a detailed prose account of a single campaign, such as that of Szigetvar (written 1568–69) or the one in Iraq and western Iran between 1534 and 1536, the subject of a manuscript produced in 1537 by Matrakci Nasuh and containing 128 largely topographical paintings – essentially a traveller's guide. The same painter recorded Suleyman's Hungarian campaign and that of his admiral Barbaros, both occurring in 1543; here again there are frequent representations of cities. These works may owe something to the widespread contemporary European fashion for topographical woodcuts of major cities. But they are also remarkably up-to-date; elaborate and richly illustrated accounts of the imperial campaigns were produced as soon as possible after the fighting had ended.

Illustrated prose histories of entire reigns, such as those of Bayezid II, Suleyman the Magnificent, Selim and Murad III, were also produced; so too were illustrated portmanteau histories of the Ottoman dynasty. In much the same vein were the books describing the various public festivals which enlivened Ottoman society, such as the 207 *Surname* (1582). Yet for all the colour and detail of Ottoman painting, and the often panoramic scope of individual pictures, something is missing. The earnestly literal bent of Ottoman painters (which may explain the popularity of elaborate maps in Ottoman painting) was fundamentally at odds with the conventions within which they were operating. Constantly refined through long use in Persian painting, those conventions were designed to keep the real world at a distance, and to transform nature into art. Thus Persian painters appealed to the imagination to decode their images. Most of these images were transferred wholesale into Ottoman painting, but in the process they lost much of the inner relationship between the figures,

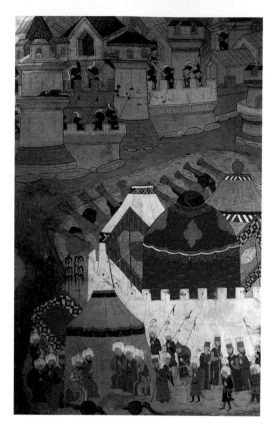

206 (*left*) The Ottoman threat to Europe. The imperial army besieging Vienna in 1529. Loqman, *Hünername*, 1588 (f.257b). The architecture, with its fanciful palette, reflects at one remove too many the influence of European topographical engravings, but the portable pomp of the great scarlet tent, complete with its flimsy battlements, is vigorously rendered.

207 (*right*) The sultan relaxes. Ahmed III watches dancers and comedians at the Hippodrome at Istanbul. *Surname-yi Vehbi*, *c.* 1720–32, illustrated by Levni. The festivities to celebrate the circumcision of the sultan's four sons in 1720 lasted fifteen days and nights, and included guild processions, firework displays, regattas, mock battles, magic shows and acrobatic performances including tightrope walkers. The variations in the scale of figures reflect social hierarchies.

or between figures and landscape or buildings, which had given the original its depth and nuance. The densely populated images of Ottoman painting describe the surface of things, and they cover a great deal of ground. But they are scarcely exploratory. Compositions manipulate groups of buildings or people or even colours *en bloc*, and these busy scenes, for all their overwhelming detail, lack finesse and attest a basic inflexibility. There is a sense of painting by the yard. Yet at its best, Ottoman painting – profiting, it seems, from the example of Italian Renaissance artists such as Costanzo da Ferrara and Gentile Bellini, who painted a memorable likeness of Mehmed the Conqueror as a brooding, self-contained intellectual – produced a series of excellent portraits which owe virtually nothing to the Persian tradition. Here a mastery of line and a series of happy inspirations in pose and colour evoke both the public and the private faces of royalty.

274

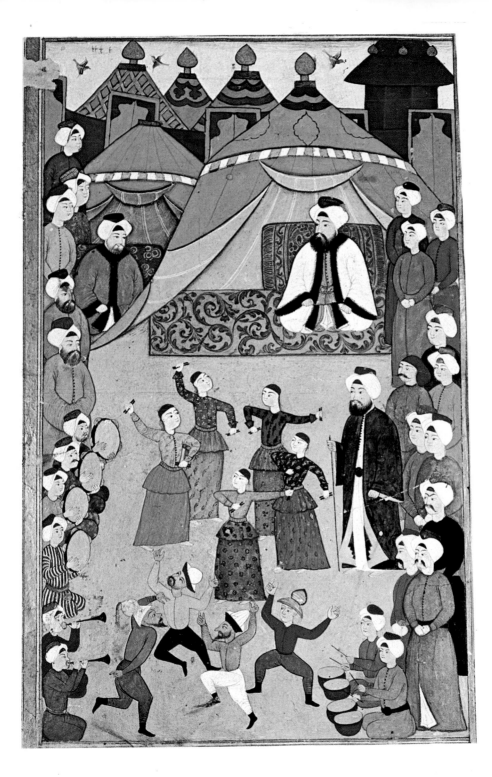

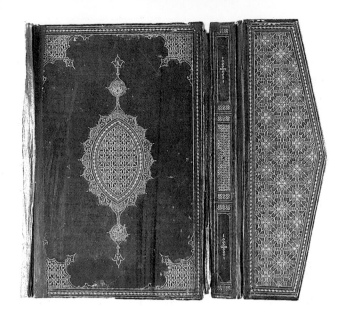

208 Thirst for learning. Back doublure of *Commentaries on the Maqasid of al-Taftazani*, made for Prince Bayezid, Amasya, 1477. Several Ottoman sultans were bibliophiles; it was a tradition for members of the élite to have libraries, and respect for knowledge found expression in luxuriously appointed manuscripts with fine bindings. Ottoman scholars wrote copiously if not originally on many topics, especially historiography and the religious sciences.

Turkish bindings, and specifically those datable between *c.* 1430 and *c.* 1510, are distinguished from most of their Arab and even Persian counterparts, both contemporary and earlier, by their visual aesthetic, which is dominated by an intense appreciation of colour and its possibilities. The imperial Ottoman binders in this period definitively forsook the all-over geometrical and vegetal designs of earlier tradition in favour of a field comprising a central medallion and cornerpieces. While the size of the field is allowed to vary dramatically according to the scale of these elements and of the borders, the dominant feature of many bindings is a serene expanse of empty space. Its strong colour ensures that this space is never neutral. Set into it at precisely determined points are the cartouches or medallions and corner-pieces which animate it. All is controlled, as in Ottoman architecture, by a matchless sense of interval, the fruit of long observation and experiment. Perhaps this instinctively satisfying placement of decorative features is the result of mathematical calculation – it may have been governed by proportional ratios of the kind seen in so much Islamic architecture and book painting.

While some of the basic stock-in-trade of these Ottoman binders came from Iran – the use of coloured leather, filigree, cartouches – they managed by dint of extreme concentration, and by setting up an imperial scriptorium on Iranian lines, to fashion their own style from these elements. Perhaps, like the Fatih mosque project in Istanbul, of unprecedented scale by Ottoman standards, and the earliest Ushak rugs, whose complexity represents a quantum leap forward in Turkish carpet design, the success of this atelier owed something to the euphoria generated by the fall of Constantinople. Some ninety manuscripts dedicated to Mehmed II survive, a record total among Islamic rulers, and this remarkable number provides a context for the rapid evolution of a distinctive imperial style. These original dated or datable bindings of the period 1450–1500 also offer precious clues to other apparently contemporary artefacts, especially in view of the total dearth of Ottoman textiles, ceramics or metalwork dated to that period. The spirit and structure of the decoration found in these bindings, as well as their detail, is therefore a benchmark for the definition of Ottoman art in the key generation after 1453. The classic balance, the seemingly effortless harmony, the chaste detailing (so curiously prophetic, despite the different idiom, of the spirit of Robert Adam) and the subdued luxury of contrasting colours and textures confer a unique éclat on these bindings. 208

Ottoman textiles of the sixteenth and seventeenth centuries survive in considerable numbers and, what is more, in the form of complete items of clothing. While Islamic textiles of the pre-Ottoman period do survive in reasonable quantity, they are nearly all incomplete. Thus, while they offer plentiful data on textile design and technique, their evidential value for the history of costume is very limited; the wider context of these fragments has gone. This depressing picture changes dramatically in the imperial Ottoman era, thanks to the holdings of the Topkapi Saray. Even entire tents have survived. The sultan's silk robes were used only once and then stored in the treasury, and a wardrobe-master was specifically charged with this task. Official protocol dictated frequent changes of apparel, thereby ensuring that these clothes did not wear out, so that the principal threat to their survival lay in the conditions of storage. Naturally, museum standards of conservation did not prevail, but the range of clothing still preserved is gratifyingly full – though very clearly not all items were stored to begin with, and the collection would require frequent sifting. Over 2,500 textiles remain, over 1,000 of them kaftans. These were woven not just for royal use but also, following an ancient Islamic custom, for distribution as gifts to foreign dignitaries and potentates or as a means of honouring high officials. But the Topkapi collections also contain a wonderfully varied assortment of embroidery work applied to objects as disparate 209 as leather boots, sharkskin boxes, bookbindings and tankards, hand-kerchiefs galore, headbands and kerchiefs for the royal ladies, gloves, sashes, purses, quilt covers, portfolios for documents or Qur'ans, cushions, and military or hunting equipment such as saddlecloths, shields, quivers and bowcases. The more expensive embroidery employing gold thread (*zerduz*) was made by specialist teams working in the palace; other types of embroidery were often produced by women in their own homes. Floor coverings comprised not merely rugs, traditionally capable of withstanding heavy wear and tear, but also brocaded satins and velvets, and sometimes silk was spread along a prince's route for him to ride over – a true 'red carpet treatment'. Thrones, sofas, litters and the like also featured elaborate textiles.

Such was the scale of the textile industry that from early Ottoman times, while the capital was still at Bursa, it required close govern-ment supervision. This extended well beyond the control of import, production and pricing of silk, for fine Ottoman textiles were exported in large quantities to Europe and were thus of importance to the Ottoman economy and state. Quality control was therefore vital. Tailors, weavers, silk-spinners, textile designers, producers of metallic thread and similar specialists were organized in guilds and their salaries were fixed by the bureaucracy. Nor was it only the court workshops that were subject to imperial control. Punishments were inflicted on those found guilty of cheating: in 1564 an imperial edict decreed that two-thirds of the looms then functioning in Istanbul for the production of textiles using gold and silver thread were to be shut down for that very reason. Lists of palace expenses

209 A tented palace. Ottoman tent, 17th century. Textile architecture, with its immemorial nomadic asso-ciations, played a vital role in Ottoman life, as can be gauged from its frequent appearance in contemporary painting. The fictive arches here themselves evoke textiles – in this case, prayer rugs.

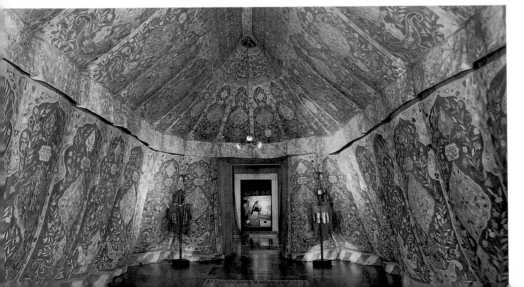

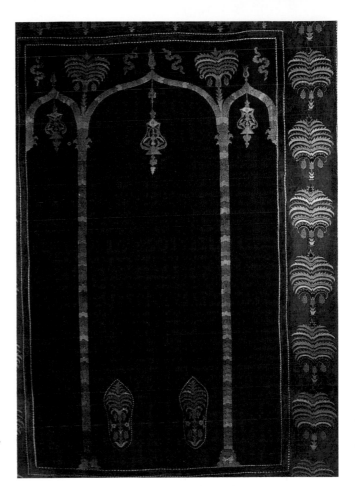

210 Portable mosque. Silk prayer cloth, 17th century. It depicts a triple *mihrab* with stylized finials in the form of tulips and date palms, openwork mosque lamps and outlines for the worshipper's feet – which contain further palms, a theme taken up again, but in lusher form, in the border; it may have paradisal associations.

specify how much craftsmen were paid in cash and kind, and even the costs of the materials they used are recorded. These were not independent craftsmen or even self-constituted teams operating a cottage industry; artists serving these gigantic state enterprises were in effect civil servants. And of course they had to conform. Clearly there was a house style to be followed, and while it developed certain motifs to a pitch of elegant assurance – the *hatayi* (Cathayan, i.e. Chinese) or *saz* ('reed pen' or 'red flower') style with its serrated leaves, *rumi*s ('Greek' spiralling arabesques), *chintamani* motifs (a combination of stripes and three dots), multiple ogives – it discouraged experimentation on a broad front.

Textiles, moreover, were only one element among many specialist luxury crafts. Every last accessory of the royal wardrobe displayed the same love for expensive, often *outré* materials and for fastidiously delicate detail. It is entirely possible that the Ottoman artefacts of this kind, far from expressing a distinctively Ottoman taste for such objects, were typical of earlier Islamic dynasties too and that it is the uniquely privileged status of Istanbul as an imperial Islamic capital that was never sacked which accounts for the sheer quantity of survivals – because, of course, such objects would be the very first to be looted. The lack of parallels, not only in the narrow chronological and stylistic sense, but in the most general typological way, makes it very hard to evaluate this Ottoman *Prachtkunst*. How can one tell – other than by stylistic analysis – what is distinctively Ottoman about the mother-of-pearl belts, turban ornaments, Qur'an boxes, leather canteens, quivers, wickerwork shields, gold-inlaid steel mirrors, bejewelled gold maces, ivory buckles, jade tankards and a host of other luxury objects, from masterpieces to elegant knick-knacks? Yet this is not the main issue. The wider significance of this material, representing both Ottoman production and centuries' worth of gifts from other Islamic states, is that it provides an unequalled visual context for the life and ceremonial of a Muslim court.

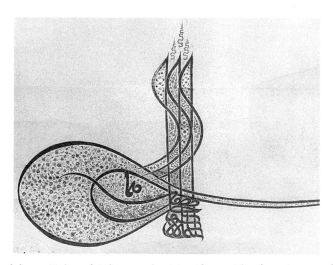

211 Royal logo. *Tughra* of Suleyman the Magnificent. The form is a standardized emblem of the ruler, and was used for centuries, but is personalized in that it accommodates his own name. Its origins have been variously interpreted as an inky handprint or a bow with the ruler's name written beneath it. It authenticated chancery documents and appeared on coins and banners; its misuse was a capital offence.

Select Bibliography

Reference Works

"Ali, "Abdallah Yusuf, *The Holy Qur'an: Text, Translation and Commentary*, repr. Brentwood, Maryland, 1989
Bacharach, Jere, *A Near East Studies Handbook*, Seattle and London, 1976
Bosworth, Clifford E., *The New Islamic Dynasties: A Chronological and Genealogical Manual*, Edinburgh, 1996
Bosworth, Clifford E. and Joseph Schacht (eds.), *The Legacy of Islam*, Oxford, 1974
Creswell, Keppel A.C., *A Bibliography of the Architecture, Arts and Crafts of Islam*, Cairo, 1961; *First Supplement*, Cairo, 1973; *Second Supplement*, Cairo, 1984
The Encyclopaedia of Islam, Leiden, 1960 onwards; 8 vols. to date
Endress, Gerhard (trans. Carole Hillenbrand), *An Introduction to Islam*, Edinburgh, 1988
Hodgson, Marshall G.S., *The Venture of Islam. Conscience and History in World Civilisation*, 3 vols., Chicago, 1974
Lewis, Bernard, *The Arabs in History*, London, 1958; many reprints
Lewis, Bernard (ed.), *The World of Islam: Faith, People, Culture*, London and New York, 1976; paperback ed. 1992
Lewis, Bernard, Ann K.S. Lambton and Peter M. Holt (eds.), *The Cambridge History of Islam*, 2 vols., Cambridge, 1970
Rahman, Fazlur, *Islam*, Chicago, 1979
Turner, Jane S. (ed.), *The Dictionary of Art*, London, 1996

Handbooks

Brend, Barbara, *Islamic Art*, London and Cambridge, Mass., 1991
Bloom, Jonathan M., and Sheila S. Blair, *Islamic Arts*, London, 1997
Bloom, Jonathan M., and Sheila S. Blair, *The Art and Architecture of Islam, 1250–1800*, New Haven and London, 1994
Ettinghausen, Richard, and Oleg Grabar, *The Art and Architecture of Islam 650–1250*, New York and Harmondsworth, 1987; paperback ed., New Haven, Conn., and London, 1992
Grabar, Oleg, *The Formation of Islamic Art*, New Haven and London, 1973, repr. 1988
Grube, Ernst J., *The World of Islam*, Feltham and New York, 1967
Irwin, Robert, *Islamic Art*, London, 1997

General

Allen, Terry, *Five Essays on Islamic Art*, Sevastopol, 1988
Baer, Eva, *Islamic Ornament*, Edinburgh, 1998
Blair, Sheila S., *Islamic Epigraphy*, Edinburgh, 1998
Burgel, Johann C., *The Feather of the Simurgh. The 'Licit Magic' of the Arts in Medieval Islam*, New York, 1988

Ettinghausen, Richard (ed. Miriam Rosen-Ayalon), *Islamic Art and Archaeology. Collected Papers*, Berlin, 1984
Ettinghausen, Richard, and Elisabeth B. MacDougall (eds.), *The Islamic Garden*, Washington, D.C., 1976
Grabar, Oleg, *The Mediation of Ornament*, Princeton, 1992
Jones, Dalu, and George Michell (eds.), *The Arts of Islam*, London, 1976
Kühnel, Ernst (trans. Richard Ettinghausen), *The Arabesque*, Graz, 1977
Kühnel, Ernst (trans. Kay Watson), *Islamic Arts*, London, 1970
Lehrman, Jonas, *Earthly Paradise. Garden and Courtyard in Islam*, London, 1980
Rogers, J. Michael, *Islamic Art and Design: 1500–1700*, London, 1983

Architecture

Creswell, Keppel A.C., *Early Muslim Architecture. II. Early 'Abbasids, Umayyads of Cordova, Aghlabids, Tulunids and Samanids, A.D. 751–905*, Oxford, 1940
Creswell, Keppel A.C., *Early Muslim Architecture. Umayyads. A.D. 622–750*, 2 vols., Oxford, 1969
Creswell, Keppel A.C., revised James W. Allan, *A short account of early Muslim architecture*, Aldershot, 1989
Hillenbrand, Robert, *Islamic Architecture. Form, Function and Meaning*, Edinburgh, 1994
Hoag, John D., *Islamic Architecture*, repr. London, 1988
Jairazbhoy, Rafique A., *An Outline of Islamic Architecture*, Bombay, 1972
Michell, George (ed.), *Architecture of the Islamic World*, London and New York, 1978; paperback ed. 1995

The Arts of the Book

Arnold, Thomas W., *Painting in Islam*, Oxford, 1928, repr. New York, 1965
Binyon, Laurence, John V.S. Wilkinson and Basil Gray, *Persian Miniature Painting*, London, 1933, repr. Toronto and London, 1971
Bosch, Gulnar, John Carswell and Guy Petherbridge, *Islamic Bindings and Bookmaking*, Chicago, 1981
Canby, Sheila, *Persian Painting*, London and New York, 1993
Ettinghausen, Richard, *Arab Painting*, Geneva, 1962; several reprints
Grabar, O., *The Illustrations of the Maqamat*, Chicago and London, 1984
Gray, Basil, *Persian Painting*, Geneva, 1961; several reprints
James, David, *Mamluk Qur'ans*, London, 1988
Lentz, Thomas, and Glenn Lowry, *Timur and the Princely Vision. Persian Art and Culture in the Fifteenth Century*, Los Angeles, 1989

Lings, Martin, *The Qur'anic art of Calligraphy*, London, 1976
Pedersen, Johannes (translated by Geoffrey French, edited by Robert Hillenbrand), *The Arabic Book*, Princeton, 1984
Safadi, Yasin H., *Islamic Calligraphy*, London, 1978
Schimmel, Annemarie, *Islamic Calligraphy*, Leiden, 1970
Schimmel, Annemarie, *Calligraphy and Islamic Culture*, New York and London, 1984
Welch, Anthony, *Calligraphy in the Arts of the Muslim World*, Austin, 1979
Welch, Stuart C., *Royal Persian Manuscripts*, London and New York, 1976
Ziauddin, M., *A Monograph on Moslem Calligraphy*, Calcutta, 1936

The Arts of the Loom

Baker, Patricia. L., *Islamic Textiles*, London, 1995
Bier, Carol (ed.), *Woven from the Soul, Spun from the Heart: Textile Arts of Safavid and Qajar Iran 16th–19th Centuries*, Washington, D.C., 1987
Black, David (ed.), *The Macmillan Atlas of Rugs & Carpets*, New York, 1985
Edwards, A. Cecil, *The Persian Carpet*, London, 1953
Erdmann, Kurt (trans. May H. Beattie and Hildegard Herzog, ed. Hanna Erdmann), *Seven Hundred Years of Oriental Carpets*, London, 1970
Folsach, Kjeld von, and Anne-Marie Keblow Bernsted, *Woven Treasures – Textiles from the World of Islam*, Copenhagen, 1993
Kühnel, Ernst, and Louise Bellinger, *Catalogue of Dated Tiraz Fabrics: Umayyad, Abbasid, Fatimid*, Washington, D.C., 1952
Mackie, Louise W., *The Splendor of Turkish Weaving: an exhibition of silks and carpets of the 13th–18th centuries*, Washington, D.C., 1973
May, Florence L., *Silk Textiles of Spain, eighth to fifteenth century*, New York, 1957
Serjeant, Robert B., *Islamic Textiles: Material for a History up to the Mongol Conquest*, Beirut, 1972

Ceramics and Glass

Allan, James W., *Islamic Ceramics*, Oxford, 1991
Atasoy, Nurhan, and Julian Raby (ed. Yanni Petsopoulos), *Iznik: The Pottery of Ottoman Turkey*, London, 1989
Atil, Esin, *Ceramics from the World of Islam*, Washington, D.C., 1975
Caiger-Smith, Alan, *Lustre Pottery: Technique, Tradition and Innovation in the Islamic and the Western World*, London, 1985
Carswell, John, *Blue and White: Chinese Porcelain and its Impact on the Western World*, Chicago, 1985
Grube, Ernst J., *Islamic Pottery of the Eighth to the Fifteenth Century in the Keir Collection*, London, 1976
Jenkins, Marilyn, 'Islamic Glass: A Brief History', *The Metropolitan Museum of Art Bulletin*, 44:2, 1986 (complete issue)
Lane, Arthur, *Early Islamic Pottery*, London, 1947
Lane, Arthur, *Later Islamic Pottery* (revised ed.), London, 1971
Philon, Helen, *Benaki Museum Athens. Early Islamic Ceramics. Ninth to Late Twelfth Centuries*, London, 1980
Porter, Venetia, *Islamic Tiles*, London, 1995
Watson, Oliver, *Persian Lustre Ware*, London, 1985
Watson, Oliver, 'Ceramics', in *Treasures of Islam* (ed. Toby Falk), London, 1985, 206–47

Metalwork

Atil, Esin, *Renaissance of Islam: Art of the Mamluks*, Washington, D.C., 1981
Dodds, Jerrilynn (ed.), *Al-Andalus: The Art of Islamic Spain*, New York, 1992
Hillenbrand, Robert (ed.), *The Art of the Saljuqs in Iran and Anatolia*, Costa Mesa, 1994
Petsopoulos, Yanni (ed.), *Tulips, Arabesques and Turbans*, London, 1982
Pope, Arthur U., and Phyllis Ackerman (eds.), *A Survey of Persian Art from Prehistoric Times to the Present*, London and New York, 1938–9
Rogers, J. Michael, and Rachel M. Ward, *Suleyman the Magnificent*, London, 1988

Glossary

'Abd servant, slave (used in many Muslim names in combination with one of the names of God, as in 'Abd al-Malik, 'Servant of the King')

ablaq literally 'piebald'; used especially of two-tone marble decoration

Abu father (of); used in many Muslim names in combination with the name of the first-born son

amir commander, prince

arabesque geometricized vegetal ornament

atabeg guardian of a prince; often a governor

b. son of (Arabic 'ibn', 'bin')

bab gate (also used in a spiritual sense)

baraka 'blessing'; a quality of divine grace dispensed by God and by those whom He selects

bismillah 'in the name of God'

caliph the name given to leaders of the Muslim community (from Arabic *khalifa*, 'successor' – to Muhammad)

cami Friday Mosque (Turkish; the Arabic form is **jami'**)

caravansarai lodging place for travellers, merchants and their goods; often fortified and situated on a trade route

chinoiserie decorative motifs derived from Chinese sources

dinar gold coin

dirham silver coin (later copper)

diwan government office or ministry; royal reception chamber; collection of poems

Fatiha opening chapter of the **Qur'an**

ghazi warrior for the faith

gunbad dome

hadiths collective body of traditions relating to Muhammad and his Companions; they constitute one of the sources of guidance for Muslims

hajj the pilgrimage to Mecca

hammam steam baths; bathing establishment for the public

hijra (hegira) Muhammad's emigration from Mecca to Medina in 622, the date which marks the beginning of the Muslim calendar

hypostyle having a roof supported by multiple columns – a standard type of mosque

ibn see *b.*

Ilkhan a Mongol ruler, subordinate to the Great Mongol Khan

imam spiritual leader; prayer leader; descendant of 'Ali, Muhammad's son-in-law; leader of the **Shi'ite** community

Islam submitting oneself to the will of Allah

Isma'ilis or **Seveners** members of a **Shi'ite** group who believe that the legitimate succession of *imams* includes the seventh *imam* Isma'il, son of the *imam* Ja'far al-Sadiq

iwan vaulted or flat-roofed hall, open at one end; often used to mean simply a covered hall in a mosque or a palace

jami' the great mosque in which the communal Friday prayer takes place and the Friday sermon is preached

jihad holy war against unbelievers

khamsa quintet of books (Persian usage)

khan lodging place for travellers and merchants; lord, prince

khanqah residential **Sufi** convent, often with an additional funerary function

khutba bidding prayer or sermon delivered in the mosque at midday prayers on Fridays

kitab book

Kufic angular style of Arabic script

külliye a typically Ottoman foundation comprising multiple buildings, centred on a mosque but with a strong educational or welfare bent

madhhab school of law

madina city

madrasa an institution for the study of the orthodox Islamic sciences

Maghrib the Muslim world in North Africa west of and including Tunisia

maidan open public square or plaza; central ceremonial space

mamluk slave (often also used of manumitted slaves)

maqsura a private enclosure in the mosque, usually for the ruler

mashhad mausoleum (of a martyr)

mashrabiya window grille or screen of turned wood, often with geometrical or interlaced designs

masjid mosque (literally 'place of prostration')

masjid-i jami' Persian term for the Friday mosque (see *jami'*)

mihrab arched niche, usually concave but sometimes flat, indicating the direction of Mecca (the *qibla*) and thus of prayer

mina'i pottery in which colours are applied both under and over the glaze

minaret the tower of a mosque from which the faithful are called to prayer

minbar stepped pulpit in a mosque, used for the pronouncement of the *khutba*

mi'raj the ascent of the Prophet Muhammad into heaven

mosque a place where Muslims worship

muhaqqaq a majestic Qur'anic cursive script

muqarnas honeycomb or stalactite vaulting made up of individual cells or small arches

muraqqa' an album of pictures

Muslim a person who follows the religion of Islam

nama a book of writing (Persian)

naskhi cursive style of Arabic script; a scribal hand

nasta'liq 'hanging' script characterized by wide sweeps and loops (Persian)

pishtaq lofty arch framing an *iwan*; hence, monumental portal

qadi a judge, usually in matters of civil law

qasr castle or palace; fort

qibla direction of prayer, i.e. to the Black Stone in the Ka'ba in Mecca

qubba dome

Qur'an God's Word revealed to the Prophet Muhammad; the primary source of Islamic law

ribat a fortified Muslim monastery or frontier post

sahn interior court, usually of a mosque

Seveners see Isma'ilis

Shahnama literally 'Book of Kings'; the Persian national epic composed by Firdausi and completed *c.* 1010

shaikh leader, whether tribal or religious (e.g. **Sufi**); highly venerated man

shari'a Islamic law

283

Shi'a (hence **Shi'ite**) generic term for a series of sects not regarded as part of orthodox Islam; they all recognize 'Ali (cousin and son-in-law of the Prophet) as the first legitimate caliph
simurgh mythical bird like a phoenix
squinch an arch spanning the corners of a square chamber and acting as a support for the dome
Sufi Islamic mystic
sultan ruler, king
Sunni orthodox Muslim (see **Shi'a**)
sura chapter of the **Qur'an**

thulth a formalized and elongated version of **naskhi** script
tiraz inscribed fabrics made in state workshop and often presented by the ruler to those he wished to honour
tughra monogram of the sultan (Turkish)
Twelvers the most numerous branch of **Shi'ites** in modern times; they believe that the legitimate succession of **imams** ended with the twelfth **imam** Muhammad al-Mahdi
'ulama 'those who possess knowledge'; scholars of Islamic theology and law; clerics; the learned class
vizier minister

Sources of Illustrations

Department of Antiquities, Amman 4, 16; Courtesy Cathedral Treasury, Apt 63; Al Araby Magazine 1; James Allan 160, 182, 183; Aga Khan Visual Archives, MIT. Walter Denny (1984) 81b; Collection Prince Sadruddin Aga Khan 189; Press Broadcasting and Tourist Department, Ankara 92; *Architectural Review* Photograph by Sheridan Cantacuzino 87; Azimut S.a.s. 136; Directorate General of Antiquities, Baghdad 90, 96, 168; Roloff Beny/National Archives of Canada/PA-198936, by permission of Nickle Arts Museum, University of Calgary 82; Staatliche Museen zu Berlin – Preußicher Kulturbesitz Museum für Islamische Kunst, © bpk 20, 25, 26, 27, 31, 36, 45, 65, 103; Sheila Blair and Jonathan Bloom 140; Helen & Alice Colburn Fund. Courtesy Museum of Fine Arts, Boston 33; Boudot-Lamotte 200; Barbara Brend 12; Courtesy of the Byzantine Institute 199; DAI, Cairo 113; Picture by kind permission of the Egyptian Publishing Company - Longman, Cairo 3, 117; Museum of Islamic Art, Cairo 51, 121; National Library, Cairo 126, 127, 176; Courtesy of the Arthur M. Sackler Museum, Harvard University Art Museums, Cambridge, MA 166 (gift of Edward W. Forbes), 188 (Grace Nichols Strong, Francis H. Burr and Friends of the Fogg Art Museum Funds), 190 (Bequest of the Estate of Abby Aldrich Rockefeller); J. Carswell 110; Kunstammlungen der Veste Coburg, Germany 62; Photo A.C. Cooper 73; The David Collection, Copenhagen, photo Ole Woldbye 159; Wawel State Collection of Art, Cracow 209; after K.A.C. Creswell *Early Muslim Architecture*, vol. I (1969) 2 (top) 14; Abbas Daneshvari 74; J.E. Dayton 153, 169; Photo Jean Dieuzade 197; Reproduced by kind permissionof the Trustees of the Chester Beatty Library, Dublin 40, 41, 75, 133; Edinburgh University Library 161, 162, 164; Olga Ford 91, 150, 205; Godfrey Goodwin 195; Alhambra, Granada 149; after E.J. Grube *The World of Islam* (1967) 53; Sonia Halliday Photography 8 (Photo by Jane Taylor), 9, 203; after Robert Hillenbrand *Islamic Architecture. Form, Function and Meaning* (1994) 2 (above top left); Keir Collection, Ham, England 58; after R.W. Hamilton *Levant I*, 1969 17; after R.W. Hamilton *Khirbat al Mafjar* (1959) 18; R. Hillenbrand *Islamic Architecture, Form, Function and Meaning* (1994) 81; Robert

Hillenbrand 189; Tiroler Landesmuseum Ferdinandeum, Innsbruck 86; Museum of Turkish and Islamic Art, Istanbul 208; Topkapi Saray Palace Museum, Istanbul 119, 206, 207, 210, 211; Dalu Jones 78; The Nelson-Atkins Museum of Art, Kansas City, Missouri (Purchase: Nelson Trust) 195; A.F. Kersting 28, 44, 54, 109, 114, 116; Kartay Madrasa Museum, Konya 45; Jonas Lehrman 145; Grassimuseum, Leipzig/Museum für Kunsthandwerk: frontispiece, 186; Lawrence Lockhardt 178, 181; By permission of the British Library, London 187; Copyright © British Museum, London 5, 6 (right), 38, 94, 104, 120, 157; Conway Library, Courtauld Institute of Art, University of London 155; From the Arcadian Group library. First published in *The Qur'an and Calligraphy*, London, Bernard Quaritch Ltd, catalogue 1213 (items 13 & 14) 46, 47; V & A Picture Library, London 59, 69, 122, 148, 158, 191, 192, 193, 194, 204; Museo Arqueologico Nacional, Madrid 134; Mas 128, 131, 138, 139, 142, 147; Viktoria Meinecke-Berg 111, 112; George Mott 130; American Numismatic Society, New York 7; Courtesy, Trustees of the Pierpont Morgan Library, New York 163; Bernard O'Kane 13, 30, 55, 56, 57, 77, 115, 129, 141, 151, 156, 174, 177, 198; Ashmolean Museum, Oxford 6 (bottom left); The Bodleian Library, University of Oxford 125; Creswell Archive, Ashmolean Museum, Oxford 15, 24, 98; Museo de Navarra, Pamplona 135; © Bibliothèque Nationale de France, Paris 99, 101, 102; Musée du Louvre, Paris 34, 39; Philadelphia Museum of Art 64; University of Pennsylvania Museum, Philadelphia 76; Josephine Powell 79, 83, 88, 89, 93, 143, 144, 172, 179, 201; Photo © RMN 105, 107, 118; National Library of Russia, courtesy B.N. Robinson 175; Photograph by J. Rock and A.J. Sutherland 48, 50; The State Hermitage Museum, St Petersburg 32, 94, 95, 85, 173; D. Talbot Rice 154; Mme. Th. Ullens de Schooten 152; Foto Biblioteca Vaticana 132; Treasury of St Mark's, Venice 61; Österreichisches Museum für angewandte Kunst, Vienna 123; Österreichische Nationalbibliothek, Vienna 124; Photo Roger-Viollet 170; Courtesy of the Freer Gallery of Art, Smithsonian Institution, Washington, D.C. 60, 68, 70, 71, 106, 165, 167; Edouard Widmer 202; Roger Wood/Corbis 29, 37.

Index